WALKING LIFE'S VALLEYS

Legacies of Faith
Volume V

WALKING LIFE'S VALLEYS

Legacies of Faith
Volume V

by Ed Erny

Devotional readings for
every day of the year

Published by OMS International, Inc.
P. O. Box A
Greenwood, Indiana 46142

Copyright © 2007

OMS International, Inc.
P. O. Box A
Greenwood, IN 46142

Legacies of Faith Volume V
Printed in the United States of America
by Evangel Press, Nappanee, IN

ISBN 10: 1-880338-41-6
ISBN 13: 978-1-880338-41-4

FOREWORD

This is the fifth in a series of devotional books entitled *Legacies of Faith*. In compiling these readings, we have for the most part focused on the subject of suffering, afflictions, sorrow, and grief. In following this plan, I am fully aware that we are running the risk of wearing the reader out with a plethora of material addressing the old question of why bad things happen to good people. Of course, since we are all sinners and the world has yet to see the first truly good person outside our incarnate Lord, many address the subject of pain in terms of a problem. How can a truly merciful and gracious God allow any one of his creatures to experience the unremitting and torturous pain we read about and witness every day in the chronicles of human life?

The older I get the more I appreciate the wisdom of Job's comforter who observed, "Man is born to trouble as the sparks fly upward." As it is in the nature of sparks to ascend, it is in the very nature of things that human beings suffer and there are few exceptions.

We have been missionaries for more than 40 years and privileged to travel to a great many parts of the world—Europe, Asia, Africa, South America and island nations—meeting and talking with people of virtually every race. All corroborate the wisdom of the sages, going back 4000 years: Yes, man is born to trouble.

We, in OMS, have a special fondness for the devotional book, *Streams in the Desert*, compiled in 1923 by Lettie Cowman. Lettie became president of The Oriental Missionary Society after her husband's untimely death and was frequently in our home. She was the soul of sweetness, albeit a staunch and unyielding stalwart in matters she judged to be of great importance, especially issues she felt commissioned of God to hold without compromise.

Streams in the Desert is today listed among the 20 most widely-read books ever written in the English language—a volume that can be found in practically every bookstore in America and has been translated into many of the world's languages.

Lettie complied and wrote many books but for popularity and world-wide appeal none approaches *Streams*. This puzzled my mother and one day she asked Lettie, "How do you account for the amazing popularity of *Streams in the Desert?*" After a moment's silence, she answered in a low voice that verged on the melodramatic. "Esther," she said, "the other books were written; *Streams in the Desert* was born." The story of the birth of the unusual volume is chronicled in *The Story Behind Streams in the Desert* (published by OMS International).

I recalled my first reading of *Streams* during my high school years. I found it less than compelling. With middle age and the first advent of great personal sorrow came the shocking discovery that not even missionaries are exempt from the usual afflictions of "ordinary folk." In those dark years of unaccountable pain and a myriad of unanswered questions, I again picked up an old, worn copy of *Streams* and began a surprising odyssey through its pages. I marveled how almost every day in some uncanny way the assigned reading was suited to our situation—in a distant land where for long, terrible months we lived under an awful grief following the death of our son.

The womb that gave birth to Lettie Cowman's famous book was six interminable years of pain beyond description. Added to that was the dark puzzle of apparently unanswered prayer. The Cowmans believed almost fanatically in divine healing. In Japan they had frequently been God's instrument of healing. Now Charles' heart condition had reduced him to the pitiful plight of a helpless invalid, in pain so severe he could not lie down but spent the long nights in a sitting position. During this long travail, he seldom, if ever, got a full night's sleep. Charles and Lettie tried to bolster their faith with the quoting of scripture and the singing of favorite old hymns. But the only answer seemed blank despair, of the kind C. S. Lewis described as the shutting of a door and "the sound of bolting and double bolting from within." The Cowmans daily looked out on a world from which on occasion, as Lewis said, "every trace of God had disappeared."

For her own survival, Lettie haunted libraries and used-book stores in quest of some word of comfort, gathered amidst heartbreak and the prospect of only everlasting pain. Those precious pages, in time, were assembled and became *Streams in the Desert.*

Are books of consolation still needed? I am inclined to think so, even in our unprecedented comfort and prosperous society. One half of all American marriages at some point sputter to an end, leaving in their wake millions of our broken countrymen and the frazzled offspring of their aborted marriages who are crushed and struggling for some meaning and identity in their shattered world.

Significantly, as I neared the completion of this volume, I was devastated by an old malady—several months of depression requiring hospitalization for weeks in a psychiatric ward. I surely learned that it is much easier to write or preach about God's sufficiency in pain than to experience that unrelenting darkness.

Finally, in compiling these pages, I have borrowed heavily from the biographies of saints who give testimony to our Father's adequacy for them, His afflicted children. For me, these testimonies provided honest windows into the mysterious shadows that God graciously admits to the life of every soul he intends to use. We offer Walking Life's Valleys to you with a prayer that these readings may bless you as they have us.

Ed Erny
Greenwood, Indiana, 2007

January 1
THE UNKNOWN JOURNEY
Hebrews 11:6-10

Abram began his journey without any knowledge of his ultimate destination. He obeyed a noble impulse without a clear grasp of its consequences. He took "one step," and did not "ask to see the distant purpose." And that is faith, to do God's will here and now, quietly leaving the results to Him. Faith is not concerned with the entire chain; its devoted attention is fixed upon the immediate link. Faith is not knowledge of a moral process; it is fidelity in a moral act. Faith leaves something to the Lord; it obeys His immediate commandment and leaves to Him direction and destiny.

And so faith is accompanied by serenity. "He that believes shall not be in haste," or more literally, "shall not get into a fuss." He shall not get into a panic, neither fetching fears from his yesterdays nor from his tomorrows. Concerning his yesterdays faith says, "You hem me in behind." Concerning his tomorrows faith says, "You hem me in before." Concerning his today faith says, "You have laid your hand upon me." That is enough, just to feel the pressure of the guiding hand.

J. H. Jowett

January 2
THE TOUCH OF THE HAND
Acts 9:15-16

"When heaven is about to confer a great office on a man, it always first exercises his mind and soul with suffering and his body to hunger and exposes him to extreme poverty and baffles all his undertakings. By these means, it stimulates his mind, hardens his nature and enables him to do acts otherwise not possible to him." Thus wrote Mencius, the Chinese sage, 2000 years ago.

The illustration of the Chladni plate beautifully shows how these agitating circumstances can be caused to work together. You sprinkle sand on a brass plate fixed in a pedestal and draw a bow across the edge of the plate, touching it at the same time with two fingers. Then, because of this touch, the sand does not fall into confusion but into an ordered pattern like music made visible. Each little grain of sand finds its place in that pattern. No one grain is forgotten and left to drift about unregarded.

There is nothing in the vibrations of the bow to make a pattern. Suffering, hunger, poverty, baffling circumstances cannot of themselves make anything but confusion. But if there be the touch of the Hand, all these things work together for good, not for ill, not for discord, but for something like the harmony of music.

Amy Carmichael

May I remind you that the great Dr. Thomas Chalmers always said that what really brought him, under God, to understand the gospel truly, was an illness which confined him to his sick chamber for nearly 12 months. He had been a brilliant "scientific" and "intellectual" preacher, but he came out of the sick chamber as a preacher of the gospel, and he thanked God for that visitation.

D. Martyn Lloyd-Jones

January 3

THE WORST THING, THE BEST
Matthew 26:45-46

> That life is not as idle ore,
> But iron dug from central gloom,
> And heated hot with burning fears,
> And batter'd with the shock of doom
> To shape and use.
>
> Selected

I would enter into the sufferings of Jesus as I sat under an olive tree (in the Garden of Gethsemane). I took a blanket and a hand lantern and my New Testament. About midnight I reread the account of Gethsemane's agony. But when I came to the last line, I nearly jumped to my feet: "Up, let us go forward" (Matthew 26:46 NEB). Forward to what? To the cross?

So the meaning of Gethsemane dawned on me anew. It was not the prostrate form and the bloody drops of sweat and the asking if the cup should pass; no, it was this last line: "Up, let us go forward"—going to meet whatever comes. Gethsemane was triumph, not tears. He at the end was perpendicular, not prostrate. His head was up, and his face set to meet and meet victoriously whatever comes.

As I have often said, he took the worst thing that could happen to him—the cross—and turned it into the best thing that could happen to the world—redemption. If you can take the worst and turn it into the best, you know how to live, if not on account of, then always in spite of. He was Lord of his own present—at Gethsemane and at Calvary. On the cross he was not resigned, he was regal. He dispensed forgiveness to his enemies, opened the gates of Paradise to a dying thief, cried, "It is finished," not "I am finished"—that thing I came to do, redeem mankind—"it is finished." He was Lord even when he was most victim.

E. Stanley Jones

January 4

LESSONS IN THE STORM
Psalm 139:11-12

I had a dear friend who had been a Methodist minister's wife. Her husband had died early, and she had become a Christian after he died. She was a soul-winner and a passionate lover of Jesus. One day I heard that she was losing her eyesight, so I made a trip to see her. I had been in her apartment for about seven minutes before she shocked me with a question. "Dennis, you came to comfort me, didn't you?"

She asked the question like it was an accusation, and I knew I was guilty, so I said, "Yes, I did."

She looked at me and said, "Would you deprive me of the privilege of walking with Christ in the dark? There are secrets I can learn in the dark that I could never learn in the light."

Not too long after our conversation, she regained her sight, and then she lost it totally. But when she walked into total darkness, she walked into darkness while embracing it because she did not walk alone.

God gives us songs in the midst of our trials and teaches us lessons in the storm that we could never learn in the sunshine. If you have the eternal God with you, you have the Source of all goodness, and if you have the Fountainhead of all goodness with you, what else do you need?

Dennis Kinlaw

January 5
AN ENIGMA TO BE UNRAVELED
II Corinthians 12:10

> Were not griefs mine, might I not come to deem
> The life eternal but a baseless dream?
> My winter and my tears and weariness,
> Even my griefs may be His way to bless;
> I call them ills, yet that can surely be
> Nothing but love that shows my Lord to me.
>
> Selected

It is difficult to find anyone in our culture who will respect us when we suffer. We live in a time when everyone's goal is to be perpetually healthy and constantly happy, and if any one of us fails to live up to the standards that are advertised as normative, we are labeled as a problem to be solved.

A host of well-intentioned people rush to try out various cures on us. Or we are looked on as an enigma to be unraveled, in which case we are subject to endless discussions in which our lives are examined by zealous researchers for the clue that will account for our lack of health or happiness.

Ivan Illich in a recent interview said: "You know, there is an American myth that denies suffering and the sense of pain. It acts as if they should not be and hence it devalues the experience of suffering. What this myth denies is our encounter with reality."

The gospel offers a different view of suffering. In suffering we enter the depths. We are at the heart of things. We are near to where Christ was on the cross. P.T. Forsyth wrote: "The depth is simply the height inverted, as sin is the index of moral grandeur. The cry is not only truly human, but divine as well."

Eugene H. Peterson

January 6

THE LOAN OF YOUR BODY
Hebrews 11:36-40

Helen Roseveare spent several years in medical missionary work in Africa, giving herself for others, until one day she fell into the hands of rebel soldiers. She was mercilessly beaten and kicked. Her teeth were broken, her mouth and nose gashed and her ribs bruised. When the rebel lieutenant pulled out his gun and pressed it to her forehead, Helen prayed he would pull the trigger; she knew that if he did not, worse pain and humiliation lay ahead.

She felt utterly alone. Had God forsaken her? In the loneliness and humiliation of that moment, His love enveloped her and an incredible peace flowed through her. Then He spoke:
> These are not your sufferings; they are not beating you. These are My sufferings. All I ask of you is the loan of your body.

Then the Lord breathed into Helen's troubled mind the word, *privilege*. Note her comment:
> For twenty years, anything I had needed, I had asked of God and He had provided. Now, this night, the Almighty had stopped to ask of *me* something that He condescended to appear to need, and He offered me the *privilege* of responding. He wanted my body in which to live, and through which to love these very rebel soldiers in the height of their wickedness. . . . He offered me the inestimable privilege of sharing with Him in some little measure, at least, in the edge of the fellowship of His sufferings. And it was all privilege.

Cost swallowed up in privilege! He does that when He sends us in His place.

Preaching in the Spirit
Dennis Kinlaw

January 7
THE TEST OF A GREAT SOUL
Psalm 23:4

To find God in our sorrows seems the test of a great soul. George Matheson was one of these saintly persons who used his sorrows to deepen his religious living. Blinded totally at 20 years of age, he was determined to prepare himself for the Christian ministry. In spite of his blindness, he earned three degrees at Glasgow in the four years following the loss of his vision. Later he received honorary degrees from Edinburgh and Aberdeen universities. Prepared to speak about "the power of God in sorrow," here is what this great Scottish theologian and preacher writes:

> My soul, if you would be enlarged into human sympathy, you must be narrowed into the limits of human suffering; Joseph's dungeon is the road to Joseph's throne. . . . It is the shadows of your life that are the real fulfillment of your dreams of glory. Murmur not at the shadows; they are better revelations than your dreams. Say not that the shades of the prison-house have fettered you; your fetters are wings—wings of flight into the bosom of humanity. The door of your prison-house is a door into the heart of the universe. God has enlarged you by the binding of sorrow's chains.

A beloved bishop once said, "Few people reach the age of 40 without having their hearts broken several times." The longer we live, the more we find the truth in these words! Our broken hearts can affect us in different ways: if we have no abiding religious philosophy, sorrow and tragedy can make us cynical, bitter, bestial; if your lives are tied with a Christian viewpoint into the heart of God, our disappointments and heartaches cannot only *teach* us some previous truth but make us sweeter.

A Journey with the Saints
Thomas S. Kepler

January 8

DENYING REALITY
I Thessalonians 5:16-18

The temptation to deny reality is the Devil's clever attempt to turn suspended judgment inside out. It goes through the same motions and makes the same gestures, but it achieves the opposite result. To deny reality does not answer the problems raised by reality; it only affirms that they are insuperable to faith and insists that they remain so.

These are elements of unhealthy repression in many areas of contemporary faith. This is true of Christian attitudes toward other emotions, such as feelings of failure, depression or grief. Over much of the stiff, tight-corseted unnaturalness that poses as Christian faith we might engrave the sound advice of Shakespeare:
> What man, ne'er pull your hat upon your brows.
> Give sorrow words; the grief that does not speak
> Whispers the o'er-fraught heart and bids it
> break.

Augustine demonstrated the honesty and freedom of a better way. Writing after his mother's death, he admitted, "The tears which I had been holding back streamed down, and I let them flow as freely as they would, making them a pillow for my heart. On them it rested, for my weeping sounded in your ears alone." He owed to his mother not only his physical birth but his spiritual birth, too, and at her death he was not ashamed to express his profound grief.

This mistake has been brought sharply into focus today by the exaggerated teaching on thanksgiving. In its extremes it strains for a praise which is unnatural. The new emphasis on praise and thanksgiving is so welcome that it seems churlish to question it. But when the Biblical injunction to "give thanks whatever happens" is taught with an insistence on literalism, it contradicts much of the Bible.

In Two Minds
Os Guinness

January 9
IT DOESN'T FIT
Proverbs 3:5

The problem with this world is that it doesn't fit. Oh, it will do for now, but it isn't tailor-made. We were made to live with God, but on earth we live by faith. We were made to live forever, but on this earth we live but for a moment. . . .

We must trust God. We must trust not only that He does what is best but that He knows what is ahead. Ponder the words of Isaiah 57:1-2: "The good men perish; the godly die before their time and no one seems to care or wonder why. No one seems to realize that God is taking them away from the evil days ahead. For the godly who die shall rest in peace" (TLB).

My, what a thought. God is taking them away from the evil days ahead. Could death be God's grace? Could the funeral wreath be God's safety ring? As horrible as the grave may be, could it be God's protection from the future?

Trust in God, Jesus urges, and trust in me.

A Gentle Thunder
Max Lucado

January 10
THROUGH THE EYES OF SUFFERERS
Galatians 6:1-5

Pain, sickness, delirium, madness are as great infringements of the laws of nature as the miracles themselves. They are such veritable presences to the human experience, that what bears no relation to their existence cannot be the God of the human race. And the man who cannot find his God in the fog of suffering, no less than he who forgets his God in the sunshine of health, has learned little either of St. Paul or St. John.

So long as men must toss in weary fancies all the dark night, crying, "Would God it were morning," to find, it may be, when it arrives but little comfort in the grey dawn, so long must we regard God as one to be seen or believed in—cried unto at least—across all the dreary flats of distress or dark mountains of pain. Therefore, those who would help their fellows must sometimes look for Him, as it were, through the eyes of those who suffer, and try to help them to think, not from ours, but from their own point of vision.

The Miracles of Our Lord
Rolland Hein

January 11

AN UGLY, ABHORRENT THING
Matthew 26:36-39

No man can love pain. It is an unlovely, an ugly, abhorrent thing. The more true and delicate the bodily and mental constitution, the more must it recoil from pain. No one, I think, could dislike pain so much as the Savior must have disliked it. God dislikes it. He is then on our side in the matter. He knows it is grievous to be borne, a thing He would cast out of His blessed universe, save for reasons.

But one will say, "How can this help me when the agony racks me, and the weariness rests on me like a gravestone?" Is it nothing, I answer, to be reminded that suffering is in its nature transitory, that it is against the first and final will of God, that it is a means only, not an end? Is it nothing to be told that it will pass away? Is not that what you would? God made man for lordly skies, great sunshine, gay colors, free winds, and delicate odors. However, the fogs may be needful for the soul, right gladly does He send them away and cause the dayspring from on high to revisit His children. While they suffer He is brooding over them an eternal day, suffering with them, but rejoicing in their future. He is the God of the individual man, or He could be no God of the race.

I believe it is possible—and that some have achieved it—so to believe in and rest upon the immutable Health that one regards his own sickness as a kind of passing aberration. The soul is thereby sustained, even as sometimes in a weary dream the man is comforted by telling himself it is but a dream and that waking is sure. God would have us reasonable and strong. Every effort of His children to rise above the invasion of evil in body or in mind is a pleasure to Him. Few, I suppose, attain to this. But there is a better thing which to many, I trust is easier—to say, "Thy will be done."

The Miracles of Our Lord
Rolland Hein

January 12
TRIBULATION, SEVERE AND PROTRACTED
Deuteronomy 4:30-31

We know that all the children of God are to have tribulation in this world. Nevertheless, we are all surprised every time tribulation comes to us. If the tribulation becomes severe and protracted, many a painful question begins to burn in our weary and wounded souls. Let us see what answer the Scriptures give.

We do not learn *obedience* without tribulation. Even Jesus had to learn obedience by the things which He suffered. We cannot learn it by anything less. And obedience is better than sacrifice. Remember this, you who seem to get nothing else done but to suffer for the Lord.

Tribulation worketh *approvedness*. The fires of tribulation purge us by melting away the dross, all that is not genuine within us. And these fires are hot, though not dangerous.

Tribulation worketh *hope*, says the apostle. We all have a tendency to allow ourselves to become attached to this world, making our heavenly fatherland seem distant and alien to us. But "our tribulations make us weary of the bondage of worldliness and, on the other hand, make it easier for us to walk in the way of life," says Brorson.

The more familiar I become with the Scriptures and with life, the clearer it becomes to me that tribulation is the silent dynamic of all Christian life. As the old wall-clock stops when we remove its weights, so also would our life in God come to a stop if the weights of tribulation were removed.

Oftentimes it seems to you that the weights are heavy. But do not forget that He who places them upon you knows of what you are made. He will make both the temptation and the way of escape such that you can endure. Remember this also: you honor God through suffering.

O. Hallesby

January 13
STRUGGLE PRODUCES CHARACTER
Hebrews 12:11-13

Question: We know that pain and struggle produce character and that often in the realm of music and art the tensions of childhood result in creative genius. Do you think the tendency in America to try to balance everyone out through self-help books, counseling, advice, and so forth, can be unhealthy? I often wonder how a psychiatrist would have handled Beethoven.

Answer: There are problems in this area. One is a trend to eliminate variety. I think variety is exciting and lovely, yet we set up norms and tend to reject people who do not match. If one does not have the proper standard of height, weight, figure, shape of nose, outgoing personality, and extroversion, the psyche is bruised and he or she loses the will to succeed. Anyone who doesn't conform to our artificial goals does badly. When a child is bookish and is clumsy with sports and doesn't shine in conversation, society tends to discard him or her. But that's the material from which research scientists come.

Another danger is the tendency of modern culture to remove risk and adventure from life. Most of our excitement happens to us vicariously, as we watch it on television. We shelter our kids, removing them from risky situations, and as a result stunt their growth. I have always maintained that of our six children, I would rather have four survivors who truly lived, with adventure and self-determination in the face of risk, then end up with six fearful, timid youngsters. This tendency to eliminate risk is compounded upon the old. . . . They lie there all day. I asked why they were not allowed to get up and walk about. He said, "Well, if they do, we find that they sometimes fall and break their hips. If they go outdoors, they catch cold, and if they meet with each other, they exchange infections."

Open Windows (Talk with Dr. Paul Brand)
Phillip Yancey

January 14

NOT ABLE TO EXPLAIN

Psalm 119:67

Doubters use suffering to force Christians against the wall: "Explain why your God of love let babies die at Dachau," they demand, "or we will not believe in him." We have not been able to explain, at least not in a way that convinces many people. We float a few guesses as to the general purpose of pain in the universe, but when it comes down to the particulars—why must this child suffer in this particular way?—we are as blind as anyone. We do not know where the blows come from or why. We can only hope and believe, through faith in God, that they have a point. Yet believers and nonbelievers still scrutinize suffering as though some lesson lies there, yet to be drawn out.

Many who have suffered in hospitals or concentration camps have written of it. None of them, to my knowledge, has offered a convincing and comprehensive reason for suffering. Yet strangely there is no more uplifting, positive, hopeful reading in any bookstore than the literature of suffering, written by those who have suffered. This literature does not justify suffering or make it worthwhile; it merely describes what suffering is like. I want to focus on one aspect of what they describe: the profound effect suffering has on relationships. Suffering affects people's relationships with themselves, with others and with God.

Suffering is lonely, and its most obvious effect is to bring the sufferer into a new relationship with himself. Suffering does not teach from a textbook; it works with the material already in a woman or man. It purifies this human material, cutting away layer after soft layer until only firmer stuff remains. All the dross goes: the ambitions, love of money, vanity about appearance, everything that sets us above others in our own mind. Suffering purges everything that is not central to life.

Knowing the Face of God
Tim Stafford

January 15
"SO WHAT IS THE ANSWER?"
John 12:25-26

The days pass and the realization grows that we may never leave the prison alive, that we may never make any semblance of fidelity out of this horrible marriage. The mind and the body cry against this outrage. Hair falls out, flesh wilts, courage fails. Past achievements mean nothing. In the present we are useless; our future does not exist. So much for all our plans. We must bid them good-by if we are to stay sane and learn to live with this new unyielding companion. We cannot afford to live in regret too long.

Solzhenitsyn speaks plainly of this need to embrace what is real. After detailing the 52 means of torture his captors took to break prisoners, he asks the ultimate question:

> So what is the answer? How can you stand your ground when you are weak and sensitive to pain, when people you love are still alive, when you are unprepared? What do you need to make you stronger than the interrogator and the whole trap? From the moment you go to prison you must put your cozy past behind you. At the very threshold, you must say to yourself: "My life is over, a little early to be sure, but there's nothing to be done about it. I shall never return to freedom. I am condemned to die—now or a little later. But later on, in truth, it will be even harder and so the sooner the better. I no longer have any property whatsoever. For me, those I love have died, and for them I have died. From today on, my body is useless and alien to me. Only my spirit and my conscience remain precious and important to me."
> Confronted by such a prisoner, the interrogator will tremble. Only the man who has renounced everything can win that victory.

Knowing the Face of God
Tim Stafford

Psalm 30

SO VERY WEARY

January 16

Charlie suffered greatly and we were at wits' end. I was so very weary. Felt perplexed till God *lifted* me in prayer. I felt I could keep on praying. It is said of Joseph "his soul entered into iron" during his prison life, but it made a strong, firm, unshaken character. I feel dumb before the mystery "of permitted suffering which none can explain."

"Unto you that fear My name shall the Son of Righteousness arise with *healing* in His wings." With what? *Healing*!

"Help thy brother's boat across, and lo, thine own hath reached the shore" (a Hindu proverb).

I have not conquered all of my negative thoughts and tendencies, but I have checked them when I found them in myself and they shall go no further.

Called two brothers from Pisgah who anointed Charles. We retired as usual but only to get right up. Charlie was very ill and asked me to call Brother Kilbourne. He came at 2:30 a.m. and stayed till morning and it was a fight for life all night. I had an *unusual* amount of strength freshly given and was kept all night. The little paper *Trust* came and on the front page was the word "Shall He find faith on earth?" God spoke through it clearly. It was *His own elect* that He was permitting to pass through such long and protracted trials and He called the *holding on*, and persistence, "faith." He said also He would "avenge them speedily." I caught for the first time in our trial the thread of God's meaning and it hushed me. In the night I asked for a word and turned to Psalm 30. A note at the top said, "See, I have given Jericho into thine hand." The Psalm speaks of healing, also verses 11-12: "Thou has turned for me my mourning into joy . . . to the end that my tongue might praise and not be silent." Praise God!

Lettie Cowman Diary, 1924

January 17
"OH, GOD, HOW COULD YOU?" (I)
John 14:29

Catastrophic loss wreaks destruction like a massive flood. It is unrelenting, unforgiving, and uncontrollable, brutally erosive to body, mind, and spirit. . . .

By 8:15 p.m., however, the children had had enough. So we returned to our van, loaded and buckled up and left for home. By then it was dark. Ten minutes into our trip home I noticed an oncoming car on a lonely stretch of highway driving extremely fast. I slowed down at a curve, but the other car did not. It jumped its lane and smashed head-on into our minivan. I learned later that the alleged driver was Native American, drunk, driving 85 miles per hour. He was accompanied by his pregnant wife, also drunk, who was killed in the accident.

I remember those first moments after the accident as everything was happening in slow motion. They are frozen into my memory with a terrible vividness. After recovering my breath, I turned around to survey the damage. The scene was chaotic. I remember the look of terror on the faces of my children and the feeling of horror that swept over me when I saw the unconscious and broken bodies of Lynda, my four-year-old daughter, Diana Jane, and my mother. I remember getting Catherine (then eight), David (seven), and John (two) out of the van through my door, the only one that would open. I remember taking pulses, doing mouth-to-mouth resuscitation, trying to save the dying and calm the living. I remember the feeling of panic that struck my soul as I watched Lynda, my mother, and Diana Jane all die before my eyes. I remember the pandemonium that followed—people gawking, lights flashing from emergency vehicles. . . . And I remember the realization sweeping over me that I would soon plunge into a darkness from which I might never emerge as a sane, normal, believing man.

A Grace Disguised
Jerry Sittser

Job 9:11-12
"OH, GOD, HOW COULD YOU?" (II)
January 18

In the hours that followed the accident, the initial shock gave way to an unspeakable agony. I felt dizzy with grief's vertigo, cut off from family and friends, tormented by the loss, nauseous from the pain. . . . . I could not rid my eyes of the vision of violence, of shattering glass and shattered bodies. All I wanted was to be dead. Only the sense of responsibility for my three surviving children and the habit of living for forty years kept me alive. That torrent of emotion swept away the life I had cherished for so many years. In one moment my family as I had known and cherished it was obliterated. The woman to whom I had been married for two decades was dead; my beloved Diana Jane, our third born, was dead; my mother, who had given birth to me and raised me, was dead. Three generations—gone in an instant!

That initial deluge of loss slowly gave way over the next months to the steady seepage of pain. . . . Life was chaotic. My children too experienced intense grief and fear. John was seriously injured; he broke his femur in the accident, which required him to be in traction for three weeks and in a body cast for another eight weeks. People from everywhere called on the telephone, sent letters, and reached out to help and mourn. Responsibilities at home and work accumulated like trash on a vacant lot, threatening to push me toward collapse. I remember sinking into my favorite chair night after night, feeling so exhausted and anguished that I wondered whether I could survive another day, whether I *wanted* to survive another day. I felt punished by simply being alive and thought death would bring welcomed relief.

A Grace Disguised
Jerry Sittser

January 19
"OH, GOD, HOW COULD YOU?" (III)

Lamentations 1:16

I remember counting the consecutive days in which I cried. Tears came for 40 days, and then they stopped, at least for a few days. I marveled at the genius of the ancient Hebrews, who set aside 40 days for mourning, as if 40 days were enough. I learned later how foolish I was. It was only *after* those 40 days that my mourning became too deep for tears. . . Of course I had no way of anticipating the adjustments I would have to make, the suffering I would have to endure in the months and years ahead. Still, on the night of the tragedy, I was given a window of time between the accident and our arrival at the hospital that presaged, at least initially, what lay ahead for me. Because the accident occurred in rural Idaho, just outside the Indian reservation, we were at the scene for well over an hour before an emergency vehicle transported the four of us to a hospital—another hour away. Those two hours between the accident and our arrival at the hospital became the most vivid, sobering, memorable moments of reflection I have ever had or will ever have. I was lifted momentarily out of space and time as I knew it and was suspended somehow between two worlds.

One was the world of my past, so wonderful to me, which was now lying in a tangle of metal on the side of the road; the other was the world of my future, which awaited me at the end of that long ride to the hospital as a vast and frightening unknown. I realized that something incomprehensible and extraordinary had just happened. By some strange twist of fate or mysterious manifestation of divine providence, I had been suddenly thrust into circumstances I had not chosen and could never have imagined. I had become the victim of a terrible tragedy. There was no way out but ahead, into the abyss.

A Grace Disguised
Jerry Sittser

January 20

IS IT NOT YET ENOUGH?
Job 13:24-28

What does it matter how this grief of mine evolves or what I do with it? What does it matter how I remember her or whether I remember her at all? None of these alternatives will either ease or aggravate her past anguish.

Her past anguish. How do I know that all her anguish is past? I never believed before—I thought it immensely improbable—that the faithfulest soul could leap straight into perfection and peace the moment death has rattled in the throat. It would be wishful thinking with a vengeance to take up that belief now. H. was a splendid thing, a soul straight, bright, and tempered like a sword. But not a perfected saint. A sinful woman married to a sinful man; two of God's patients, not yet cured. I know there are not only tears to be dried but stains to be scoured. The sword will be made even brighter.

But oh God, tenderly, tenderly. Already, month by month and week by week you broke her body on the wheel whilst she still wore it. Is it not yet enough?

The terrible thing is that a perfectly good God is in this matter hardly less formidable than a Cosmic Sadist. The more we believe that God hurts only to heal, the less we can believe that there is any use in begging for tenderness. A cruel man might be bribed—might grow tired of his vile sport—might have a temporary fit of mercy, as alcoholics have fits of sobriety. But suppose that what you are up against is a surgeon whose intentions are wholly good. The kinder and more conscientious he is, the more inexorably he will go on cutting.

A Grief Observed
C. S. Lewis

TREE SHAKERS

January 21

Romans 5:3-4

How many of us count it joy when we face trials? I don't. I don't know if it's my personality or the way I was raised or living in America or a combination of all the above, but I'm spoiled. I don't like it when things are too hard, when circumstances or relationships are difficult, when I struggle to keep going because I'm hurting.

A couple of months ago, Nelson and I went with the Oklahoma Native Plant Association to visit the tropical rainforest at the zoo. The building is filled with trees, plants, animals, and birds that are natives of tropical areas. As we walked through the rainforest exhibit the director, Chris Gabbard, pointed out and described the characteristics of many of the inhabitants. Some of the trees had grown to the ceiling of the building and as he spoke of the trimming, pruning, and maintenance they required, someone asked him if he could climb the larger and taller trees to make it easier to reach his work. His answer was no, because the trees don't have a strong root system and can't handle the weight and trauma of a person climbing them. He said that it takes wind for trees to develop a strong root system and because the trees are protected by the building they don't have any wind. He told us . . . they have volunteer "tree shakers," people who volunteer to come in and shake the trees periodically in order for the trees to develop a strong root system.

Maybe our trials and sufferings are for us like tree shakers are for the trees. Maybe they are to help us build a strong root system. A tree doesn't have much of a choice as to how to react to its trials or tree shaking, but we do. When we have trials or suffering, we have a choice as to how we react to the situation and to life in general. We can turn away from God and become bitter, or we can turn to God and allow Him to work good in our lives.

Jean Nelson

Hebrews 5:2 ## THANKFUL FOR PAIN **January 22**

In the last resort it is highly improbable that there could ever be a therapy which gets rid of all difficulties. Man needs difficulties; they are necessary for health.

Carl Jung

I am quite sure that "the angel's slackened hand" allowed that fall because of the immense help it would be later on. This sounds illogical, but Love has amazing ways of leading us to the place where we can help most.

The one person who stands out in my memory as one incapable of ever helping others was one who never suffered—never even had a headache. She had beautiful children, but apparently never even suffered then. She was incapable of understanding pain in others.

I have often thought of her and been thankful for pain. In a similar way, though of course different, a slip on the upward climb is sometimes the one way by which we can be led into Hebrews 5:2. For if one doesn't know by startling experience the peril of such things—such subtle things—one might not be able to enter into the experience with others. And we would not be quick and aware to come to the rescue *before* the wolf has leaped.

Amy Carmichael

January 23
GOD HAS WILLED TO TAKE YOU ASIDE
I Kings 17:1-6

A serene fortitude in the face of disappointment and chagrin should be our goal. If you have evaded all unpleasantness in life, your happiness is placed in unstable equilibrium by the constant dread that some unavoidable disappointment is just around the corner. If you have faced pain and disappointment, you not only value your happiness more highly, but you are prepared for unpredictable exigencies. Just as we can immunize ourselves against certain bodily diseases by stimulating our reserves to overactivity by taking graduated doses of toxin into our bodies, so we can immunize ourselves against adversity by meeting and facing the unavoidable chagrins of life, as they occur. There may be happy human vegetables who have succeeded in avoiding unhappiness and pain, but they cannot call themselves men.

W. Beran Wolfe

It can happen that a sick person undergoes experiences that are more valuable than all the successes of the healthy. Just because illness has brought a man up short in the rat race for worldly success, it can become an opportunity for withdrawal, for fruitful self-examination, for meeting God. "You know, my lord," Calvin wrote to an illustrious invalid, "how difficult it is amidst the honours, riches and influences of the world to lend an ear to God. . . . God has willed to take you aside, as it were, so as to be heard more clearly. . . . He has given you this opportunity to profit in His school, as if He wanted to speak to you privately, in your ear."

The Adventure of Living
Paul Tournier

January 24
THE HAMMER, FILE AND FURNACE
I Samuel 30:6

Heartaches and disappointments are like the hammer, the file and the furnace. They come in all shapes and sizes: an unfulfilled romance, a lingering illness, an untimely death, an unachieved goal in life, a broken home or marriage, a severed friendship, a wayward and rebellious child, a personal medical report that advises "immediate surgery," a failing grade at school, a depression that simply won't go away, a habit you can't seem to break. Sometimes heartaches come suddenly . . . other times they appear over the passing of many months, slowly as the erosion of earth.

Do I write to a "nail" that has begun to resent the blows of the hammer? Are you at the brink of despair, thinking that you cannot bear another day of heartache? Is that what's gotten you down?

As difficult as it may be for you to believe this today, the Master knows what He's doing. Your Savior knows your breaking point. The bruising and crushing and melting process is designed to reshape you, *not ruin you.* Your value is increasing the longer He lingers over you.

A. W. Tozer agrees: *It is doubtful whether God can bless a man greatly until He has hurt him deeply.*

Aching friend—stand fast. Like David when calamity caved in, strengthen yourself in the Lord your God. God's hand is in your heartache. Yes, it is!

If you weren't important, do you think He would take this long and work this hard on your life? Those whom God uses most effectively have been hammered, filed and tempered in the furnace of trials and heartache.

Charles R. Swindoll

January 25
LET NOT YOUR HEART BE TROUBLED
John 13:38-14:1
Ezekiel 36:24-27

Perhaps two of the most amazing verses in all of Scripture are John 13:38 and 14:1. Have you ever put these verses together? The chapter division obscures a hidden gem of truth. I never even dreamed that the verse acknowledging Peter's failure and sin would be followed by one of deepest comfort. Jesus knew the desire of Peter's heart. He knew Peter did not want to deny Him, that Peter dreamed of being a hero and dying for the Messiah. But Jesus also recognized that as much as Peter wanted to do what is right, he would not. His response to Peter's failure was comfort. He was going to send One to Peter who would enable him to do what he longed to do, to be faithful. The Holy Spirit would make Peter all he wanted to be.

All the valor and heroic spirit in the world will not equal the Spirit of God in a person's life. Jesus knows your heart and your willingness to accept the Spirit, and He also sees your failures. He knows whether you are hungry for Him, and if you are, He says, "Let not your heart be troubled. Believe in Me. I will set you free so you can follow Me with all your heart, all your soul, all your mind, and all your strength. I will set you free to be faithful."

The promise in Ezekiel 36:27 holds true. "And I will put My Spirit within you and cause you to walk in My statues, and you will be careful to observe My ordinances" (NASB). Those are not commands to obey; they are promises that we will obey when we are filled with the Holy Spirit.

Dennis Kinlaw

Genesis 6:9

A GROWING FAITH

January 26

Noah's faith is exactly like our own—a growing faith. As the flood destroyed and buried every living thing, Noah's faith grew and bore him high above the abodes of catastrophe. And this is the miracle and wonder of faith—that the very thing that kills and buries and overwhelms is now compelled to bear him up. Anybody who has made this venture of faith and knows it from his own experience knows that this is just simple truth. Everything that comes to us like an assault of fate—dread of the future, human disappointments, embroilments in our life, trials and afflictions—all this becomes for him who has faith an element which can no longer swamp and bury him, but mysteriously bears him up, as Noah was borne up by the flood.

Many a person who has experienced this has also testified that faith actually needs the perilous elements to prove its lifting and sustaining power.

And that's why Jesus Christ does not say, in the face of trouble to come: "When these things come upon you, then take cover, dig yourself in, lie flat on the ground!" No, he says: "When things grow really hard for you, 'look up and raise your heads, because your redemption is drawing near.'"

Why does faith rise up and take heart like this? Why does it go striding through the storms with head held high? Because it hears the footsteps of Another, striding toward us in these storms, because the tempests never come unaccompanied, because there is a voice that calls to us in every gale and a hand that holds us in every dark and dismal place.

Helmut Thielicke

DECEITFUL BLESSINGS

January 27

II Peter 3:8

As for me, I regard the centuries as a minute because I know that the centuries are less than a minute to thee. This sequence of centuries, which we call the duration of the world, is only a shifting scene which is going to disappear, as a figure which passes and vanishes. A little while, O man who sees nothing, a little while and you will see what God is preparing. You will see him himself treading all his enemies under his feet. What! You find this horrible waiting too long!

Whatever happens, it is God who has brought it about, and who has brought it about so that he may turn it to our good. We shall see in his light, in eternity, that what we were desiring would have been fatal for us, and that what we sought to avoid was essential to our happiness.

O deceitful blessings, I will never call you blessings because you only made me wicked and unhappy! O crosses with which God has weighted me and by which weak human nature thinks me overwhelmed, you which the blind world calls evils, you will never be evils to me! Rather never speak, than speak the cursed language of the children of this time! You are my true blessings. It is you which humble me, which detach me, which make me feel my wretchedness and the vanity of all that I tried to love here below. Blessed be thou forever, O God of truth, that thou hast attached me to the cross with thy Son, to make me like the eternal object of thy love!

Fenelon

STORE UP COMFORT

Isaiah 40:1

January 28

> They tell me I must bruise
> The rose's leaf
> Ere I can keep and use
> Its fragrance brief.
>
> — Selected

Store up comfort—this was the prophet Isaiah's mission. The world is full of hurting and comfortless hearts. But before you will be competent for this lofty ministry, you must be trained. And your training is extremely costly, for to make it complete, you too must endure the same afflictions that are wringing countless hearts of tears and blood.

Consequently, your own life becomes the hospital ward where you are taught the divine art of comfort. You will be wounded so that in the binding up of your wounds by the Great Physician, you may learn how to render first aid to the wounded everywhere. Do you wonder why you are having to experience some great sorrow? Over the next ten years you will find many others afflicted in the same way. You will tell them how you suffered and were comforted. As the story unfolds, God will apply the anesthetic He once used on you to them. Then in the eager look followed by the gleam of hope that chases the shadow of despair from the soul, you will know why you were afflicted. And you will bless God for the discipline that filled your life with such a treasure of experience and helpfulness.

— Selected

God comforts us not to make us comfortable but to make us comforters.

— John Henry Jowett

January 29
LET THE GLORY OUT
II Corinthians 2:14

God wins His greatest victories through apparent defeats. Very often the enemy seems to triumph for a season, and God allows it. But then He comes in and upsets the work of the enemy, overthrows the apparent victory, and as the Bible says, "frustrates the ways of the wicked" (Psalm 146:9). Consequently, He gives us a much greater victory than we would have known had He not allowed the enemy seemingly to triumph in the first place.

The story of the three Hebrew young men who were thrown into the fiery furnace is a familiar one. There was an apparent victory for the enemy. It *looked* as if the servants of the living God were going to suffer a terrible defeat. We have all been in situations where it seemed as though we were defeated, and the enemy rejoiced. We can only imagine what a complete defeat this appeared to be for Daniel's friends. They were thrown into the terrible flames which their enemies watched to see them burn. Yet the enemy was greatly astonished to see them walking around in the fire, enjoying themselves. Then King Nebuchadnezzar told them to come out of the fire. The enemy "crowded around them. They saw that the fire had not harmed their bodies, nor was a hair on their heads singed; their robes were not scorched, and there was no smell of fire on them. . . . for no other god can save in this way" (Daniel 3:27, 29).

Life of Praise

> Defeat may serve as well as victory
> To shake the soul and let the glory out.
> When the great oak is straining in the wind,
> The limbs drink in new beauty, and the trunk
> Sends down a deeper root on the windward side.
> Only the soul that knows the mighty grief
> Can know the mighty rapture. Sorrows come
> To stretch out spaces in the heart for joy.

Selected

Psalm 23 **"MY SHEPHERD"** January 30

When Dr. J. Wilbur Chapman was traveling through the Scottish highlands, he met a little shepherd boy tending his sheep. "Do you know the Twenty-third Psalm?" he asked the boy. He did not and so Dr. Chapman gave him the first five words, "The Lord is my shepherd" and told him to have a word for each finger of his hand. Months later Dr. Chapman traveled through the same section and decided to visit the boy. Not finding him, he inquired at a nearby hut, where he found the lad's mother. She told him how her boy had perished in a fearful blizzard during the winter. He had always treasured the words and, holding onto his fourth finger, would repeat: "My Shepherd, My Shepherd." "When his body was found in the deep snow," said his mother, "his two hands were seen projecting from the snow. He was clasping his fourth finger—and we knew what that meant."

In a children's hospital, I stood with my hand in a mother's hand. Her little girl had died. She looked like an angel. On the little girl's dead face there was such an expression of peace! "Oh, what joy it must be for that child to be with Jesus! She will be so happy in heaven," I said.

"I believe that, too," the mother said, "but Corrie, why did the Lord take her away from me?"

"I do not know, but God knows. He understands you. He loves you and He loves that little girl."

There are moments when the suffering is so deep that one can hardly talk to a person. What a joy it is then to know that the Lord understands. No pit is so deep that the Lord is not deeper still. Underneath us are the everlasting arms—and the Lord understands.

Corrie Ten Boom

January 31
THE VERY SUBSTANCE OF LIFE
Mark 8:34

The Cross of Christ should become the very substance of our life. No doubt this is what Christ meant when he advised his friends to bear their cross each day, and not, as people seem to think nowadays, simply that one should be resigned about one's little daily troubles—which, by an almost sacrilegious abuse of language, people sometimes refer to as crosses.

It is possible for a perfectly happy man—if he recognizes, truly, concretely, and all the time, the possibility of affliction—to enjoy happiness completely and at the same time bear his cross. But it is not enough to be aware of this possibility; one must love it. One must tenderly love the harshness of that necessity which is like a coin with two faces, the one turned towards us being domination, and the one turned towards God, obedience. We must embrace it closely even it if offers its roughest surface and the roughness cuts into us.

Simone Weil

If Jesus Christ were only a martyr, His cross would be of no significance; but if the cross of Jesus Christ is the expression of the secret heart of God, the lever by which God lifts back the human race to what it was deigned to be, then there is a new attitude to things.

Oswald Chambers

February 1

ALL SUFFER LOSS

II Kings 4:32-35

All people suffer loss. Being alive means suffering loss. Sometimes the loss is natural, predictable, and even reversible. It occurs at regular intervals, like the seasons. We experience the loss, but after days or months of discomfort we recover and resume life as usual, the life that we wanted and expected. The winter's loss leads to the spring of recovery. Such losses characterize what it means to live as normal human beings. Living means changing, and change requires that we lose one thing before we gain something else.

Thus we lose our youth but gain adulthood. We lose the security of home but gain the independence of being on our own. We lose the freedom of singleness but gain the intimacy of marriage. We lose a daughter but gain a son-in-law. Life is a constant succession of losses and gains. There is continuity and even security in this process. We remember the losses that lie behind us, and we look forward to the gains that lie ahead. We live suspended between the familiar past and the expected future. . . .

But there is a different kind of loss that inevitably occurs in all of our lives, though less frequently and certainly less predictably. This kind of loss has more devastating results and it is irreversible. Such loss includes terminal illness, disability, divorce, rape, emotional abuse, physical and sexual abuse, chronic unemployment, crushing disappointment, mental illness, and ultimately death. If normal, natural, reversible loss is like a broken limb, then catastrophic loss is like an amputation. The results are permanent, the impact incalculable, the consequences cumulative. Each new day forces one to face some new and devastating dimension of the loss. It creates a whole new context for one's life.

A Grace Disguised
Jerry Sittser

February 2
THESE THINGS HAPPEN TO OTHER PEOPLE
Job 6:1-3

When we arrived at the hospital the next morning, we were directed down a long hall to a small emergency center. A blood test would precede the biopsy. Danny screamed as the nurse pricked his finger with a scalpel and caused blood to spurt. Then we waited for hours, it seemed.

Finally Dr. Mooi appeared, beckoning us into his office. "We are canceling the biopsy because we believe we have already diagnosed the problem," he said. Then, slowly and in measured, professional tones, he went on. "The white blood count is very high, and we suspect that your son has acute lymphatic leukemia. However, we are hoping our diagnosis is wrong, and we would like you to take Danny to Ann Arbor University Hospital."

There was a long, awkward pause, then in a voice, gentle and subdued, Dr. Mooi continued. "Telling you this is one of the hardest things I have ever had to do. We don't know why many children from good homes develop this disease. Unfortunately, it is not curable at this time. All we can do is offer you treatments which could extend his time to five or six months, maybe more." His voice trailed off. "Or maybe we'll find a cure."

We sat there stunned, struggling to take in the import of what the doctor had said. And yet, at the same time, we somehow wanted to erase the whole conversation from our consciousnesses. Surely these words had not been spoken to *us*. He was speaking about someone else, not *our* son, not Danny. These things happen only to other people in faraway places: people you read about in newspapers, strangers or perhaps even people in the church, but not to you.

Thrice Through the Valley
Valetta Steel Crumley

February 3

BEHIND THE MASK

Job 5:7

One of the oldest books in the world states, "Man is born to trouble as surely as sparks fly upward."

Never have these words been truer than today. The whole world is sighing and suffering on a scale perhaps not known in human history: the refugees, the starving, the "new slaves," the psychological woes, the emotional turmoils, the broken marriages, the rebellious children, the terrorism, the hostages, the wars, and a thousand other troubles which beset every country in the world. There are no people anywhere that are immune. The rich and famous suffer as well as the poor and obscure. As the late actor Peter Sellers said, "Behind the mask of all us clowns is sadness and broken hearts."

It seems that the human race may well be heading toward the climax of the tears, hurts, and wounds of the centuries—Armageddon!

Suffering is the common lot of all people everywhere—believers and non-believers alike. But Christians often have their own particular types of sufferings in addition to the normal range of human miseries. Many times they suffer because they are followers of Jesus Christ. And many times they cry out with the psalmist, "Has God forgotten to be gracious?"

Billy Graham

God could have kept Daniel out of the lion's den. . . . But God has never promised to keep us out of hard places. . . . What He has promised is to go with us through every hard place and bring us through victoriously.

Merv Rosell

February 4

ANYWHERE, LORD

Philippians 2:17

Don't be surprised if temptations come. The one way is to throw yourself, everything you have to give, into the service to which you have been called. Paul spoke of himself as an offering poured out on "the sacrifice and service of your faith." That's what you must be, nothing kept back. And as you give all, you find all.

Often His call is to following paths we would not have chosen. But if in truth we say, "Anywhere, Lord," He takes us at our word and orders our goings and then He puts a new song in our mouths, even a thanksgiving unto our God (Psalm 40:2-3). There is wonderful joy to be had from knowing that we are *not* in the way of our own choice. At least I have found it so. It gives a peculiar sort of confidence that even we—we who are nothings—are being "ordered" in our goings. It is very good to be "ordered" by our beloved Lord. . . .

I woke between one and two o'clock and prayed, oh such poor prayers for you. I was troubled about their poorness till I suddenly remembered in whose Name I prayed. That was enough. The Father so loves His beloved Son that the poorest little word that rises in His name touches His heart. So you woke into a prayer.

Go with an open mind to be led at the time—not with all arranged beforehand. It is great to be faced with the impossible, for nothing is impossible if one is meant to do it. Wisdom will be given and strength. When the Lord leads He *always* strengthens.

Amy Carmichael

February 5
DANGERS ON EVERY SIDE
II Corinthians 11:26

We have to trust to God to guide us and really we have no fear for in everything yet we have been protected so often when it really appeared to us miraculous. We are truly in the midst of famine, pestilence and war. Dangers are on every side. If we women were to walk on the streets, I suppose to say the least we would be insulted and perhaps worse. We meet with all kinds of disease, smallpox and cholera, especially now. Hundreds die every day here of cholera. In two days there were three hundred funerals passed out from the city gate which is nearest to us. All died from cholera.

When the gentlemen go out on the street, they see people in the agonies of cholera and dying. They come to the hospital in the Compound for medicine. You know when the Chinese find that anyone is dying, they cruelly take him out and lay him on the ground. They won't let him die in the house.

In Mr. Cunningham's school right here where the boys come into his study to recite, we had three cases and one poor boy died. Dr. Coltman and Mr. Cunningham worked night and day to save them. We have practically no fear. We drink a little sulphuric acid in our water at meals, for the doctor recommended it, but we hardly ever thought of it ourselves. Now, of course, if there were two or three cases of cholera in America, you would all be greatly frightened, but here we live with it all about us and never fear.

The Tragedy of Paotingfu

February 6
WATCHING FOR HIS IMAGE
Jeremiah 1:18-20

What a night! Who but God can measure all we have passed through in a few brief hours. Charles was taken with violent pain. I gave him his nitro tablets, but he writhed in agony. I called Brothers Clark and Prescott and we wrestled in prayer for three hours, and God brought him through. I felt so stunned as if someone had hit me on the head and God had forsaken. We lay down and he slept some. I did not—was too weary.

Got up at 4:30 when away down in the very depth of my being Jesus whispered,
> Never a trial that He is not there,
> Never a burden that He doth not share.
> Moment by moment I'm kept in His love,
> Moment by moment I've life from above.
> Looking to Jesus, 'til glory doth shine,
> Moment by moment, O Lord I am thine.

Our God is sitting by the furnace waiting and watching for His image to be reflected 'ere the fire can be put out. He is bringing forth an instrument for *His* work, but it must be without a flaw. I somehow feel that these prolonged chastenings are but God's hand on the self life and they cannot be removed 'til self is consumed. I am praying anew this a.m. for another time of healing—cleansing of self first. When self, not sin, is fully consumed then the Holy Spirit can come in and sit on the throne of our beings. He "sits" as a refiner and purifier of silver—takes His time till He sees the moment has come for deliverance. Ezekiel 14 gives light that no matter how many saints pray there comes a time when each must get deliverance for himself by his own standing before God.

Lettie Cowman Diary, 1924

February 7
MOVING TOWARDS DAYBREAK
Lamentations 3:1-9

But a man may be in darkness and yet in motion toward the light. I was in the darkness of the subway, and it was close and oppressive, but I was moving toward the light and fragrance of the open country. I entered into a tunnel in the Black Country in England, but the motion was continued and we emerged into fields of loveliness. And, therefore, the great thing to remember is that God's darknesses are not His goals; His tunnels are means to get somewhere else. Yes, His darknesses are appointed ways to His light. In God's keeping we are always moving, and we are moving towards Emmanuel's land, where the sun shines and the birds sing night and day.

There is no stagnancy for the God-directed soul. He is ever guiding us, sometimes with the delicacy of a glance, sometimes with the firmer ministry of a grip, and He moves with us always, even through "the valley of the shadow of death." Therefore, be patient, my soul! The darkness is not your goal, the tunnel is not your abiding home! He will bring you out into a large place where you shall know "the liberty of the glory of the children of God."

J. H. Jowett

February 8

IMPRISONED MUSIC

Ephesians 6:12

(At a time of great affliction and diabolical accusations in the life of Francis Xavier.)

The explanation for these assertions probably was his shuddering horror of the almost universal vice prevalent in that warlike society, and of which some monasteries and schools were hotbeds. Then, too, "the care of the churches" weighed on him as it had done with St. Paul; and always the anxiety about Gomez was like the hurt of a thorn in a festering wound. Perhaps, too, that night struggle with the powers of darkness had left wounds not yet wholly healed, if they ever would be in this life. Yet the words from *El Conde Lucanor* rang in his ears, as they had done in Paris days: "Let us not leave the battle for the wounds we have; those we shall receive will make us forget the old ones."

St. Francis Xavier – Apostle of the East
Margaret Yeo

At the end of a dreary London day, she lay suffering on her couch, some of the darkness in her soul. Why did her Lord thus deal with His child? "For a while," she writes, "silence reigned in the little room broken only by the crackling of an oak log on the fireplace. Suddenly I heard a sweet, soft sound, a little clear musical note, like the tender trill of a robin. 'What can that be?' I said to my companion. We listened and again the soft plaintive note. Tirshatha exclaimed, 'It comes from the log on the fire.' The fire was letting loose the imprisoned music, garnered up by the old oak when soft sunlight flecked his tender leaves with gold. We are like this old log. We should give forth no melodious sounds were it not for the fire!"

Life of Spurgeon
Richard Ellsworth Day

February 9
MADE PERFECT THROUGH SUFFERING
Romans 8:19-21

I once kept a bottle-shaped cocoon of an emperor moth for nearly one year. The cocoon was very strange in its construction. The neck of the "bottle" had a narrow opening through which the mature insect forces its way. Therefore, the abandoned cocoon is as perfect as one still inhabited, with no tearing of the interwoven fibers having taken place. The great disparity between the size of the opening and the size of the imprisoned insect makes a person wonder how the moth ever exits at all. Of course, it is never accomplished without great labor and difficulty. It is believed the pressure to which the moth's body is subjected when passing through such a narrow opening is nature's way of forcing fluids into the wings, since they are less developed at the time of emerging from the cocoon than in other insects.

I happened to witness the first efforts of my imprisoned moth to escape from its long confinement. All morning I watched it patiently striving and struggling to be free. It never seemed able to get beyond a certain point, and at last my patience was exhausted. The confining fibers were probably drier and less elastic than if the cocoon had been left all winter in its native habitat, as nature meant it to be. In any case, I thought I was wiser and more compassionate than its Maker so I resolved to give it a helping hand. With the point of my scissors, I snipped the confining threads to make the exit just a little easier. Immediately and with perfect ease, my moth crawled out, dragging a huge swollen body and little shriveled wings! I watch in vain to see the marvelous process of expansion in which these wings would silently and swiftly develop before my eyes. As I examined the delicately beautiful spots and markings of various colors that were all there in miniature, I longed to see them assume their ultimate size. I looked for my moth, one of the loveliest of its kind, to appear in all its perfect beauty. But I looked in vain. My misplaced tenderness had proved to be its ruin. The moth suffered an aborted life, crawling painfully through its brief existence instead of flying through the air on rainbow wings.

I have thought of my moth often, especially when watching with tearful eyes those who were struggling with sorrow, suffering and distress. My tendency would be to quickly alleviate the discipline and bring deliverance. O shortsighted person that I am! How do I know that one of these pains or groans should be relieved? The farsighted, perfect love that seeks the perfection of its object does not weakly shrink away from present, momentary sufferings. Our Father's love is too steadfast to be weak. Because He loves His children, He "disciplines us . . . that we may share in His holiness" (Hebrews 12:10). With this glorious purpose in sight, He does not relieve our crying. Made perfect through suffering, as our Elder Brother was, we children of God are disciplined to make us obedient and brought to glory through much tribulation.

From a tract

February 10
QUESTIONS THAT INTRUDE
Romans 8:22

The room was full of youngsters, most of them apparently normal. I soon learned, however, that they too were on death's row, under the sentence of that terrible disease.

In the examining room the nurse reached for Danny's finger and made a quick incision. Danny screamed, and each childish wail found an echo in my own wounded spirit and brought a huge lump to the throat. *We will love him so much and take such good care of him,* I thought. *Certainly he will be different. He will get well. We'll find the best physicians in the world, and, of course, God will help.* Soon enough we got the report which only confirmed Dr. Mooi's diagnosis—leukemia. Apart from a miracle, Danny had no more than a few months to live.

I've tried many times to analyze the phenomenon—how a single moment, a single word, can forever alter the shape of one's world. The mind struggles to comprehend, yet it revolts. The heart will not accept what reason insists is fact. Then, slowly, at intervals, the facts begin to seep down from the numbed brain into the heart, bringing a kind of paralysis. At the same time comes a vague, nagging sense of guilt. Why me? Why us? Are the questions that intrude again and again. Where did we fail? Was there something we could have done that we didn't do? Is God punishing us?

Thrice Through the Valley
Valetta Steel Crumley

February 11
TOO BUSY FOR THE PRESENT
Psalm 90:12

When the remissions came, providing a brief reprieve from the relentless march of the disease, a slight recovery of strength would come to Danny. These were golden hours we savored to the fullest. I would strap on Danny's six-guns, find the battered cowboy hat, and soon it would be time for cowboys and Indians again. Henry had bought him an oversized plastic bat. The two of them would tumble out on the lawn for "baseball." As I stood watching from the window, their shouts and laughter came to my ears with a terrible sweetness.

We were learning something new about the preciousness of time. With the doctor's words, "a few months," we had begun mentally to tick off the days. We could no longer think of Danny's life, our time together with him, as stretching out into a distant future. We could no longer project in our minds' eyes scenes of childhood, teenage years, college, adulthood. In a moment, our perspective had changed. Time now was seen as a priceless commodity, so fragile and fleeting. How important that we treasure every hour with our son.

It was as though the joys of a normal life span were being distilled and poured into a few dwindling golden days. Thus, strange as it may seem those last months were studded with good times, laughter and fun. When Danny was able to respond, how willingly I would drop everything. I would think, *I can't let this opportunity pass.*

Gradually, I began to understand that this is the way one should view every moment, every day of his life, as an infinitely precious commodity. How often in our frenzied plans for the future are we too busy for the present?

Thrice Through the Valley
Valetta Steel

February 12

IN THE FURNACE
Psalm 1

Someone asked me if there ever was a time when I thought I just couldn't take it anymore. I could honestly answer, "No." My reason was simple.

Psalm 1 describes the person who is "like a tree planted by rivers of water." Not only does he "bring forth his fruit in his season" but "his leaf also shall not wither." The Psalmist tells us that this person meditates upon the Word of God, day and night.

During the trying times with Danny, I was discovering in my life this profound truth: that meditating on the Word of God had made me strong—like the Psalmist's tree. As a teenager I had tried to imitate my father and his love for the Bible. When I went away to school at Spring Arbor, I had determined that no matter how busy my daily schedule became nothing would crowd out my time alone with the Lord. Though I occasionally missed my devotions, God enabled me for the most part to keep my pledge to end each day in the Word with him.

It was never my habit to read long passages of Scripture at one time, but rather to take shorter portions, meditate upon them, turn them over and over in my mind. The Holy Spirit seemed to guide me to certain passages which became precious favorites. I marked verses that seemed to apply to my life and returned to them often.

And now I was discovering that in the withering furnace of affliction, my leaf was not withering. But those precious streams of living water kept rising up into my heart, refreshing me daily, hourly, moment by moment.

Thrice Through the Valley
Valetta Steel

February 13
THE FLAME THAT BURNS DIVINE COLORS
Matthew 26:42

Monday, September 1. I had a real nerve collapse this evening, just felt my nerves slipping from me. I had Dr. Crouse come and give me an adjustment which helped me much. Feel so worn and so broken, unable for anything.

Tuesday, September 2. Charlie is passing through a strange battle and it seems the most unexplainable thing imaginable. I have no light on his case and can but "stay" upon God. I have left him in God's hand entirely. The safest thing always is to pray, "Thy will be done."

Lettie Cowman Diary, 1924

Now again, as it happened during the long vigil with Danny, day by day God opened to me the sweet resources of his Word in special ways. Through the Word, the Holy Spirit can work a curious alchemy which transmutes pain into comfort and crushing sorrow into sweetness. Romans 8:28, a verse so time-worn it has almost become a cliché, was expounded anew to my heart by the Comforter. God would bring good out of this. How? I could not fathom but he would. I would keep watching for that good. Yes, I would look for miracles, and it would be an adventure.

Thrice Through the Valley
Valetta Steel

February 14
A VALE OF SOUL MAKING
Mark 11:22

The Scripture's counsel has relevance not only to the sense of sin, but also to *Perplexity*. I have in mind particularly the perplexity which arises out of dark experiences. Few travelers on life's highway escape the challenge to faith that comes to them from some stark happening. At such an hour of crisis we can do one of three things. We can follow the way of stoicism which hurls defiance at fate "or whatever gods there be" and cries, "My head is bloody but unbowed." But not thus is the "deep thunder" of our "want and woe" silenced. Or, as we may allow to happen far too often, we may yield place to doubt. Let it be said quite frankly that, in such a reaction, there is nothing but weakness and folly. It means either crumpling up or becoming cynical; and the strong are ashamed to crumple up whilst the wise avoid cynicism as they do all nasty things.

The difficulty created by the "Giant agony of the world" has engaged the attention of the greatest minds of the ages, yet no complete answer of an intellectual kind has ever been given. But if intellectual theory does not provide an answer, the experience of life does; and, since life is larger than logic, the practical answer is of great value. An answer that satisfies the heart is worth more than one that does no more than inform and convince the mind. The fact is that we find the solution to life's problems only when the problems vanish. God has not given us the full explanation of the presence of evil in the world. We understand a good deal when we realize that this world, in which there is so much pain, is a "vale of soul making," but that only takes us part of the way towards an explanation. But, we repeat, there is a solution that comes out of life. It is this; that when faith bravely, patiently, trustingly faces its personal problem, it finds that the problem disappears in an experience of God which dispels all doubts and resentments.

The Quest for Serentiy
G. H. Morling

February 15
"YOU HAVE MET A CRISIS"
Psalm 18:2

(Charles Cowman writes) Forgive me if I write plainly right out of my heart. You have met a life crisis to be sure, but should such a man as you, redeemed, sanctified, called of God to be an ambassador to the heathen, flee from your corner of the field, just because the battle waxed hot?

The other day I read a really good thing which I shall pass on. It said that an American traveler was in Italy when one day he stood watching a lumberman, who, as the logs floated down the swift mountain stream, occasionally jabbed his hook into one and drew it carefully aside. He said to the man, "Why do you pick out these few, for they all look alike?" The lumberman replied, "They all look alike, but they are not all alike, signior. The logs I let pass are grown in the valley where they have been protected all their lives. But these logs grew on the mountains. From the time they were sprouts and saplings they were lashed and buffeted by the winds, and so they grew strong with fine grain. We save them for choice work; they are not lumber, signior."

I somehow believe that the Lord has chosen you for some "fine work," which the devil wants to thwart. Hold steady a bit longer. You tell me there is darkness in your soul. Here is a rule that I copied in my Bible when I first found the Lord. It is a safe rule.

"In times of darkness, be concerned about two things. First, is my consecration entire? Second, do I this moment trust in Jesus as my perfect Savior and Sanctifier? Yes. Then all is well. I am on the Rock."

Missionary Warrior
Charles Cowman

"ALL" MEANS ALL
February 16

Psalm 25:10

"All the paths of the Lord are loving kindness." I found that in RV lately (Psalm 25:10) and have found it feeds. *All* does not mean "all but these paths we are in now" or "nearly all, but perhaps not just this specially difficult painful one." All must mean *all*. So your path with its unexplained sorrow and mine with its unexplained sharp flints and briers and both with their unexplained perplexity of guidance, their sheer mystery are just loving kindness, nothing less. I am resting my heart on that word. It bears one up on eagle's wings; it give courage and song and sweetness, too, that sweetness of spirit which it is death to lose even for one half hour.

God bless you and utterly satisfy your heart with Himself. I remember in old days almost desperately repeating to myself these lines from Tersteegen:

> Am I not enough, Mine own?
> Enough Mine own for thee? . . .
> Am I not enough, Mine own?
> I forever and alone,
> I, needing thee?

It was a long time before I could say honestly "Yes" to that question. I remember the turmoil of soul as if it were yesterday, but at last, oh the rest, "for in acceptance lieth peace" . . . .

It doesn't much matter what happens to us. The one thing that matters is how we meet what happens. Limitations, frustrations—they can't cast the smallest handful of dust on the glory of God. So let us be of good courage. He is leading us through and on, and as for God, His way is perfect.

Amy Carmichel

February 17
THE PIT
Psalm 40:2

A man fell into a pit and couldn't get himself out.

A SUBJECTIVE person came along and said, "I feel for you, down there."

An OBJECTIVE person came along and said, "It's logical that someone would fall down there."

A PHARISEE said, "Only bad people fall into a pit."

A MATHEMATICIAN calculated how he fell into the pit.

A NEWS REPORTER wanted the exclusive story on his pit.

A FUNDAMENTALIST said, "You deserve your pit."

An I.R.S. man asked if he was paying taxes on the pit.

A SELF-PITYING person said, "You haven't seen anything until you've seen MY PIT."

A CHARISMATIC said, "Just confess that you're not in a pit."

An OPTIMIST said, "Things could be worse."

A PESSIMIST said, "Things will get worse!"

JESUS, seeing the man, took him by the hand and LIFTED HIM OUT of the pit.

Source Unknown

Hebrews 12:7-8 "I WAS SPOILED" **February 18**

"I am grateful that fate has hit me so hard," she told me. "In my former life I was spoiled and did not take spiritual accomplishments seriously." Pointing through the window of the hut, she said, "This tree here is the only friend I have in my loneliness." Through that window she could see just one branch of a chestnut tree, and on the branch were two blossoms. "I often talk to this tree," she said to me. I was startled and didn't quite know how to take her words. Was she delirious? Did she have occasional hallucinations? Anxiously I asked her if the tree replied. "Yes." What did it say to her? She answered, "It said to me, 'I am here—I am here—I am life, eternal life.'"

We have stated that that which was ultimately responsible for the state of the prisoner's inner self was not so much the enumerated psychophysical causes as it was the result of a free decision. Psychological observations of the prisoners have shown that only the men who allowed their inner hold on their moral and spiritual selves to subside eventually fell victim to the camp's degenerating influences. The question now arises, what could, or should, have constituted this "inner hold"?

Man's Search for Meaning
Victor E. Frankl

February 19
AN IMMENSE AND DARK LOAD
II Samuel 22:29

John of the Cross, like Teresa, grew up in difficult circumstances. His father died when he was three, and John's family was cast into hunger and poverty. John eventually received a proper education but still chose to enter a religious order. Because of his connection with Teresa and her teachings, he was arrested, classified as a rebel and given the usual penalties for such offenses—imprisonment, flogging and fasting on bread and water. John was kept in a small room, six feet wide by ten feet long, with one tiny, two-inch window for his only source of light. For nine months, he lived in darkness with little food and hardly a change of clothing.

Yet a divine light pierced the darkness of that prison cell, and John's teaching on the dark night of the soul has inspired many Christians to persevere through the spiritual desert. Read what John wrote about difficulty: "The darknesses and trials, spiritual and temporal, that fortunate (notice, he says *fortunate*) souls ordinarily undergo on their way to the high state of perfection are so numerous and profound that human science cannot understand them adequately." He added later, "Both the sense and the spirit, as though under an immense and dark load, undergo such agony and pain that the soul would consider death a relief."

Remember, John's life was not easy, but he didn't mention the physical pain, the cold, the hunger, or the loneliness. Instead, he was concerned about the difficult war within, the battle for his soul. This was the struggle he focused on.

In John's mind, internal pain became the "doorkeeper" to further growth. He wrote that often souls do not advance because they are unwilling to face the "dark night" that would lead to a closer walk with God.

Seeking the Face of God
Gary L. Thomas

February 20
THE WAY THEY SUFFER
Job 23:10

The more we suffer, the more we need to do so.
Fenelon

How many saints has adversity sent to Heaven? And how many poor sinners has prosperity plunged into everlasting misery?
William Law

I would not consider any spirituality worthwhile that wants to walk in sweetness and ease and run from the imitation of Christ.
John Climacus

If he lavished them (good gifts) on all who asked, we might have the impression that God is to be served only for the gifts He bestows. In that case, the service of God would not make us religious, but rather covetous and greedy. In view of all that, when good and bad men suffer alike, they are not, for that reason indistinguishable because what they suffer is similar. The sufferers are different even though the sufferings are the same trials; though what they endure is the same, their virtue and vice are different.

For, in the same fire, gold gleams and straw smokes; under the same flail the stalk is crushed and the grain threshed; the lees are not mistaken for oil because they have issued from the same press. So, too, the tide of trouble will test, purify, and improve the good, but beat, crush, and wash away the wicked. So it is that, under the weight of the same affliction, the wicked deny and blaspheme God, and the good pray to Him and praise Him. The difference is not in what people suffer but in the way they suffer. The same shaking that makes fetid water stink makes perfume issue a more pleasant odor.
The City of God
St. Augustine

February 21

GRASPING TRUTH

Psalm 15:2

(Edward Wilson went with Scott on his last expedition to the Antarctic as doctor and zoologist. He endured the terrible winter journey with Bowers and Cherry-Garrard when they went in search of Emperor Penguin eggs. He was one of the five who reached the South Pole in January 1912. These words are from his diary.)

The more we try the clearer becomes our insight, and the more we use our thinking faculties the quicker they become in their power of grasping points of truth.

Truths are not things we can pick up without taking trouble to hunt for them. And when we find a truth we really possess it, because it is bound to our heart by the process by which we reached it . . . through trouble, difficulty or sorrow . . . a man binds it into his life. But what is easily come by is easily lost.

Every bit of truth that comes into a man's heart burns in him and forces its way out, either in his actions or in his words. Truth is like a lighted lamp in that it cannot be hidden away in the darkness because it carries its own light.

Edward Wilson (1872-1912)

February 22
EMBRACE IT WILLINGLY
Romans 8:35

Love is subject and obedient to its superiors, to itself mean and despised, unto God devout and thankful, trusting and hoping always in Him, even when God is not sweet unto it: for without sorrow none lives in love. He that is not prepared to suffer all things, and to do the will of his Beloved, is not worthy to be called a lover. A lover ought to embrace willingly all that is hard and bitter, for the sake of his Beloved; nor to turn away from Him for things that fall out against one.

Thomas a Kempis

Here is the final fact of vast practical importance and a door of unending opportunity. If I am Christ's, then voluntary "deaths" to the normal advantages in the flesh, comforts, loved ones, material advancement, enlarged income, pleasures, leisure, give me the right to claim and receive the harvest in the Spirit. Instead of regarding such as losses and deprivations to be endured if necessary but avoided if possible, we deliberately embrace them and glory in them as the way of the harvest. Equally we turn all life's unsought "trials" to the same use: tragedies, injustices, slights, insults, losses. As a matter of fact, although unsought, none are unsuited. Each comes because it just fits our case, and each is resisted as an impudent gatecrasher or welcomed as friend and ally, with corresponding destructive or constructive effect. "Awake, O north wind; blow upon my garden that the spices thereof may flow out." By the practice of this principle of the Cross, losses and trials, whether unsought or deliberately chosen, become positive weapons of offense in destroying the works of the devil and loosening his grip on humanity; even as Christ's death thus embraced, destroyed him who had the power of death and led captivity captive.

Touching the Invisible
Norman P. Grubb

February 23
THE FELLOWSHIP OF SUFFERERS
II Corinthians 4:7-11

A careful study of the New Testament is bound to give one a shock when he sees the contrast between the oft-repeated insistence on the necessity of suffering on the one hand and our colossal efforts in the Church to eliminate suffering on the other. Indeed we very often ignore and forget the clear scriptural message on this point. I feel that I must clarify the point before going on to its treatment.

First of all let me cite a half dozen or more texts in which the absolutely essential place of suffering in a Christian life is set forth.

" . . . joint-heirs with Christ; if so be that we suffer with him." Romans 8:17

" . . . not only to believe on him but also to suffer for his sake." Philippians 1:29

"That I may know him and the power of his resurrection and the fellowship of his sufferings, being made conformable unto his death." Philippians 3:10

"Strengthened with all might, according to his glorious power unto all patience and longsuffering with joyfulness." Colossians 1:11

"Who now rejoice in my sufferings for you and fill up that which is behind of the afflictions of Christ in my flesh for his body's sake, which is the church." Colossians 1:24

"For this is thankworthy, if a man for conscience toward God endure grief, suffering wrongfully." I Peter 2:19

"For even hereunto were ye called; because Christ also suffered for us, leaving us an example, that ye should follow his steps." I Peter 2:21

" . . . if ye suffer for righteousness sake, happy are ye." I Peter 3:14

"Beloved, think it not strange concerning the fiery trial which is to try you, as though some strange thing happened unto you, but rejoice, insasmuch as ye are partakers of Christ's suffering." I Peter 4:12-13.

This body of teaching leaves no doubt about the basic necessity of suffering in the work of the Kingdom. Have you ever daydreamed about what Christian work you would do with a million dollars if you had that much? Many of us would be glad to serve the Lord in the form of a sort of corporation president with a beautiful office in a tall building where we could receive bulletins on the progress of the missionary crusade and allot vast sums here and there as needed with the signing of allocation forms. But this is not the way the Kingdom goes forward. It is only by sacrifice and suffering. This is a fundamental of the faith for which we must contend by the surrender of our lives. This does not mean to court suffering. But is does mean that if we individually follow the will of God we will inevitably be led into suffering and rather than trying to escape it we shall accept it as a means of grace.

Keswick in Kashmir
Eugene Erny

February 24
THOSE WHO ESCAPE DIFFICULTIES
Psalm 119:71

I think that people who are poor and have to live modestly and bring up children at considerable sacrifice to themselves are fortunate, not unfortunate. It is the others who are unfortunate. They are missing out on something very exhilarating and delightful. . . . Judging from my own friends and people I have known, those who escape these difficulties miss a great deal.

Christians are often accused of being morbid when they talk of the joy of sacrificing. I think it is one of the deepest truths of the Christian religion. . . . It is a source of illumination—perhaps the greatest of all. I also think that to live modestly is always a richer experience because you are living like the majority of people; the trouble with the rich, as I have known them, is not really that they are bad people, but that they are cut off from an essential experience they don't understand.

Malcolm Muggeridge

Can you say that you thank God for things that have gone against you? That is a very good test of our whole profession. Can you see why certain things—things which were unpleasant and which made you feel very unhappy at the time they happened to you—benefitted you? Can you look back and say, "It is good for me that I was afflicted," like the Psalmist in Psalm 119:71?

. . . . It is very difficult to be humble if you are always successful, so God chastises us with failure at times in order to humble us, to keep us in a state of humility. Examine your life and see this kind of thing happening.

D. Martyn Lloyd-Jones

Romans 8:17   **FOR HIS SAKE**   **February 25**

I was in prayer one night when it was time to go to sleep. I was in very great pain, and my usual sickness was coming on. (This was a sickness which prevented her for over 20 years from eating any food until after midday.) I saw myself so much a slave to my own weakness, and yet my spirit sought to own liberty to enjoy God. This distressed me so much that I wept copiously, feeling very sorry for myself. This happened to me, not just once, but very many times. It made me feel so weary with myself, so that I felt repugnance about myself. Habitually, I know, I do not have self-hate for I seek to do what is good for myself. May the Lord grant that I do not indulge myself with doing more for myself than is necessary! But I am afraid I do.

When I was thus distressed, our Lord appeared to me. He comforted me greatly and told me I must accept this affliction for His sake and bear it for love of Him. My thorn in the flesh now became relevant to me. And since then, I have not known any real pain, since I resolved to serve my Lord and my Comforter with all my strength.

Although God would permit me to suffer for a little, yet He would also console me in such a way that I now even long for troubles. Now it seems to me that there is nothing more worth living for than this, so now suffering is what I most heartily pray God may give me. Sometimes I say to God with all my heart, "O Lord, I ask of You nothing else than to die or to suffer! I ask for nothing else for myself." It is a comfort to hear the clock strike another hour, for it is an hour nearer when I shall have the vision of God, and another hour of this life has passed away.

St. Teresa of Avila

February 26

A DEADLY SILENCE

I Thessalonians 2:4

We want to avoid sorrow and to keep the peace. And it is precisely our desire to avoid sorrow and to possess peace that causes us to keep quiet over things we don't like, and to avoid any kind of confrontation. But . . . silence in the face of wrong-doing is going to lead us to sorrow, and the courage to stir up a little trouble by objecting is, in fact, what will lead to peace. Most of us are unwilling to recognize that the power of silence in the cause of evil is one of Satan's most formidable weapons.

We look at much of the evil and sin that is portrayed in modern literature or movies. We praise the ardor and candor with which "honesty" is portrayed. Somebody said to me recently that she thought pornography was one of the very honest things and that the church should become more honest. I wonder if pornography is really honesty, and if our silence is really detachment. Karl Olsson said in one of his editorials in the *Covenant Companion* that all this silent acceptance of honesty in literature and movies today would be all right if he didn't see a wink in the eyes of those who keep quiet. That wink betrays tacit participation. Silence is seldom neutrality.

Nor can we excuse ourselves by saying that we are not influenced by what we see on the screen or read in a book. The whole premise of our educational system is that what we read and hear and see does influence us.

Paul Larsen

February 27
THINGS MISSING IN HEAVEN
Revelation 21:5-7

What a number of "conspicuous absences" there are to be in the "homeland!" No more sea! John was in Patmos, and the sea rolled between him and his kinsmen. The sea was minister of estrangement. But in the home-country every cause of separation is to be done away, and the family life is to be one of inconceivable intimacy. No longer any sea!

And no more pain! Its work is done, and, therefore, the worker is put away. When the building is completed, the scaffolding may be removed. When the patient is in good health, the medicine bottles can be dispensed with. And so shall it be with pain and all its attendants. The inhabitant never says, "I am sick!"

And no more death! The last enemy to be destroyed is death. Yes, he, too, shall drop his scythe, and his lax hand shall destroy no more forever. Death itself shall die! And all things that have shared his work shall die with him. "The old order of things has passed away." The wedding peal which welcomes the Lamb's bride will ring the funeral knell of death and all his sable company.

J. H. Jowett

February 28

CAN FAITH BEAR IT?

I Peter 4:12

Suffering is the most acute trial that faith can face, and the questions it raises are the sharpest, the most insistent and the most damaging that faith will meet. Here as nowhere else the supreme challenge is issued to suspend judgment. The basic principle is the same (we do not know why but we know why we trust God who knows why) and our basic prayer is the same, "Father, I do not understand you, but I trust you," but the price we are asked to pay is unique.

Can faith bear the pain and trust God, suspending judgment and resting in the knowledge that God is there, God is good and God knows best? Or will the pain be so great that only meaning will make it endurable so that reason must be pressed further and further and judgments must be made? To suspend judgment not only seems hard but ridiculous. At first it makes the problem worse. To suffer is one thing, to suffer without meaning is another, but to suffer and choose not to press for any meaning is different again. Yet that is the suicidal submission that faith's suspension of judgment seems to involve.

As suffering continues, the fire heats, the temperature mounts, the pressure increases, and the unbearable anguish threatens to choke faith and turn its cry into a scream of doubt. To suspend judgment and to simply trust is the hardest thing. Faith must reach deep into its reserves of courage and endurance if the rising panic of incomprehensible pain is not to be overwhelming.

In Two Minds
Os Guinness

February 29

LIVE IN FACTS
Hebrews 11:26

Charles had to sit up much of the night. It is a lovely a.m. full of sunshine. The resurrection is a fact and we need to live in *facts*, not feelings. We went to the Kilbournes in afternoon and on return I went to prayer and Hebrews 11—"By faith he forsook Egypt." He might have encamped on the banks of the Red Sea, but only as he went *forward* was the way opened. Christ is the *Way*.

> The test of the heart is trouble,
> And it always comes with the years;
> And the smile that is worth the praise of earth,
> Is the smile that comes through tears.

The windows of my soul, I throw wide open to the sun.

Lettie Cowman Diary, 1924

While I was prisoner at Vincennes and Monsieur De La Reine examined me, I passed my time in great peace, content to pass the rest of my life there, if such were the will of God. I sang songs of joy, which the maid who served me learned by heart, as fast as I made them; and we together sang thy praises, O, my God! The stones of my prison looked in my eyes like rubies; I esteemed them more than all the gaudy brilliancies of a vain world. My heart was full of that joy which thou givest to them who love thee, in the midst of their greatest crosses.

When things were carried to the greatest extremities, being then in the Bastille, I said to thee, "O, my God, if thou art pleased to render me a new spectacle to men and angels, thy holy will be done!"

Madame Guyon

Genesis 15:12 **SUDDEN, TRAGIC LOSS** **March 1**

Sudden and tragic loss leads to terrible darkness. It is as inescapable as nightmares during a high fever. The darkness comes, no matter how hard we try to hold it off. However threatening, we must face it, and we must face it alone.

Darkness descended on me shortly after the accident. I spent the first seventy-two hours caring for John, my two-year-old son, who was screaming from the pain of a broken femur and fighting the confinement of traction. I was inundated with telephone calls and visitors. Every voice and face called forth more tears and demanded the retelling of the story. I had to plan memorial services. I also had to care for my two older children, who were terrified and confused by the accident, having been pushed, as it were, out of their cozy home into a blizzard of pain. During those first busy days, however, I was rational enough to know that darkness loomed ahead and that I would soon descend into it. . . . The next morning I visited the funeral home and stared in disbelief at three open coffins before me. At that moment I felt myself slipping into a black hole of dread and oblivion. I was afloat in space, utterly alone among billions of nameless, distant stars. People seemed to recede from sight until they appeared to be standing far away, on some distant horizon. I had trouble hearing what people were saying, their voices were so faint. Never have I experienced such anguish and emptiness. It was my first encounter with existential darkness, though it would not be my last.

A Grace Disguised
Jerry Sittser

Jean Valjean, my brother, you no longer belong to evil; but to good. It is your soul I am buying for you. I withdraw it from dark thoughts and from the spirit of perdition, and I give it to God!

Les Miserables
Victor Hugo

March 2

IMPLICATIONS OF ATHEISM
Psalm 14:1

The implications of atheism are intolerable to me. However difficult belief in God can sometimes be, belief in atheism is more difficult still. It deprives us of the objective view of reality we need to validate our feelings about the losses we suffer. Sorrow, anger, and depression—these are genuine expressions of a soul that has a valid reason to convulse. The soul suffers because bad has appeared to triumph over good. It is the existence of God that provides categories by which we make moral judgments and respond with appropriate emotions.

We have good reason, then, to mourn our losses. Tears at a funeral, hospital, divorce court, or therapist's office manifest sadness in the face of legitimate loss. What we lost was good; what we lost rightfully makes us feel bad. The system of meaning that makes us feel bad about the losses and gives us the *right* to feel bad—reflects a universe that has God at the center of it. There may be other explanations, but this one makes the most sense to me.

The trail of atheism I followed, therefore, led me right back to belief in God. But I still found myself bewildered by His sovereignty. It still towered over me like a huge, granite cliff. I have not yet found a simple explanation, nor am I sure I ever will or even want to. There is too much mystery to make God's ways easy to explain. Still, I keep circling this mystery, exploring it from a variety of perspectives.

A Grace Disguised
Jerry Sittser

March 3

ENCOMPASSING ALL OF LIFE
Romans 9:10-14

Since the accident . . . I have started to broaden my understanding of God's sovereignty so that it includes rather than nullifies human freedom. I have come to realize that I can affirm God's sovereignty and still be a person instead of a puppet. I believe now that my view of God's sovereignty was once far too small. His sovereignty encompasses all of life—for example, not simply tragic experiences but also our responses to them. It envelops all of human experience and integrates it into a greater whole. Even human freedom, then, becomes a dimension of God's sovereignty, as if God were a novelist who had invented characters so real that the decisions they made are genuinely their decisions. As the novelist, God stands outside the story and "controls" it as the writer. But as characters in the novel, humans are free to act and to determine their own destiny. God's sovereignty then transcends human freedom but does not nullify it. Both are real—only real in different ways and on different planes.

Belief in God's sovereignty thus gives us the security of knowing God is in control, but it also assigns us the responsibility of using our freedom to make wise choices and to remain faithful to him. It assures us that God is transcendent without canceling out the important role we play. God's sovereignty allows us to believe that he is bigger than our circumstances and will make our lives better through those circumstances.

A Grace Disguised
Jerry Sittser

March 4

A NECESSARY WORK

James 1:3-4

Without a rich background of understanding of the gentleness, compassion, kindness, goodness, and love of our Heavenly Father, the seed fertilized by tribulation will not begin to send down roots and put up shoots of the "plant of patience!" In this particular picture, one needs to recognize the continually necessary work of soil preparation. We do have something to do with the richness of this particular soil. We, the children of the Living God, are already in this picture. In this imaginary garden, in which I am one plot and you another, one of the things we are meant to be growing is a plant called "patience." The fertilizer for this plant seems to be carefully described to us as "tribulation." I would like to suggest, however, that before the fertilizer is added, the soil preparation needs to be an hour-by-hour, day-by-day digging into the Word of God. This preparation involves having as a part of our whole being a growing understanding of the love of God and of His marvelous kindness which surpasses any kindness we could imagine from our knowledge of human beings or ourselves. We need to be trusting Him in an increasing manner, so that our reactions and actions are slowly, slowly changing through the months and years. One of the points of discovery—akin to the discovery of the sprout of a most difficult seed to germinate in our physical gardens—is the discovery of patience starting to sprout!

There is a fertilizer that speeds up a spurt of growth, causes heads to form in the cabbages that were too loose-leafed and peas to burst forth in their pods. Something has to be there to start with, but this is a "pusher" for fruitful growth. Tribulation, all by itself, without a ground to work in and without a seed planted there—without a "base," so to speak—would not bring about patience. There is a very basic need to be "rooted and grounded" in the love of God.

Affliction
Edith Schaeffer

March 5

DON'T CRY OVER YOUR LAMB
I Thessalonians 4:13

In the early days of February, 1892, Suzannah (Spurgeon) returned from Mentone with the casket of her beloved husband. Westwood seemed strangely large and empty. Memories everywhere! Then in her grief, she remembered a time of lesser heart-break, long ago when her world was young.

In one of the "dear dead days beyond recall," as her boyish husband was leaving Helensburgh, tears would trickle down her cheeks in spite of her efforts; everything seemed so empty when he was away.

"Seeing me look so sad, he tenderly said, 'What! Crying over your lamb, wifie? Do you think the children of Israel stood and wept over the lamb they laid on His altar?'"

Then the heart of Susannah found peace in tears. She looked at the great portrait of Tirshatha over the mantel and sobbed: "Ah, sweetheart! Was there ever one like thee? In all these forty years I knew thee, thou wert most tender, gracious! And now I am parted from thee, not for a few days only, as in the long ago time, but 'until the day break and the shadows flee away!' I think I hear thy loving voice saying again, 'Don't cry over the lamb, wifie,' as I try to give thee up, ungrudgingly to God—not without tears—ah, no, that is not possible; but with the full surrender of heart which makes the sacrifice acceptable in His sight."

Life of Spurgeon
Richard Ellsworth Day

March 6
THE WOUND WILL HEAL
Exodus 33:19

We may be sure that time *does* bring healing, and that by the passing of the days the wound will heal, bringing with it the deeper understanding of life and a deeper sense of urgency in seeking fellowship with God Himself. "Weeping may endure for a night, but joy cometh in the morning."

Of Jesus Christ Himself it has been said, "that His body should die was not defeat. Defeat for Him was to have taken the form of cursing His enemies or sinking into self concern. But through all His anguish, love was supremely unshaken. To die thus was to conquer." And we may rejoice because of such a Christ. We are persuaded that "neither death, nor life, nor angels, nor principalities, nor powers, nor things present, nor things to come, nor height, nor depth, nor any other creature shall be able to separate us from the love of God which is in Christ Jesus our Lord." And in the goodness of what He does, we see the goodness of God as kindness. "The earth is full of the goodness of the Lord." A God who is abundant in goodness and truth; a God who says, "I will cause all of my goodness to pass before you;" a God who crowneth His people with loving-kindness or with goodness and tender mercies, that in the ages to comes He might show the exceeding riches of His grace in His goodness toward us in Christ Jesus.

Evangeline Booth, the daughter of the founder of The Salvation Army, learned to discover the goodness of God in bitterness of personal sorrow. She writes, "Yes, I have known my dark moments. I have wondered why my mother had to die of cancer and my father go blind. I have wondered about the suffering everywhere in the world and why there is so much more sorrow than joy. But I have said to myself, 'God would not be much of a God if I could understand Him.'"

The Wonder of Worship
David McKee

March 7
NOTHING BUT PAIN AND BURDEN
Genesis 47:9

The poet Goethe wrote, "I will say nothing against the course of my existence, but at the bottom it has been nothing but pain and burden, and I can affirm that, during the whole of my 75 years, I have not had four weeks of genuine well-being. It has been the perpetual rolling of a rock that must be raised up again."

Robert Louis Stevenson said that three hours out of every five he was insane with misery. John Stuart Mill said that life was not worth living after you were a boy.

This is not fiction, these are human facts. What does Christian Science do—ignores them! New Thought—ignores them! Mind Cure—ignores them! Jesus Christ opens our eyes to these facts, but here comes the difficulty; how am I to get Jesus Christ in contact with these sick souls?

In the first place, will you realize that you do not know how to do it? I want to lay that one principle down very strongly. If you think you know how to present Jesus Christ to a soul, you will never be able to do it. But if you will learn how to rely on the Holy Ghost, believing that Jesus Christ can do it, then I make bold to state that He will do it. If you get your little compartment of texts and search them out and say, "I know how to deal with this soul," you will never be able to deal with it; but if you realize your absolute helplessness and say, "My God, I cannot touch this life, I do not know where to begin, but I believe that Thou canst do it," then you can do something.

Oswald Chambers

March 8
NO CONSTRAINTS, NO CONDITIONS
Matthew 6:28

Many years ago there was a monk who needed olive oil, so he planted an olive tree sapling. After he finished planting it, he prayed, "Lord, my tree needs rain so its tender roots may drink and grow. Send gentle showers." And the Lord sent gentle showers. Then the monk prayed, "Lord my tree needs sun. Please send it sun." And the sun shone, gilding the once-dripping clouds. "Now send frost, dear Lord, to strengthen its branches," cried the monk. And soon the little tree was covered in sparking frost, but by evening it had died. Then the monk sought out a brother monk in his cell and told him of his strange experience. After hearing the story the other monk said, "I also have planted a little tree. See how it is thriving! But I entrust my tree to its God. He who made it knows better than a man like me what it needs. I gave God no constraints or conditions, except to pray, 'Lord, send what it needs. You made it, and you know best what it needs.'"

> Yes, leave it with Him
> The lilies all do,
>   And they grow—
> They grow in the rain,
> And they grow in the dew—
>   Yes, they grow.
> They grow in the darkness, all his in the night—
> They grow in the sunshine, revealed by the light—
>   Still they grow.
> Yes, leave it with Him
> It's more dear to His heart,
>   You will know,
> Than the lilies that bloom,
> Or the flowers that start
>   'Neath the snow;
> Whatever you need, if you seek it in prayer,
> You can leave it with Him—for you are His care.
>   You, you know.

Selected

March 9
QUESTIONS WHICH REMAIN UNANSWERED
Job 38:1-11

At the very time that we are asking questions of God, questions which remain unanswered, he is ever asking other questions which we fail to heed. Yes, questions altogether different, which we elude, because we know what obedience would cost us. We know what should be changed in our lives, that which is nobody's responsibility but our own. Let us open the Bible—it is clearly evident from one end to the other. Men throw out questions to God which remain unanswered. But they change and find unexpected solutions when they begin to listen to the questions God asks of them and to answer him. Jesus did not answer the weighted questions of his contradictors; he always asked them other questions, embarrassing ones, capable of making them take stock of themselves.

The book of Job is a striking example. Job, in the midst of undeserved suffering, shouts to God, barraging him with countless "why's?" The book ends without God ever having answered. Thus the problem of unjust suffering has remained unresolved all through these centuries, that is, in its form of a syllogism over which all logical minds stumble: either God is all-powerful and therefore unjust, or else he is just but not all-powerful. Job, however, received his answer—an altogether different kind. It was not an intellectual reply, but an experience of God, once he paid attention to the questions God was asking. The philosophical problem of unjust suffering remains unsolved, but Job's attitude completely altered because he met God: "I had heard of thee by the hearing of the ear, but now my eye sees thee" (Job 42:5). As long as men remain in a strictly intellectual frame of mind, they will always brandish their problems as so many challenges to which no satisfactory answers come.

To Resist or To Surrender
Paul Tournier

Exodus 3:4-6 ## A DEEPER LEVEL **March 10**

There are, then, two distinct levels: the level of logic and reason, of dilemma, of all our insoluble questions and problems. Then there is the deeper level of the personal, of life, of a living and personal encounter with God and with men. The solution of our problems is to be found always on the deeper level. Just as precious as reason is, in solving technical and scientific problems, it is powerless to settle the problems of life.

Not only is reason powerless; far worse, it is dangerous. For the end result of every logical dilemma, conflict of ideas or conflict of feelings, is to shut us up in an immovable position. It seems to be a strong position, unanswerable and triumphant: it permits us to throw out our challenges and to reduce to silence all those who would try to give us advice. Oh, how dangerous it is to be right and to be sure of it! We can no longer change or modify our viewpoint. On the other hand, by abandoning our intellectual defense, by going down to the deeper, personal level, by coming to see what we have not yet understood of the mysteries of life, and by willingly coming to see ourselves as we really are, with our real problems, we always enter into an experience fruitful and renewing.

To Resist or To Surrender
Paul Tournier

Give yourself a chance. Let yourself mentally alone. Go away with your thoughts somewhere and leave yourself behind. There is no rest for the one who thinks about his troubles all the time. There is no hope for the one who eats his heart out with self-pity. If you have nothing to think about, *find* something. Oh, the world is full of interesting things. If it is not, why should you wish to *stay* here?

Harold Bell Wright

Psalm 10:12 THE "RED SEA" PLACE **March 11**

Finishing her high school, Annie spent one year at normal school and had a position offered to her. It was a great temptation to begin earning money and as her mother was failing in health and already had had one slight stroke. She felt that she was really needed at home, so she started teaching the primary class in the same school that she had attended as a girl. According to her contract with the normal school, she taught for three years, though early in the second year arthritis began to show itself. She tried several doctors in turn, but it steadily grew worse until it became difficult for her to walk at all, and she had a hard time finishing out the third year. After that she was obliged to give up her work, and there followed three years of increasing helplessness. The death of both her adopted parents within a few months of each other left the two girls alone again. There was little money in the bank and the twice-orphaned children had come to a real "Red Sea Place" in their lives.

(Her aunt Susie arranged for Annie to go to a Sanitarium for help.) Picture if you can the hopelessness of Annie's position when she finally received the verdict of the doctors of the Clifton Springs Sanitarium, that henceforth she would be a helpless invalid. Her own parents had been taken from her in childhood, and her foster parents both passed away. Her one sister was very frail and struggling to meet her own situation bravely. Annie was in a condition where she was compelled to be dependent upon the care of others who could not afford to minister to her except as compensated by her. In after years she always stated that her poems were born of the needs of others and not from her own need; but one knows full well that she never could have written as she did for the comfort and help of thousands of others if she had not had the background of facing those very crises in hew own life.

The Story of Annie Johnson Flint
Roland Bingham

March 12
WHEN YOU PASS THROUGH THE WATERS
Isaiah 43:2

God does not open paths for us before we come to them or provide help before help is needed. He does not remove obstacles out of our way before we reach them. Yet when we are at our point of need, God's hand is outstretched.

J.R.M.

"When you pass through the waters"
  Deep the waves may be and cold,
But Jehovah is our refuge,
  And His promise is our hold;
For the Lord Himself has said it,
  He, the faithful God and true:
"When you come to the waters
  You will not go down, *BUT THROUGH.*"

Seas of sorrow, seas of trial,
  Bitter anguish, fiercest pain,
Rolling surges of temptation
  Sweeping over heart and brain—
They will never overflow us
  For we know His word is true;
All His waves and all His billows
  He will lead us safely *THROUGH.*

Threatening breakers of destruction,
  Doubt's insidious undertow,
Will not sink us, will not drag us
  Out to ocean depths of woe;
For His promise will sustain us,
  Praise the Lord, whose Word is true!
We will not go down, or under,
  For He says, "You will pass *THROUGH.*"

Annie Johnson Flint

March 13

IN ADVERSE TIMES
Song of Solomon 1:13

I have been careful to collect this bundle of myrrh and to lay it upon my breast, gathered from all the anxieties and the bitternesses suffered by my Lord; as first, of the needs of His infant years; then of the labors which He performed in preaching, His fatigues in journeying, His vigils of prayer, His temptations in fasting, His tears of sympathy, the snares laid for Him in His speech; finally, of His perils among false brethren, of the revilings, spittings, blows, derisions, the insults, and nails, and like bitter things, endured for the salvation of our race. . . . Such meditations uplift my spirit in adverse times; they moderate it when things are prosperous; and they offer safe leadership to one trying to walk in the King's highway, between the sorrows and joys of the present life.

St. Bernard of Clairvoux

Francis Asbury had no bed on board ship. His friends had raised money to provide him two blankets; these he spread on the ship's bare planks to sleep the fifty-three nights of his voyage. Even to the bones of a man of 26, the nights were cold and the floor unyielding. "I found it hard to lodge on little more than boards. I want faith, courage, patience, meekness, love. When others suffer so much for their temporal interests, surely I may suffer a little for the glory of God and the good of souls."

Francis Asbury
L. C. Rudolph

This evening I finished Robert Louis Stevenson's letters which I have been reading alternately with de Pontis. What a man! Always on the verge of death, hard up, for many years at least, and yet so buoyant and whimsical and full of fun—his is a life to make most of us ashamed of ourselves.

Marjorie Lamb Mead

II Corinthians 5:14   **CONSUMING ZEAL**   **March 14**

One hundred forty years have now elapsed since Henry Martyn's premature death in those lonely wastes of Armenia. But his life still speaks to the world with a message as vital and urgent as that proclaimed by his own lips or pen. He belongs to that band of missionary saints, devoured by a consuming zeal, which gave them no rest, but drove them ever onwards to greater endeavors for the furtherance of the kingdom of God

It was the constraining love of Christ and the vision of souls eternally lost which led Henry Martyn to the shores of India. But until his *Journals* were read after his death, few realized how strong was that constraining power, how clear that vision, or how careful had been his preparation for his Master's service. For example, there are constant references in his *Journals* to physical endurance, for the future missionary was determined to "bring his body into subjection."

"I was pleased with the thought of being alone, exposed to the inclemencies of the weather, and deprived of earthly comforts, thinking I should be a gainer on the whole by having more of the presence of God and experiencing the power of Christ resting upon me."

He would deliberately expose his body to the cold in winter, walking without an overcoat or sitting in an unheated room, to harden himself that he might learn to forgo such comforts while in England so as to be ready for the days when it might be impossible to obtain sufficient clothing.

Life of Henry Martyn
Constance E. Padwick

March 15

OBSTACLES

Isaiah 49:11

God will make our obstacles serve His purposes. We all have mountains in our lives, and often they are people and things that threaten to block the progress of our spiritual life. The obstacles may be untruths told about us; a difficult occupation; "a thorn in the flesh" (II Corinthians 12:7); or our daily cross. And often we pray for their removal, for we tend to think that if only these were removed, we would live a more tender, pure and holy life.

"How foolish you are and how slow of heart . . .!" (Luke 24:25). These are the very conditions we need for achievement and they have been put in our lives as the means of producing the gifts and qualities for which we have been praying so long. We pray for patience for many years, and when some thing begins to test us beyond our endurance, we run from it. We try to avoid it, we see it as some insurmountable obstacle to our desired goal, and we believe that if it was removed we would experience immediate deliverance and victory. This is not true! We would simply see the temptations to an impatient end. This would not be patience. The only way genuine patience can be acquired is by enduring the very trials that seem so unbearable today.

Turn from your running and submit. Claim by faith to be a partaker in the patience of Jesus and face your trials in Him. There is nothing in your life that distresses or concerns you that cannot become submissive to the highest purpose. Remember, they are *God's* mountains. He puts them there for a reason, and we know He will never fail to keep His promise. "God understands the way to it and he alone knows where it dwells, for he views the end of the earth and sees everything under the heavens" (Job 28:23-24). So when we come to the foot of the mountains, we will find our way *from* Christ in Isaiah.

F. B. Meyer

March 16
NOT IN THE STILL CALM OF LIFE
Psalm 37:39

Some author that I have met with compares a judicious traveler to a river that increases its stream the farther it flows from its source, or to certain springs which running through rich veins of minerals improve their qualities as they pass along. It will be expected of you, my son, that as you are favored with superior advantages under the instructive eye of a tender parent, that your improvements should bear some proportion to your advantages. Nothing is wanting with you, but attention, diligence and steady application. Nature has not been deficient.

These are times in which a genius would wish to live. It is not in the still calm of life or the repose of a peaceful situation that great characters are formed. Would Cicero have shone so distinguished an orator if he had not been roused, kindled and enflamed by the tyranny of Catiline, Millo, Verres and Mark Anthony. The habits of a vigorous mind are formed in contending with difficulties. All history will convince you of this and that wisdom and penetration are the fruits of experience, not the lessons of retirement and leisure. Great necessities call out great virtues. When a mind is raised and animated by scenes that engage the heart, then those qualities which would otherways lay dormant, wake into life and form the character of the hero and the statesman. War, tyranny and desolation are the scourges of the Almighty and ought no doubt to be deprecated. Yet it is your lot, my son, to be an eyewitness of these calamities in your own native land, and at the same time to owe your existence among a people who have made a glorious defense of the invaded liberties, and who, aided by a generous and powerful Ally with the blessing of heaven, will transmit this inheritance to ages yet unborn.

The Book of Abigail and John
John Adams

IT PRODUCES SOMETHING

March 17

I Peter 1:5-7

How do the suggestions in the Bible differ from the uncompassionate hospital visitor who brings a smile and a "look on the bright side!" pep talk. At first glance the references sound like a pep talk, especially the words "Rejoice!" and "Be glad!" But look closer. Each admonition is followed by a productive result. Suffering *produces* something. It is of value; it changes us. The passages quoted . . . emphasize different products: rewards, perseverance, patience, character. This fact, that our response can be a productive response, brings a new understanding to our experience of suffering. We are often willing to undergo productive suffering; athletes and pregnant women volunteer to suffer because of what it will produce. The Bible says that a proper Christian response to suffering gives this same hope to the person on the hospital bed. He can become a better person because of his pain.

The rest of the Bible sheds some light on the words "rejoice" and "be glad." By those words, the apostles did not intend a grin-and-bear-it or act-tough-like-nothing-happened attitude. No trace of those attitudes can be found in Christ's response to suffering, or in Paul's. If those attitudes were the goals, self-sufficiency would be the quickest way to attain them, not trust in God. Nor is there any masochistic hint of enjoying the pain. "Rejoicing in suffering" does not mean Christians should act happy about tragedy and pain when they feel like crying. Such a view distorts honesty and true expression of feelings. Christianity is not phony. The Bible's spotlight is on the end result, the use God can make of suffering in our lives. Before He can produce that result, however, He first needs our commitment of trust in Him, and the process of giving Him that commitment can be described as rejoicing.

Where Is God When It Hurts?
Philip Yancey

March 18

IS THERE PURPOSE?

John 9:1-3

I found myself confronted with the question whether under such circumstances (imprisonment in a Nazi death camp) my life was ultimately void of any meaning. Not yet did I notice that an answer to this question with which I was wrestling so passionately was already in store for me, and that soon thereafter this answer would be given to me. This was the case when I had to surrender my clothes and in turn inherited the worn-out rags of an inmate who had already been sent to the gas chamber immediately after his arrival at the Auschwitz railway station. Instead of the many pages of my manuscript, I found in a pocket of the newly acquired coat one single page torn out of a Hebrew prayer book, containing the main Jewish prayer, *Shema Yisrel*. How should I have interpreted such a "coincidence" other than as a challenge to *live* my thoughts instead of merely putting them on paper? A bit later, I remember, it seemed to me that I would die in the near future. In this critical situation, however, my concern was different from that of most of my comrades. Their question was, "Will we survive the camp? For, if not, all this suffering has no meaning." The question which beset me was, "Has all this suffering, this dying around us, a meaning? For, if not, then ultimately there is no meaning to survival; for a life whose meaning depends upon such a happenstance—as whether one escapes or not—ultimately would not be worth living at all."

Man's Search for Meaning
Viktor E. Frankl

In the coming days your Heavenly Father may say to you, "Now we are going to get down to the business of straightening you out until you grow up in every way into Christ." When He does this, it will hurt. Always keep in mind, God will hurt you, but He will never harm you.

Oswald Chambers

PESTILENCE TO PRAISE
March 19
Genesis 45:4-8

I believe that God both can and will bring good out of evil. For that purpose he needs men who make the best use of everything. I believe God will give us all the power we need to resist in all time of distress. But he never gives it in advance, lest we should rely upon ourselves and not on him alone. A faith as strong as this should allay all our fears for the future. I believe that even our errors and mistakes are turned to good account. It is no harder for God to cope with them than with what we imagine to be our good deeds. I believe God is not just timeless fate, but that he waits upon and answers sincere prayer and responsible action.

Letters from Prison
Dedrick Bonhoeffer

In 1989 I held a healing seminar at the military base in Fort Rucker, Alabama. One day we went for the noon meal to the nearby town of Enterprise. They showed me the only monument in the world built in the shape of a bug to honor a bug! Back in 1915 the Mexican boll weevil invaded southeast Alabama and destroyed 60 percent of the cotton crop, the mainstay of the area. In desperation the farmers turned to diversified farming with an emphasis on peanuts. The new crop brought a great wave of unexpected prosperity. By 1917 the county harvested more peanuts than any other county in the nation. The citizens were so grateful that they erected a monument and on December 11, 1919, dedicated the public marker with this inscription: "In profound appreciation of the boll weevil, and what it has done as the herald of prosperity." What began as a *pestilence* ended in *praise*. What they thought was a great *tragedy* turned out to be a great *blessing*. Yes, sometimes the tears of history are changed into laughter, after we see the big picture.

Living With Your Dreams
David A Seamands

Genesis 50:19-21

THE SHOCK TEST

March 20

It was only when I lay there on rotting prison straw that I sensed within myself the first stirring of good. Gradually, it was disclosed to me that the line separating good and evil passes, not through states, nor between classes, nor between political parties either, but right through all human hearts. So, bless, you, prison, for having been in my life.

Alexander Solzhenitzen

Redemption does not amount to anything to a man until he meets an agony. Until that time he may have been indifferent but knock the bottom board out of his wits, bring him to the limit of his moral life, produce the supreme suffering worthy of the name of agony, and he will begin to realize that there is more in Redemption than he had ever dreamed, and it is at that phase that he is prepared to hear Jesus Christ say, "Come unto Me." Our Lord said, "I did not come to call the man who is all right; I came to call the man who is at his wits' end, the man who has reached the moral frontier."

Oswald Chambers

A British general once said, "The first quality of a man in war must be robustness—the ability to stand the shocks and horrors of combat." I heard about a nation that has an interesting test for new weapons to be used in mountain warfare. If a new machine gun is under consideration, they take it to the top of a 100-foot tower and throw it down on the concrete below. If it will still fire, they also test it for accuracy and see if it can be dismantled and reassembled easily. But it must first pass the shock test. They have learned the delicate weapons are of little value in actual combat. Combat weapons must be solid. They must have an above average breaking strength. In the Christian life we must be able to overcome the difficult tests we face by the power of God.

Disciples in Action
LeRoy Eims

March 21

A VITAL PURPOSE

I Kings 19:12

What is mirrored in the unique, solitary figure of Elijah is not something we all experience, although it explains what we experience. An expositor must deal with exceptional cases, but we blunder if we look in our own experience for the exceptional and sensational. There are ways in our lives about which we cannot be articulate, they go beyond our exact expression, we do not know why we are moved as we are; the explanation for it is not to be found in ourselves but in the experience of some greater soul.

Interior desolation serves a vital purpose in the life of a Christian. At the beginning of the spiritual life the consciousness of God is so wonderful that we are apt to imagine our communion with God depends upon our being conscious of His presence. Then when God begins to withdraw us into Himself, and things become mysterious, we lose our faith and get into the dark and say, "I must have backslidden," and yet we know we have not. All we know is that we have lost our consciousness of God's presence. Madame Guyon, in commenting on her own experience, puts it thus, "To complete my distress I seemed to be left without God Himself who alone could support me in such a distressing state. The misfortune," she adds, "is that people wish to direct God instead of resigning themselves to be directed by Him." Out of this experience of desolation, Madame Guyon learned this truth: that our faith must be built on the reality of being taken up into God's consciousness in Christ, not on our taking God into our consciousness. This means entering into a relationship with God whereby our will becomes one with the will of God. To the thought of the saints God is never far enough away to think about them, there is no separation; He thinks them. How we get there, I cannot tell you, but it is by the processes of God's training.

Oswald Chambers

March 22

A VERY PRESENT HELP
Matthew 16:22

Which is harder, to do or to endure? I think to endure is much the harder, and our Father loves us too much to let us pass through life without learning to endure. So I want you to welcome the little difficult things, the tiny pricks and ruffles that are sure to come almost every day. For they give you a chance to say "No" to yourself, and by doing so you will become strong not only to do but also to endure.

Whatever happens, don't be sorry for yourselves. You know how our Lord met the tempting "Pity thyself" (Matthew 16:22 AV margin). After all, what is anything we have to bear in comparison with what our Lord bore for us?

I know that each of you is in need of continual help if you are continually to conquer. I have splendid words to give you. They are from the first verse of Psalm 46—*"a very present help."*

Our loving Lord is not just present, but nearer than thought can imagine, so near that a whisper can reach Him. You know the story of the man who had a quick temper and had not time to go away and pray for help. His habit was to send up a little telegraph prayer, "Thy sweetness, Lord!" and sweetness came.

Do you need courage? "Thy courage, Lord!" Patience? "Thy patience, Lord!" Love? "Thy love, Lord!" A quiet mind? "Thy quietness, Lord!" Shall we all practice this swift and simple way of prayer more and more? If we do, our Very Present Help will not disappoint us for thou, Lord, hast never failed them that seek Thee.

Amy Carmichael

John 14:27   **HILL COUNTRY OF THE SOUL**   **March 23**

There should be a hill country in every life, some great uptowering peaks which dominate the common plain. There should be an upland district, where springs are born and where rivers of inspiration have their birth. "I will lift up my eyes to the hills."

The soul that knows no hills is sure to be oppressed with the monotony of the road. The inspiration to do little things comes from the presence of big things. It is amazing what dull trifles we can get through when a radiant love is near. A noble companionship glorifies the dingiest road. And what if the Companion be God? Then, surely, "the trivial round, the common task" have a light thrown upon them from "the beauty of His countenance."

J. H. Jowett

I am convinced that there are some things we learn through failure that we could never learn through success. We can never be adequate witnesses until we have failed at some point, because the majority of people to whom we will minister will know what failure is. No person will ever be an adequate shepherd of souls (a Sunday school teacher, a mother, a neighbor, or a pastor) without having known the bitter spots in life. If we are not willing to face the Cross in our own lives, we limit our ability to glorify Jesus. I am convinced that Abraham Lincoln was a great president because he failed so many times. He failed at almost everything he ever tried until he became president. He failed enough that he was no longer interested in winning but wanted to do what was right. There is a spiritual peer pressure among Christians. It is the pressure to do spiritual things for the wrong reasons, so we can look good. This has the same moral value as sin. We must come to the place where we do what is right whether the world views us as a success or a failure.

Dennis Kinlaw

March 24

PEOPLE WHO UNDERSTAND
Isaiah 53:3

There is nothing more comforting than to have people who understand one. This is what drove many soldiers who had been at the front, and then on their leave enjoyed a good soft bed for a few nights, back to their comrades in the Russian steppe. When a person is pressed hard by dread and terror, then home and fulfillment and the people who are fortunate and have everything—these suddenly become alien. This also has something to do with the fact that of all people it is the poets who have become the pastors of our time, who do not hand out idylls, fulfillments, and solutions to problems, but rather cry out their dread, their nothingness, and their despair to the world. . . . Gottfried Benn's poem "Song of the Passion" says: "Wounds must heal wounds. The wounded seek refuge with the wounded. There they are understood, and that by itself means a lot."

Every year around Christmastime thoughts like these come to me. People strain themselves to the utmost to give themselves and others a few hours of joy. . . . We remember our mothers in whose protecting care we once lived, the mothers who told us about the Christ Child and Father Christmas. The hardest men sing touching little songs, and in the soft light of candles our hearts leap up. We seek these hours in the same way that years ago I sought out the quiet, secure little village, in the same way that the Hungarians may yearn for the shores of freedom. And then when the candles burn down, leaving only blackened stumps or nothing at all, there comes a secret feeling of uneasiness: we have to go back behind the counter again in the big store, back to our examinations, the flurry in the office, or a clattering machine. This quiet world around the candles is so different from our ordinary life that we cannot connect the two, and in a short time the brightness vanishes behind us—like the lights of the station when we pass the curve.

Christ and the Meaning of Life
Helmut Thielicke

March 25
HAMMERING HOME A SINGLE LESSON
II Timothy 2:8-13

Looking back over the first half of this chapter (verses 1-13), the apostle Paul seems to have been hammering home a single lesson. From secular analogy (soldiers, athletes, farmers) and from spiritual experience (Christ's, his own, every Christian's) he has been insisting that blessing comes through pain, fruit through toil, life through death, and glory through suffering. It is an invariable law of Christian life and service. So why should we expect things to be easy for us or promise an easy time to others? Neither human wisdom nor divine revelation gives us such an expectation. Why then do we deceive ourselves and others? The truth is the reverse, namely "no pains, no gains" or "no cross, no crown." It is this principle which took Jesus Christ through a lowly birth and a shameful death to his glorious resurrection and heavenly reign. It is this principle which had brought Paul his chains and prison cell, in order that the elect might obtain salvation and glory. It is the same principle which makes the soldier willing to endure hardship, the athlete discipline and the farmer toil. It would be ridiculous, therefore, to expect our Christian life and service to cost us nothing.

Guard the Gospel
John R. W. Stott

If one may judge of a good by the trouble which precedes it, I leave mine to be judged of by the sorrows I had undergone before my attaining it. The Apostle Paul tells us, that "the sufferings of this life are not to be compared with the glory that is prepared for us." How true is that even of this life? One day of this happiness was worth more than years of suffering. It was indeed, at that time, well worth all I had undergone, though it was then only dawning. An alacrity for doing good was restored to me, greater than ever. It seemed to me all quiet, free and natural.

Madame Guyon

Acts 7:54-60

A MARTYR CHURCH

March 26

The history of the church in China since 1949 has been a history of suffering. Yet by going through different stages of suffering, the church in China has been transformed from a timid, foreign-colored institutional church into a bold, indigenous institutionless church, and it has been changed from a dependent mission church to an independent missionary church. It is a church that has gone through the steps of the cross, following the footsteps of her Lord: betrayal, trial, humiliation, abandonment, suffering, death, burial, resurrection, and the gift of Pentecost. . . . Christians in China interpret the last 34 years of prolonged suffering as a gift of God's profound grace to the Chinese church to cleanse her from her impurities, to test the genuineness of her faith and loyalty, to train her for obedience and progress unto greater maturity, and to enable her to gain a deeper experience of Christ.

It has been said the "the Chinese church has from the beginning been a martyr church," but never a church with a martyr spirit. It is not eaten up with self-pity because of its hard lot, but is joyful and triumphant. Again and again the consistent joy of believers has been a powerful magnet attracting fellow Chinese to a forbidden faith. Take this eyewitness account of believers being driven away to prison:

"The people of the street could not see the people inside the cart, but they thought that they were awful criminals to be dragged away like animals. The authorities did not want us to see them. 'Are they really that sinful?' we asked. Then we found out the truth. These were Christians on their way to jail. They were all handcuffed together and they were happy. There was no dissatisfaction or resentment on their faces. We could hear them singing as they went by, 'Lord, you are worthy to receive praise. Praise the Lord.'"

China Miracle
Arthur Wallis

March 27
"IT DOESN'T MATTER"
Acts 5:41-42

The story of a Chinese sister:

She was in prayer when the authorities arrived to arrest her. She was not surprised, as the Lord had already prepared her heart. In fact, just as they arrested her, the Holy Spirit came and filled her with an uncontainable joy. As the cart in which she was being taken away jostled down the road, she was overflowing with joy and sang all the way. The authorities naturally suspected that she was demented.

As she was being registered at the prison, she had time to witness at length to one of the officials. So powerful was her anointed witness that right then and there he accepted Christ. As he registered her, she said to him, "Today is not the day I came to register myself, and I will never really be a prisoner here—Christ will constantly be with me. I am free. This is the day when you have registered your residency in the kingdom of God."

Some time later, all the inmates were given an envelope containing the length of their sentence. The other inmates asked her how long her sentence was. She answered, "I don't know. I just put the edict away without looking at it." "Why?" they asked. "Don't you want to know how many years you are getting?" "It doesn't matter," she replied. "Whether it is 10 years or 100 years, each day will be a day with my Lord."

China Miracle
Arthur Wallis

March 28

A BIT OF SORROW
I Corinthians 10:13-14

It was during the Great Depression of the thirties. A devoted group of ladies in our city conducted a Sunday afternoon meeting for wives of the unemployed, many of whom were in great need and distress. On the first Sunday of the month, husbands were invited, too, and I was asked to bring the message each month.

One afternoon after the meeting, I was in one room and two godly ladies for whom I had a great respect were in the adjoining room. I had no option but to overhear their conversation, and this is what I heard: "What did you think of his message this afternoon?" said one. "Oh, it was quite good," said the other. "He'll be all right when he has had a bit of sorrow."

In later years the Lord supplied that lack in abundant measure. But her words impressed on me the fact that it is only through sorrow and suffering that one can minister in depth to those who sorrow and suffer. Our words carry peculiar weight when we have sat where our hearers sit.

My father was full of aphorisms. He once said to me: "If in coming days, God entrusts you with severe testings that is His vote of confidence, not evidence of His displeasure."

It is a favorite ploy of Satan to make Christians think that because they are passing through a time of trial and testing, they are therefore necessarily the objects of God's displeasure. There may indeed be some cause in our lives for the trial coming upon us, but if the sky is clear above us, it may be viewed not so much a sign of God's displeasure as His vote of confidence in our ability to come through the test with flying colors.

This I Remember
J. Oswald Sanders

March 29

"YOU'VE HAD IT"

Hebrews 12:9-10

You know, the strangest thing happened to me this very morning. I want to share it with you. Actually, it didn't happen to me; it was something I saw. I was working in the garden, pulling weeds and throwing them onto our compost pile, when my eyes fell on a potted plant lying beside it—an African violet. For four years I had tended it, watered and nourished it, put it in this window and that window, with more light or less light. It just would *not* bloom. I got advice from others and tried it all, but after all had failed to produce flowers, I threw pot and all out back. It was as though I had said, "You've had it and I've had it, and that's that!" Can you believe that today that stubborn plant was full of bloom? I must go out and check again . . . I did, and brought the pot back to the house, and it *is* full of bloom—white!

I am full of questions, and somewhere in this episode lies a parable, very delicate, not to be pressed at all points, but something. What had I done wrong? Why bloom in obscurity, in the dark and in rejection, when nothing happened in the limelight of attention, care and concern? What did the backyard behind the garage have that my home did not? I don't know the answers. But, in adversity and unobserved, untended and alone, the plant came to life and burst forth into bloom.

Come to think of it, I know people like that. Right now, one very dear to me is suffering pangs of deep hurt, rejection and a growing obscurity. She said, "I would never have known the deeper things of the Spirit had I been allowed the luxury of life as it had always been." Growing deeper has brought forth sweetness and blossoms of rare fragrance.

Over the Teacup
Catherine Cattell

Psalm 18:28   **AN ILLUMINATION**   **March 30**

I have never doubted since then that in all circumstances, whatever one's condition may be, or the condition of the society one lives in, or the condition of the world, life is good, and that to gain from this experience of living what has to be gained, and to learn what has to be learned, it is necessary to live out one's life to the end until the moment comes for one's release. Then, and only then, can one truly rejoice in that moment. There is no catastrophe, as it seems to me, that can befall human beings which is not an illumination, and no illumination which is not in some sense a catastrophe.

It's in an age like ours, an age of great superficiality of thought, that people ask how, if God makes a Mongol, he can be a loving God. It's a very superficial thought, because a Mongol child is part of the process wherby man exists, and we can't judge how that comes about, or what are its full consequences. All we can say is that it's a part of the experience of living, and, like all other parts, it can shed light or it can shed darkness.

Suffering is an essential element in the Christian religion, as it is in life. After all, the cross itself is the supreme example. If Christ hadn't suffered, do you imagine that anyone would have paid the slightest attention to the religion he founded? Not at all.

Jesus Rediscovered
Malcolm Muggeridge

March 31

THE FIRST VISIT OF GOD
Matthew 10:34

And all that time it was God near her that was making her unhappy. For as the Son of Man came not to send peace on the earth but a sword, so the first visit of God to the human soul is generally in a cloud of fear and doubt, rising from the soul itself at His approach. The sun is the cloud dispeller, yet often he must look through a fog if he would visit the earth at all.

George MacDonald

A difficult lesson for me to learn was that surrender is never a once-in-a-lifetime activity; it is the continual worship of a growing Christian. This means that I must be willing to part with anything on a regular basis, even those good things that come from God. As part of our discipline of surrender, God will often ask us to let go of something very precious, even something He has given us. This is because as Fenelon wrote:

> There is not a single gift, noble as it may be which, after having been a means of advancement, does not generally become, later on, a trap and an obstacle—the return of self which soils the soul. For this reason God takes away what he has given. But he does not take it away to deprive us of it forever. He takes it away so that he can better give it, so that he can give it back without the impurity of this evil sense of ownership which we mingle with it without noticing it in ourselves. The loss of the gift takes away our ownership. . . . Then the gift is no longer the gift of God. It is God himself in the soul. It is no more a gift of God because we consider it no longer as something apart from him, and something which the soul can possess.

Seeking the Face of God
Gary L. Thomas

Psalm 23:4 ## A LONG, DARK HAND **April 1**

Life was settling again into a comfortable routine. It had never been so promising for us. But again the shadow began to approach. First, it hardly seemed to be a shadow at all, but gradually it began to extend like a long, dark hand, reaching around the circumference of our lives.

The following fall, after we had been in Kalamazoo one year, Henry was troubled by a persistent cough—a mere chest cold, he told himself. At the same time, while driving, he found it difficult to turn the steering wheel with his left arm. A few mornings later as he shaved, he was puzzled because one side of his neck appeared considerably larger than the other. I insisted he see a doctor. After a cursory exam, the doctor concluded that the problem was a glandular infection. When antibiotics produced no effect, however, the doctor decided to do a biopsy. Though the report was negative, Henry felt strangely apprehensive.

During the winter months the swelling increased. Lea, now a registered nurse, urged Henry to see a specialist. A month later Henry visited Dr. Liddig, who after examining Henry's neck scheduled him for tests at the nearby Bronson Methodist Hospital. I was told to meet him there. Stepping outside into the heavenly, gentle snow, I walked up the hill three blocks to the hospital, past the reception desk, onto the elevator, through the nurses' station, to Henry's room. Carefully opening the door, I looked in. There sat Henry, on a chair in a white sheet-like hospital gown. He looked so different without his usual suit and tie, and I said, "You sure look funny in that outfit." "Valetta, I want you to sit down," he said. "I need to talk to you, and I couldn't wait. I think I'll be out of here soon. Actually, they got the reports back, and I told the doctor to level with me. I wasn't prepared, however, for the results."

Thrice Through the Valley
Valetta Steel

April 2
"HOW WOULD YOU LIKE TO PREACH MY FUNERAL"
Psalm 22:24

I sensed a numbness rising somewhere from the pit of my stomach, that same numbness I had felt listening to Danny's diagnosis. "Valetta," Henry continued, "that little lump on my neck is Hodgkin's disease." "Hodgkin's?" I echoed. "What's that?" Henry drew a deep breath. "A type of cancer—cancer of the lymph glands. There may be remissions for a time, but it is fatal. Don't be alarmed because there is a lot of hope, and God is on our side."

That Sunday night, as Henry had sat on his hospital bed pondering his clouded future, he suddenly felt that he and Pastor Larry must talk. Larry had been holding a rally at Vicksburg, a small town a few miles from Kalamazoo. Henry reached him there and said, "Larry, how would you like to preach my funeral sermon?" Larry had known Henry long enough to take this kind of banter without flinching. "Why sure, Henry, anytime. You name the place and time, and I'll be there." "No, Larry, this time I'm serious. I'm in the hospital right now, and the doctors have diagnosed my problem as Hodgkin's disease, cancer of the lymph glands." There was a long silence. "Look, Henry, I will be right over to see you after this service." That evening the two men who had already shared so much together talked in subdued voices, as men do when awed with a view of life in an entirely new perspective. "The doctors say I may have no more than a year or two to live, and perhaps as little as six months," Henry said. "How do you think I should spend them?" "Well, Henry," Larry proposed, "if you have the strength, I think you should take a trip to some mission field, preach to those who have never heard, and you will rejoice to see those faces in eternity." "Pray with me about it, Larry," Henry said. "This may be just what God wants me to do."

Thrice Through the Valley
Valetta Steel

April 3

"WHATEVER GOD HAS FOR ME"
I Peter 4:19

The doctor's prognosis, six months, perhaps a year, drastically altered our perspective on the future career of Reverend and Mrs. Henry Steel. As we turned to the Word for guidance, God gave us I Peter 4:19: "So if you are suffering according to God's will, keep on doing what is right and trust yourself to God who made you, for he will never fail you" (TLB). For the present, at least, we believed that God would have us carry on in what we were doing. We determined to take each day as it came, to live in "day-tight compartments," giving ourselves to the things that mattered. It had never been so easy to sort through the mundane affairs of life and focus on the "important." As Samuel Johnson once said, "The prospect of immediate death wonderfully concentrates the mind."

"Maybe God wants to heal Henry for his glory," many suggested. We believed in healing, had seen God heal others. Now, certainly, if anyone had the right to ask for divine healing as his children, we too had that right. A group of ministers came and prayed for Henry, anointing him with oil as instructed in Scripture (James 5:14). After they prayed, Henry began responding to treatments and strength returned. "Do you feel that God has touched you?" Dale Cryderman asked Henry one day. "I don't doubt that God has touched me," Henry responded, "but I don't feel that I can say it will be permanent. The doctors say the disease is in remission. Whatever God has for me, though, I pray I'll accept it. My desire is that God will do with my life whatever will bring him the most glory." Listening to Henry's response, it dawned on me that some deep change was taking place in my husband. There was a quiet poise, yes, a nobility in his sincere, unaffected response that was foreign to the old Henry I had known.

Thrice Through the Valley
Valetta Steel

April 4

TRANSMUTING PAIN INTO COMFORT
Psalm 107:28-29

"Henry," Larry responded thoughtfully, "if God has put that kind of a desire in your heart, there is no doubt that he is right now preparing you for a future in missionary work. Perhaps, when your work is finished here in Kalamazoo, he will lead you to OMS."

With Henry back home, looking and sounding little different from the Henry I had always known, my mind was numb. But now the whole sequence of events had an awful familiarity. We had been through the "countdown" with Danny, and here it was on us again. Somehow the heart cannot accept what the mind insists is true. I found myself struggling to awaken from a bad dream.

The following Sunday, Henry stood before the congregation. His voice sounded strong and even. Calmly, he announced the results of the hospital tests, concluding, "We can only go ahead and do the work God has given us to do. This is all any of us can do."

Now again, as it happened during the long vigil with Danny, day by day God opened to me the sweet resources of his Word in special ways. Through the Word, the Holy Spirit can work a curious alchemy which transmutes pain into comfort, and crushing sorrow into sweetness. Romans 8:28, a verse so time-worn it has almost become a cliché, was expounded anew to my heart by the Comforter. God would bring good out of this. How? I could not fathom but he would. I would keep watching for that good. Yes, I would look for miracles, and it would be an adventure.

Thrice Through the Valley
Valetta Steel

Matthew 19:27 ## THE ONLY SECURITY April 5

The next week a group of key laymen invited Henry to lunch in one of the city's finest restaurants. After a sumptuous meal, a spokesman turned to Henry. "Look at it this way, Pastor," he began, "we want you, we need you. We believe that God still has work for you in Kalamazoo. If your life is cut short by illness, Valetta and the kids will need security, and we can give that to them here." There was a calculated pause while the man waited for his words to register. Then he went on. "We're prepared to make you an offer. If you remain here in Kalamazoo, we will guarantee that your children will be provided for through college. What do you say?"

Later, in addressing a group of missionaries about what it means to cast oneself in faith on God, Henry recalled that moment. "Don't think that it didn't come as a tremendous temptation," he said. "The devil told me I was a fool to turn down an offer like that. But as I looked into the faces of those generous men with their promises of security, an answer came to me. It wasn't my answer but God's. 'There is no security,' I told them, 'outside the will of God.'"

Thrice Through the Valley
Valetta Steel

April 6

AN INCREASINGLY SWEET DISCOVERY
John 14:18-19

Another by-product of pain is the increasingly sweet discovery of the Holy Spirit as a Comforter in the life of God's child. Many Christians are timid and ineffective because they have not grasped this truth. I like to think of it this way: We all have had times when we have felt low in spirit, despondent, discouraged. Then we have entered a room and found a group of friends who know us, understand us and love us. As we've sat there in that company, we've felt warmed by their friendship and love, reaching out to us with invisible arms to embrace, soothe, and uplift. That is parallel to the ministry of the Holy Spirit in our lives. If we recognize him and meditate on God's words of wisdom, allowing him to perform his divine work, he will be there always, teaching, encouraging, comforting, uplifting.

Why does he do this? We read in II Corinthians 1:4 that he is the one "who comforteth us in all our tribulation, that we may be able to comfort them which are in any trouble. . . ." We also read, "You can be sure that the more we undergo sufferings for Christ, the more he will shower us with his comfort and encouragement" (II Corinthians 1:5 TLB).

Without the presence of Christ and his Word, I would at one time have viewed suffering as punishment. I would have responded with anger, resentment, bitterness, self-pity, and depression. However, since the Word has taught me that suffering is positive, I have looked for those positive results so I can follow God's directions in I Thessalonians 5:16-18 TLB: "Always be joyful. Always keep on praying. No matter what happens, always be thankful, for this is God's will for you who belong to Christ Jesus."

Thrice Through the Valley
Valetta Steel

April 7

AGONY ALL NIGHT
Mark 11:24

Friday, January 10 I awakened from a dream of Charles and me being in Tibet on horse and on a trail. My heart was filled with singing and as we galloped along I sang, "We're on the homeward trail." At prayers was impressed with Mark 11:24—"believing that ye have received" and "ye shall have." This is God's way. "He shall give thee the *desires* of thine heart" (Psalm 37:4) was so impressed upon my heart, also "The *desires* of the righteous shall be granted" and "He will fulfill the *desire* of them that fear Him" (Psalm 145:19).

Saturday, January 11 Poor Charles suffered agony all night. We were up before the dawn. Was so impressed with Exodus 14, 15. The enemy kept up a hot pursuit after the children of Israel. They "pursued" and all with united effort, but God just blew upon them and that was the end. "Mighty to save and strong to *deliver*." All they had to do was to "*trust and obey.*" If we try to fight the enemy we will get the worst of it. But when God does it He does it perfectly "*and the waters were divided.*"

Phoebe Pierce came to tea with us in the afternoon and we had a long talk over China. Charles bought for me McKenzie's new book, *Our Physical Heritage in Christ*. It is very helpful. A. B. Simpson writes, "All precious things are guarded by obstacles and adverse conditions. Even the kernel of the nut is hidden in a rugged shell. The gem is buried in the rocks and mountains. The pearl is found in the ocean depths, and in the spiritual world the richest prizes must be wrested from the hardest places."

Lettie Cowman Diary, 1924

April 8

PITY THYSELF
Isaiah 53:3

Pile up thy griefs; cherish thine *accidie*
And weep; for preference, apart,
But copiously; that those who keep in heart,
(Barbarians though they be)
A certain care for thee,
May, noticing the pathos in thine eyes,
Be filled with penitence, and, being wise
Henceforth to antidate thy woe,
Compassionately flow
Fluid with feeling to prepare for thee
Sweet ministration, maudlin sympathy.

Yea, pity thy dear self. Thy soul is torn
With much emotion over that which after all
Is but the common lot; for great or small
Must suffer. What though overborne
No heart need be, unless it magnify
Its griefs and choose to fly
Its comforts, still thou art forlorn;
And thou dost mourn,
Perceiving the anticipated grief
(For which is no relief
Obtained or promised) with sharp talons tear
Thy very vitals; rare
And precious such a prescience. Not a crumb
Of comfort can I find thee; but a jest
Intrudes itself: what if th' expected guest
Though thus punctiliously met
Should quite forget
To come?

O Man of sorrows, didst Thou ever feel
Thus towards Thyself?

Amy Carmichael

April 9
BEING BEFORE GOD'S THRONE
Psalm 91:11-12

(On learning of the abduction of her daughter). We finished our list and then went to prayer. I have experienced the feeling of being before God's throne in intercession before, but never as much as at this time.

"Oh, Lord God, every day I give you that day and everything either comes directly from You or from Satan and passes through You to reach us. This day is no different, even though it seems to be, so I know you allowed this. I know You have not lost your grip on our world. I know You still have Your hand over us. You are a God of order so You have a purpose and though I can't see how any purpose or any good could come from this, O God, I know You can. Please bring good out of it. Don't let her suffering be wasted. You've promised You will never allow more to come to us than we can bear. I can't see how any of us can bear this, but I claim this promise, knowing You have already put the power in us to meet our needs. Lord God, I don't know how to voice Dana's needs, but what I don't say, Holy Spirit, You say for me. Make Yourself known to her in a real way; let Your angels be made visible to her as they bring Your comfort. In her innocence, she cannot understand this act, so do not let her experience what is happening to her body. Lord, only let her hear Your voice, only let her feel Your touch, only let her see You. Lord, if she is alive, but hurt, please don't let her be lying somewhere out in the weather. Let her be covered, for if she is needing help she would never seek it if she is uncovered. You are in her, so You share her pain. Thank You for that truth, Lord. Others are hurting because they are sharing our pain. Show us how to comfort them. Give us such a peace that everyone will know it could come only from You."

Night of Anguish, Morning of Hope
Jean Mize

Philippians 4:7   "I WAS AT PEACE"   **April 10**

As we stood, I had a feeling of peace that is beyond my ability to describe. I don't know if it was the assurance that God would honor His promises, the confidence that when we are submissive to His plan He takes control, or whatever, but I was at peace. Nothing had changed, but deep down inside of me I felt He had already solved everything so I could rest. . . . With eyes closed, I let the Bible open where it would. When I opened my eyes, the verse I first saw was Jeremiah 22:10, "Weep ye not for the dead, neither bemoan him." I sobbed, "Lord, God, I thank you and praise Your name for taking her unto Yourself!" In my mind's eye, I saw her being comforted by Jesus Himself. Then, as I realized the permanent separation, I said, "O Precious Lord, I don't question Your calling her unto Yourself, but You are a God of order and purpose. Help me understand Your purpose in this so I can bear the separation." With closed eyes, I again opened my Bible as God guided my fumbling hands—and there it was, His message, clearly and unmistakably in Isaiah 55:8. "For my thoughts are not your thoughts, neither are your ways my ways, saith the Lord." I cried, "No, Lord, no matter what good could come of it, I could never have willingly given her up. I'm not like you, in that love You bore us, that I could freely give her." For the first time, I could understand a little about God's pain in giving up Jesus, His son. "Thank you for being willing to give Your son so that through His death and resurrection Dana is now with You and some day I'll see her again." Then I continued to read, "For as the heavens are higher than the earth, so are my ways higher than your way, and my thoughts than your thoughts." Sobbing, I said, "Yes, Lord, You see the overall plan where I can only see the part where my pain is. O, God, I think I understand. Through her death some will come to life and even though I don't understand it all."

Night of Anguish, Morning of Hope
Jean Mize

April 11

"OH! DO NOT FEAR IT"
Psalm 56:9

>Soul! Wouldst thou from the battle shrink
> And flee before the foe?
>Dost thou beneath the burden sink,
> And in the dust lie low?
>Oh! Waste not there vain tears and sighs;
> The trumpet soundeth clear;
>O'ercome, and to My glory rise!
> O'ercome, and triumph here!
>
>   Thomas H. Gill

Be not discouraged because of your soul's enemies. Are you troubled with thoughts, fears, doubts, imaginations, reasonings? Yea, do you see yet much in you unsubdued to the power of life? Oh! Do not fear it; but look to Him! Look up to the power which is over all their strength; wait for the descendings of the power upon you; abide in faith of the Lord's help and wait in patience till the Lord arise and see if His arm does not scatter what yours could not. So, be still before Him, and, in your stillness, believe in His name; yea, enter not into the hurryings of the enemy, though they fill the soul; for there is yet somewhat to which they cannot enter, from whence patience, faith and hope will spring up in you, even in the midst of all they can do.

                                              Isaac Penington

April 12

PAIN HAS A MINISTRY

I Peter 2:19

In his meditation "Pain Has a Ministry," Thurman raises the possibility that "pain has a ministry which adds to the sum total of life's meaning and, more importantly, to its fulfillment." Nevertheless, he sees as a danger the idea that a specific kind of pain might be sent into the life of an individual in order to perform a ministry in his or her life. Indulged, this idea can lead to fatalism and despair. God certainly did not give me AIDS. Still, Thurman writes, "any tragedy has inherent in it positive good. . . . The pain of life may teach us to understand life and, in our understanding of life, to love life."

Believing that pain has a purpose, I do not question either its place in the universe or my fate in becoming so familiar with pain through disease. Quite often, people who mean well will inquire of me whether I ever ask myself, in the face of my diseases, "Why me?" I never do. If I ask "Why me?" as I am assaulted by heart disease and AIDS, I must ask "Why me?" about my blessings and question my right to enjoy them. The morning after I won Wimbledon in 1974, I should have asked "Why me?" and doubted that I deserved the victory. If I don't ask "Why me?" after my victories, I cannot ask "Why me?" after my setbacks and disasters. I also do not waste time pleading with God to make me well. I was brought up to believe that prayer is not to be invoked to ask God for things for oneself, or even for others. Rather, prayer is a medium through which I ask God to show me God's will and to give me strength to carry out that will. . . .

I do not brood on the prospect of dying soon. I am not afraid of death. Perhaps fear will come to haunt me when the moment of death is closer. On the other hand, perhaps I will be even less fearful, more calm and at peace.

Days of Grace
Arthur Ash

April 13

WAITING FOR GOD

Deuteronomy 2:31

The Bible has a great deal to say about waiting for God, and the teaching cannot be too strongly emphasized. We so easily become impatient with God's delays. Yet much of our trouble in life is the result of our restless, and sometimes reckless, haste. We cannot *wait* for the answers to our prayers, although it may take many years for the things we pray for to be prepared for us. We are encouraged to walk with God, but often God walks very slowly. Yet there is also another side to this teaching: *God often waits for us.*

Quite often we fail to receive the blessing He has ready for us because we are not moving forward with Him. While it is true we miss many blessings by not waiting for God, we also lose numerous blessings by *overwaiting.* There are times when it takes strength simply to sit still, but there are also times when we are to move forward with a confident step.

Many of God's promises are conditional, requiring some initial action on our part. Once we begin to obey, He will begin to bless us. Great things were promised to Abraham, but not one of them could have been obtained had he waited in Chaldea. He had to leave his home, friends and country, travel unfamiliar paths, and press on in unwavering obedience in order to receive the promises. The ten lepers Jesus healed were told to show themselves to the priest, and *"as they went, they were cleansed"* (Luke 17:14). If they had waited to *see the cleansing* come to their bodies before leaving, they would never have seen it. God was waiting to heal them, and the moment their faith began to work, the blessing came. When the Israelites were entrapped by Pharaoh's pursuing army at the Red Sea, they were commanded to "go forward" (Exodus 14:15 KJV). No longer was it their duty to wait, but to rise up from bended knees and "go forward" with heroic faith.

J. R. Miller

April 14
WITHOUT RESERVATION OR REVERSAL
I Peter 5:10

Before we can establish a new and deeper relationship with Christ, we must first acquire enough intellectual light to satisfy our mind that we have been given the right to stand in this new relationship. Even the shadow of a doubt there will destroy our confidence. Then, having seen the light, we must advance. We must make our choice, commit to it, and take our rightful place as confidently as a tree is planted in the ground. As a bride entrusts herself to the groom at the marriage altar, our commitment to Christ must be once and for all, without reservation or reversal.

Then there follows a time of establishing and testing, during which we must stand still until the new relationship becomes so ingrained in us that it becomes a permanent habit. It is comparable to a surgeon setting a broken arm by splinting it to keep it from moving. God too has His spiritual splints He wants to put on His children to keep them quiet and still until they pass the first stage of faith. Sometimes the trial will be difficult, but "the God of all grace, who called you to his eternal glory in Christ, after you have suffered a little while will himself restore you and make you strong, firm and steadfast (I Peter 5:10). There is a natural law at work in sin and in sickness, and if we just drift along following the flow of our circumstances, we will sink under the power of the Tempter. But there is another law of spiritual and physical life in Christ Jesus to which we can rise and through which we can counterbalance and overcome the natural law that weighs us down.

There is a spiritual law of choosing, believing, abiding, and remaining steadfast in our walk with God. This law is essential to the working of the Holy Spirit in our sanctification and in our healing.

Days of Heaven Upon Earth
A. B. Simpson

April 15

"GRACE IS TRANSFORMING ME"
I Timothy 1:14

If I have learned anything over the past three years, it is that I desperately need and desire the grace of God. Grace has come to me in ways I did not expect. Friends have remained loyal and supportive, in spite of my struggles. Quietness, contentment and simplicity have gradually found a place in the center of my soul, though I have never been busier. I go to bed at night grateful for the events of the day, which I try to review and reflect on until I fall asleep, and I wake up in the morning eager to begin a new day. My life is rich and productive, like Iowa farmland in late summer. My children have become a constant source of joy to me, however demanding my role as a single parent. Almost every day I take a few moments to listen to them practice their instruments, play a game with them, shoot a few baskets, talk about the day, and read aloud to them. When they go to bed, I always follow them down to their rooms and tuck them in. And just before I crawl into bed, I sneak into their bedrooms and pray God's blessing upon them, a practice I learned from Lynda. For four years now I have coached David's soccer team, and I occasionally take Catherine out to dinner or a concert. John, my youngest, is my constant companion; friends call him my clone and shadow.

Despite the fact that I had been a Christian for many years before the accident, since then God has become a living reality to me as never before. My confidence in God is somehow quieter but stronger. I feel little pressure to impress God or prove myself to him; yet I want to serve him with all my heart and strength. My life is full of bounty, even as I continue to feel the pain of loss. Grace is transforming me, and it is wonderful. I have slowly learned where God belongs and have allowed him to assume that place—at the center of life rather than at the periphery.

A Grace Disguised
Jerry Sittser

April 16

THEIR SON CAME HOME
I Corinthians 13:4a

I ran across a story in my reading which I wish to pass along to you. I think it has something of a moral in it.

Back during the Second World War, the parents of a sailor went for several weeks without hearing anything from their son. Finally, they gave up on their son and considered him a war victim. However, near the end of the war, the parents, who lived in New Jersey, received a phone call from someone in San Diego, California. After a moment on the phone, the parents recognized the voice as that of their son. He was alive! During the course of the conversation, the son explained to his parents that for the past several months he had found it difficult to write because he had been taking care of a war victim. He told them that the person had been wounded in the war and had lost a leg, an arm, an eye, and part of his face.

His parents expressed concern over the poor sailor and then bragged on their son for taking care of him during all those months. The boy then asked his parents for permission to bring the boy home to live with them. He explained that the boy didn't have another home nor anyone to care for him. His parents expressed their concern for the wounded sailor and also told their son that they thought it was very noble of him to want to bring the sailor home with him. But after some conversation, the parents expressed their desire to their son that he not bring the boy home with him. They simply didn't want the job of taking care of such a battle-scarred sailor. Their son said he understood their feelings and that he would not bring the boy home. Expressing his love for the parents, the sailor son hung up.

You know, I guess it is hard to fulfill such a request as the sailor son made. For most of us don't want a disfigured person around the house, do we? None of us like to look at ugly things, and most of us judge a person's beauty by his physical appearance. We appreciate the good that those who are disfigured have done. But we would just rather not have to be burdened with them around the house.

Many times we feel sorry for the physically handicapped. So we give some little something that requires no effort on our part and does them little good. But I think what the handicapped person wants more than anything else is to be treated like a human being.

The morning after they spoke with their son, the couple in New Jersey received a telegram from the Naval officials stating that their son had jumped from a window to his death. The parents couldn't understand why their son had reacted so to their request until the body arrived and the casket was opened. Their son had only one arm, one leg, one eye, and a badly disfigured face.

Maybe we should try a little harder to love those who want to be treated like a human being.

Author Unknown

April 17
"IT PERVADED EVERYTHING"
Psalm 17:15

The five years (of Amy Carmichael's illness) lengthened out to sixteen and a half. Sometimes, half humorously but with a trace of seriousness, she would question the code whereby doctors and nurses use every possible means to keep the spark of life alight, or, to change the metaphor—and these are her own words—"you dear doctor people have something to answer for sometimes, I think, when you shut that shining door, at least don't give it even the gentlest push open."

All those who were privileged to nurse her speak of her sense of humor. "It pervaded everything," says one of them, "except when she was in severe pain. She gave appropriate names to her bad leg and arm, etc., and she would make up nonsense verses on the spot." But Amma was always like that. She writes of a subject that was perhaps nearer to her heart than any other—the danger of "unlove," and then immediately goes on: "How it hurts the heart to be out of love. I couldn't bear to be out of love with a hedgehog—if there was any way of getting into it again."

Acceptance of her helplessness never became easy. "The greatest difficulty," she writes, "is to readjust, to see others daily worn down by the Warfare of the Service, and to be oneself sheltered from all the hardest things. . . . Bring me out of this fog of the spirit. . . . Quicken Thou me. And till this prayer is fully answered, let no shadow of mine shadow any who come to this room. No, never, Lord." That prayer was heard. There must have been few indeed who did not see the Lord when they entered the Room of Peace. She, on her part, rejoiced in the visits of members of the Family because she saw Christ in them. "It is not only human love, it is something different that quickens the joy. I do truly see Him Whom we love best, in each one as he or she comes into the room."

Amy Carmichael of Dohnavur
Frank Houghton

April 18

LIKE BROKEN TOYS

John 16:13

C. S. Lewis, in his interesting book on "The Problem of Pain," gives us a wonderfully clear picture of the second stage, but is perhaps too humble to point us to the third stage. He writes, "My own experience is something like this. I am progressing along the path of life . . . when suddenly a stab of abdominal pain threatens serious disease and all my little happinesses look like broken toys. I remind myself that all these toys were never intended to possess my heart, that my true good is in another world, and my only real treasure is Christ. And perhaps, by God's grace, I succeed and for a day or two become a creature consciously dependent on God and drawing its strength from the right sources. But the moment the threat is withdrawn my whole nature leaps back to the toys. Thus the terrible necessity of tribulation is only too clear. God has had me only by dint of taking everything else away from me. Let Him but sheath that sword for a moment and I behave like a puppy when the hated bath is over. I shake myself as dry as I can and race off to reacquire my comfortable dirtiness . . . in the nearest flower bed. And that is why tribulations cannot cease, until God either sees us remade or sees that our remaking is now hopeless."

Wise words and full of truth and yet not the whole truth. For if it is true that man can only for a few days live the life of dependence upon God, then the Gospel is a failure and unable to give us victory over sin and the world. But, praise God, there is a third stage in Christian experience—the anointing or filling of the Holy Spirit—when dependence upon God becomes our daily attitude, a stage to which few of us seem to reach but a stage to which each one of us is called by our Heavenly Father. It is on this third stage, the filling or anointing of the Spirit, that I want us to meditate tonight.

Keswick in Kashmir
Eugene Erny

April 19
FACING THE FUNDAMENTAL THINGS
Isaiah 30:20

"Strip off your commonplace moods," God says; "if you are going to see into this thing, you must put on the right mood for discerning it." The agony of a man's affliction is often necessary to put him into the right mood to face the fundamental things of life. The Psalmist says, "Before I was afflicted I went astray, but now have I kept thy word." The Bible is full of the fact that there has to be an approach to the holy ground. If I am not willing to be lifted up, it is no use talking about the higher heights. In putting John the Baptist to death, Herod committed moral suicide. He ordered the voice of God to be silent in his life, and when Jesus Christ stood before him, "he questioned with Him in many words," for "he hoped to have seen some miracle done by Him"; but we read that Jesus "answered him nothing." It is quite possible for any man amongst us to get to a place where there is no such thing as truth or purity, and no man gets there without himself being to blame. Every man ought to be intellectually skeptical, but that is different from moral doubt which springs from a moral twist. No man can do wrong in his heart and see right afterwards. If I am going to approach the holy ground, I must get into the right frame of mind—the excellency of a broken heart.

The war has upset every man's nest, and we are face to face with a terrific upheaval in life; there is no civilized security anywhere on the globe. We have seen that there is no such thing as a Christian nation, and we have seen the unutterable futility of the organized Christian Church; and many a man who has had no tension in his life has been suddenly dumped "into the soup" and been obliged to face things that he never thought he would have to face.

The Shadow of an Agony
Oswald Chambers

April 20
TAKE AWAY THE SHARPS AND FLATS
II Corinthians 1:6

For many people suffering is the major stumbling block on the road to Christian faith. It has never been so for Muggeridge. Although his family circumstances were comfortable enough, he is no stranger to poverty or affliction; in fact he has been surrounded by both for most of his life. Muggeridge sees suffering as something basic and integral to human life, like sharps and flats are to music. Take away sharps and flats and there is no music; take away suffering and there is no life. The point is not to single out individual notes and debate their why and wherefores, but rather to catch the melody of the whole composition. Life is, to use his friend Anthony Powell's evocative phrase, a dance to the music of time in which he who strains may hear secret harmonies.

The key to Muggeridge's attitude is that he envisages life not as a *scientific*, but as an *artistic* creation. God's action in making us and our world and our universe was, as it were, comparable to Shakespeare's writing *King Lear*. As one cannot fully understand drama apart from the dramatist, so one cannot understand life, in all its vicissitudes, apart from God. This is not to suggest that we can now, or perhaps ever, fully grasp our Creator's mysterious purposes, any more than one sees the denouement of a play midway through the third act. But from the first moment when King Lear's folly leads him to mistake Regan's and Goneril's humbug for Cordelia's genuine love, the discerning eye senses rather than sees the outlines of a dark, foreboding future. So one may sense or, as Saint Paul put it—"see through a glass darkly," how contemporary man who turns his back on a drama in which suffering is an essential part and harkens instead to the sedulous voices of doctors and eugenicists who promise to eliminate suffering, perhaps even death itself, is fashioning a tragedy by his own hand.

Malcom Muggeridge A Life
Ian Hunter

April 21

A STRANGE KIND OF COMFORT
I Timothy 6:12

There is a strange kind of comfort which is nevertheless very real. If anyone reading my words is in trouble, let me say this: The fact that you are unhappy or troubled is no indication that you are not a Christian. Indeed, I would go further and say that if you have never had any trouble in your Christian life I should very much doubt whether you are a Christian at all. There is such a thing as false peace; there is such a thing as believing delusions. The whole of the New Testament and the history of the Church throughout the centuries bear eloquent testimony to the fact that this is a "fight of faith," and not to have any troubles in your soul is, therefore, far from being a good sign. It is, indeed, a serious sign that there is something radically wrong, and there is a very good reason for saying that. For from the moment we become Christians, we become the special objects of the attention of the devil. As he besieged and attacked our Lord, so does he besiege and attack all the Lord's people. "Count it joy," says James, "when ye fall into diverse temptations" or trials. That is the way your faith is proved, for not only is it a test of your faith, in a sense it is a proof that you have faith.

Spiritual Depression
D. Martyn Lloyd-Jones

Disturb us O Lord when we are too well pleased with ourselves; When our dreams come true only because we have dreamed too little; When we arrive safely only because we sailed too close to the shore; When with the abundance of things we are losing our thirst for more of God; When in loving time, we have ceased to dream of eternity; When in our desire to build on this earth we have lost our vision of a new heaven. We need to venture on wider seas where the storms show God's mastery; Where losing sight of land we see the stars. God is inviting the brave to follow him.

Author Unknown

April 22

I SHALL LISTEN
I Samuel 3:9

If I can learn some lesson through this pain,
If I can hear God's voice above the storm,
And catch His words and pass them on again
To other suffering ones, if I can warm
Some troubled heart with cheer and sympathy,
And help it find a haven of release,
If I can speak the words God speaks to me
To one soul that has lost its poise, its peace,
This, even this, shall not have been in vain!
God keep me quiet, keep me very still,
That through the heavy darkness and the rain,
The thunder crashing loud upon my sill,
I may discern Your voice, that I may hear
The gentle, helpful, loving words You say.
The storm runs high, God make the words quite clear,
And I shall listen carefully today.

Grace Noll Crowell

The ladies now supplied him (Watchman Nee) with milk and good food and such medicines as were available, and the brothers waited on him. The dark days dragged on into weeks as he continued to lose weight and feel his strength ebb away. "He was so humble," Luke recalls, "so desirous to be healed. He asked me every day to anoint him in the Lord's name and pray." When he was too exhausted to read, his memory of Scripture came to the rescue: "Humble yourself under the mighty hand of God"—but he dared not yet complete the sentence. "For two months," he observed, "I lived daily in the very jaws of Satan."

Against the Tide
Angus I. Kinnear

I Corinthians 1:27 **O MY WEAKNESS** **April 23**

My weakness! My weakness! Oh, that I had the ability of a Paul, the eloquence of an Apollos, the strength of a Peter, the courage of a Daniel, the burden of a Jeremiah, the triumphant faith of an Isaiah, the power of a Moses . . . above all, if I had the divine compassion of my Master Himself, then, hear and be ashamed, O earth! I could not, in some places, do many mighty works, because of their unbelief! I conclude that my own weakness reproaches me, perhaps, when it should not, but this does not always hinder me from accusing myself of being a failure. Is not this the common experience of the God-fearing, God-bearing, burden-bearing servants of God? . . .

Jeremy Taylor likens us to the fabled lamps in the tomb of Terentia which burned underground for many ages, but as soon as they were brought out and saw a brighter light, went out in darkness. Then he adds, "So long as we are in the retirements of sorrow, of want, of fear, of sickness, we are burning and shining lamps; but when God lifts us up from the gates of death and carries us abroad into the open air, to converse with prosperity and temptations, we go out in darkness." There is beauty and some truth in all this, but the danger is that such a life would produce only a morbid and ghastly piety, and these bright lights would irradiate—"only a tomb." But God knows how to temper the sunshine and the rain. He who made us, and who tutors us, alone knows what is the exact measure of light and shade, sun and cloud, frost and heat, which will best tend to mature those flowers which are the object of His celestial husbandry; and which, when transplanted into the paradise of God, are to bloom there forever in exquisite loveliness.

Holiness and the Human Element
H. A. Baldwin

April 24

A STAGNANT SOUL

Romans 15:30

Then, who is it that has reached a place in his religious experience where he is completely satisfied? He may be satisfied with the quality, and he is if his heart is cleansed, but the quantity is another question. Show us the man who has reached a place of complete satisfaction, and we will show you a man who has become stagnant in soul. The Psalmist declares that he will be satisfied when he awakes in the likeness of God. There is a possibility that present attainments when measured by the attainments of others, and the vast possibilities of grace will seem so meager that there will be danger of the soul sinking in despair unless strenuous effort is immediately made for further advancement.

Just a note here in passing: Do not attempt to gage your own experience by the reported experiences of men whose lives have been written, such as Bramwell, Carvosso, Fletcher, etc. Why? Simply because the biographer has often omitted the struggles and losses and inserted the victories and good things. They want to make a hero of their favorite. God only know the struggles of soul through which these great men passed before they gained the victories which are recorded. Are you, too, willing to struggle? Then you can be great—in God's sight, if not in man's.

Holiness and the Human Element
H. A. Baldwin

April 25

THE FURNACE

Isaiah 48:10

One of the purposes of suffering is the building of character. Certainly Job was a better man for having gone through the furnace. James explained this process to us (1:2-12). If words are a test of character, than oaths would indicate there is yet work to be done. When Peter poured out those oaths in the courtyard (Matthew 26:72), he was giving evidence that his character was still in need of a transformation.

James wanted to encourage us to be patient in times of suffering. Like the farmer, we are waiting for a spiritual harvest, for fruit that will glorify God. Like the prophets, we look for opportunities for witness, to share the truth of God. And, like Job, we wait for the Lord to fulfill His loving purpose, knowing that He will never cause His children to suffer needlessly. And, like Job, we shall have a clearer vision of the Lord and come to know Him better for having been in the furnace of affliction. "Be patient, for the coming of the Lord draweth nigh!"

Be Mature
Warren Wiersbe

Considering how little thou art worth, what great matter is that? Yes, thou wilt lose thyself if thou wilt abandon thyself to God, but thou wilt lose thyself in *Him*. Alas, people are so blind. They consider this as unsuitable for great minds. It is something too low for them. This path is very little known because most are so wise, and prudent. It is "hid . . . from the wise and prudent, and . . . revealed . . . unto babes" (Matthew 11:25 AV). By what route does God lead to Himself? By ways quite opposite to those we should imagine for ourselves. He builds up by casting down. He gives life by taking it away.

Spiritual Torrents
Madame Guyon

April 26

PERIODS OF DRYNESS
Job 16:12; 29:2-3

He knows the bitter weary way;
  He knows the endless striving day by day;
He knows how hard the fight has been;
  The clouds that come our lives between,
The wounds the world hath never seen,
  He knows.
He knows! O thought so full of bliss!
  For though our joys on earth we miss,
We still can bear it, feeling this,
    HE KNOWS!

Author Unknown

The soul had been in such deep peace that it had not thought of ever losing it. It becomes inactive and ceases to advance. God has to move it on. He does this by withdrawing the old experience. To its astonishment instead of *manifestly* advancing from strength to strength in the spiritual life or at least maintaining its ground, the calm it thought it possessed forever seems gone and the *will* appears powerless to control. The soul is always "accepted in the Beloved" when it draws near in full assurance of faith (Hebrews 10:19-23). It will then be kept free from all "oppression of the enemy," and overcome him and all his accusations "because of the blood of the Lamb" (Revelation 12:10-11). Moreover as the soul is led on, by the Holy Spirit, from "faith to faith" in the knowledge of God (Romans 1:17), and the word of God effectually works to the dividing of soul and spirit (Hebrews 4:12), it must cast itself more and more, in faith, upon the life of Him who is a life-giving Spirit (I Corinthians 15:45), for "we are made partakers of Christ, if we hold fast the beginning of our confidence firm unto the end" (Hebrews 3:14).

Spiritual Torrents
Madame Guyon

April 27

A BRUISED REED

Isaiah 42:3

Because he loves you, even your glimmering little wick He will trim to give light in the surrounding darkness. Only recently when we asked a man why he was seeking conversion, he said that he could hold out no longer against the life and witness of a Christian workmate who could scarcely speak for stammering. . . . "The Lord was looking for a man weak enough to use and He found me," said Hudson Taylor. "We may easily be too big for God to use, but never too small," Moody observed.

Awake My Heart
Sidlow Baxter

You enter the Christian life by faith in Christ, you walk by faith in Christ and you grow by faith in Christ. Everything you receive in the Christian life is from Christ by faith. That's why Paul says in another place that it is from "faith to faith" that you progress in the Christian life (Romans 1:17). Faith establishes, not tests.

When a trial confronts you—a death in the family, a financial reversal, a schedule delay—it is actually a test of your faith in God. God said He would comfort you (II Corinthians 1:3-4), lovingly provide for all your needs (Philippians 4:19), and work things together for your good (Romans 8:28). What then, is being tested? Your character? Are you patient enough, content enough, secure enough? NO! Your confidence that God will keep His Word is tested. This is the way faith is stabilized and matured: by the repeated experience of God fulfilling His Word when it appears He won't come through.

Josh McDowell and Dale Bellis

April 28

DRIVEN TO DESPAIR

I Kings 19:3-5

Some of God's most successful ministers are most beset with discouragement because they feel their labors are producing so little results. It is said that at one time Bishop Asbury had fully made up his mind that his work was a failure and that he would quit. In this frame of mind he slipped into a meeting, taking a seat unobserved near the door. During the testimony meeting, a sister arose and stated that she owed her salvation to Bishop Asbury, giving time and particulars. When she was seated, the bishop arose, told of his temptation and decision, but declared that if he had been instrumental in the salvation of one soul he would continue to preach the gospel.

Some of the best of God's people have almost been driven to despair in their very dying moments. A notable example of this is found in the annals of early Methodism. Thomas Walsh, a Methodist minister, was so holy and devoted that even Wesley stood in awe of him, but his biographer says that in his dying hour "his great soul lay thus, as it were, in ruins for some considerable time, and poured out many a heavy groan and speechless fear from an oppressed heart and dying body. He sadly bewailed the absence of Him whose wanted presence had so often given him the victory over the manifold contradictions and troubles which he endured for His name's sake." The characters of neither good nor bad men can be surely inferred from their dying words—it is the life that tells.

The discouragement which blasts the soul: When I yield, in the midst of the pressures, to a distrustful spirit; when I become despondent concerning God's power or willingness to help me. . . . Then and only then is my spiritual strength stolen away. No man can be his whole bigness for God when he is looking sadly at his weaknesses, or despondently viewing his temptations.

Holiness and the Human Element
H. A. Baldwin

April 29

SUFFERINGS UNEXPLAINED
John 11:17-22

We accept life's mysteries and sufferings unexplained because they are known to God, and we know Him. Of course we seek answers from the Bible and from experience, our own and that of others. But when no answer is forthcoming, we don't attempt to rationalize ("It could have been worse," "Look at how many people heard the gospel through the funeral service," or "Things are getting so bad on earth; think of what he's been spared by not growing up"). Reason, we believe, is a deceptively weak crutch for faith. Reason gropes in the dark for answers, while faith waits for God. But we also believe that God is love. He is kind. "He does not lightly afflict the children of men." I cannot explain it, but my wife and I have never been more convinced of His love for us and our children than when we have returned from a fresh grave.

Jesus wept with the suffering sisters of Lazarus, who had died. He suffered anguish of soul the night before His execution; He cried, "My God, My God, why have you forsaken me?" on the cross. He shared our humanity, our grief, our pain. But He also taught that God is sovereign, and He was the personification of His love on earth. Here is the mystery: the kind and sovereign God permits suffering and agony. One thing we must remember is that this is not "the best of all possible worlds." It is a world in rebellion against the kind God, a world of evil and sin and pain. It is a world, as Jesus explained, where God's enemy is at work. In such a world, it is easy to forget God, to live only to enjoy the banquet hall without thinking about the painful exit door. But God will not permit this; He interrupts the banquet with suffering. "God whispers to us in our pleasures," C. S. Lewis wrote, "speaks in our conscience, but shouts in our pain. Pain is God's megaphone to rouse a deaf world."

The View from the Hearse
Joseph Bayly

Psalm 42:7   **"YES, FATHER, YES!"**   **April 30**

Job never took his sufferings from the Sabeans, nor the Chaldeans, nor from "natural causes." He took them from God via Satan. "The Lord gave and the Lord hath taken away. Blessed be the name of the Lord." Or was it the psalmist who taught (the saints) this truth? When the storm smote the psalmist, he refused to accept it just as a storm. He must find God in it! With mighty faith he plants God in its heart and, as that icy green water engulfs him, he cries: "All thy waves and thy billows are gone over me." Somewhere, at the heart of this awful experience, he holds that there is a loving purpose of God. They are God's waves and God's billows.

Or was it from the Savior Himself that the saint learned this secret transformation of suffering? Every saint knows Gethsemane. He has overheard his Lord say, "Father, if it be possible, let this cup pass from me," and has overheard Him also say later, "The cup which my Father hath given me, shall I not drink it?" One can transform the contents of a cup if one can change the hand from which one takes it. It is as though the Lord said, "If I must drink it, I will not take it from Judas, Pilate, Caiaphas, or the people. I will take it only from my Father. . . ." The saint always takes the cup from his Father. He reckons little of secondary causes. Half the secret of his triumph over suffering is there.

Here, too, you have the secret of Etienne Mattier reeling beneath an awful blow and crying, "No questions, Lord! No questions! Only Amens!" Here also we understand St. Francis de Sales's beloved phrase: "Yes, Father, Yes!—and always Yes!" By this means, I learned to understand the repetitive word of a little saint of my own acquaintance. . . . "Have it your own way, Father."

The Pure of Heart
W. E. Sangster

May 1
AN ACCIDENT WAITING TO HAPPEN
Romans 5:1-4

Affliction is anonymous . . .; it deprives its victims of their personality and makes them into things. It is indifferent; and it is the coldness of this indifference—a metallic coldness—that freezes all those it touches right to the depths of their souls. They will never find warmth again. They will never believe any more that they are anyone.

Simone Weil

My brother-in-law Jack said that life in this world is an accident waiting to happen, and there is not much we can do about it. Common sense, of course, tells us to wear seatbelts, drive the speed limit, eat healthy food, exercise regularly, get sufficient rest, and make wise decisions. These good habits will minimize accidents but not eliminate them. Did I really want to know what was going to happen in the future so that I could protect myself from the accidents that inevitably and randomly occur in every person's life? And if I knew what accidents were looming ahead and could change the course of my life, would I then want to know what accidents would befall me as a result of the new course I had set for myself? What I really wanted, he said, was to be God—an option obviously closed to me. So, if I really wanted to protect myself from accidents, he continued, I should lock myself inside an antiseptic bubble and live there for the rest of my life. But who would want that? Better, he concluded, to brace myself for accidents and endure them as best I can. Better to give up my quest for control and live in hope. Maybe that is why most people seem to weather loss so well. They learn to live in hope. It is a wonder, considering the suffering that awaits us all, how few of us live in constant dread, utterly immobilized by what may happen to us. Somehow we manage to live reasonably well, expecting the best and, when the time comes to face the worst, accepting it as part of the bargain of living in a fallen world.

A Grace Disguised
Jerry Sittser

May 2

"THE CROSS IS MY WEAPON"
Matthew 24:9

(Testimony of a Formosan tribesman during World War II) "We were discovered by Japanese government policemen. They took us to the police station and forced us to stand before their judge. One of the Christian women was Chi Oang, who was the first to take the Gospel to the Tayal tribe. The policemen especially hated her because she had been responsible for leading multitudes of her tribesmen out of darkness into the light of God's love.

"We were all put into a dark cell for four days and were given nothing to eat. When they could not force us to recant and deny the Lord who bought us with His own blood, they again brought us before the judge. Chi Oang was the first to undergo torture. They forced her to kneel while they poured water into her nose so she could not breathe. The rest of us were severely beaten in an effort to force us to renounce our Lord Christ. But with the courage given to us by God Himself, we all firmly said that if we died for Jesus we would not regret it. This firm stand seemed to reduce their hatred for us. Even while they tortured and persecuted us, we continued to pray for the judge and for the policemen. On the fifth day, they realized that we were immovable in our faith and would not retract, so they released us. We were weak and wounded but still rejoicing in the Lord." Many of the believers died as a result of such ill treatment, but Chief Ga Tzao continued to travel and preach. He was fearless, believing that God would spare his life as long as He wanted him to bear the message of salvation to those who had never heard. His fortitude was like that of Philip Melanchthon who, at the time of the Reformation, said, "The cross is my weapon of defense and the Bible is my weapon of attack." Most certainly the tribal domains were passing through a great reformation from devil worship to Christianity.

From Headhunters to Hallelujahs/
Doris Trefren

May 3
STUMBLING BLOCKS INTO STEPPING STONES
John 5:27

Nor would I have you ignorant that the Day of Judgment is coming and you will be expected to give account. We do not know of what character the Judgment will be . . . but there can be no doubt of the fact. Nor is there any doubt as to the identity of the Judge. John tells us that all Judgment has been committed unto Jesus. How are you preparing for that Judgment? Are you polishing your excuses? Look at the face of your Judge! Remember what He suffered! Can you possibly offer that excuse to Him?

Will you plead a physical disability with Paul and Helen Keller and Frances Ridley Havergal standing at His side? . . . Will you come up and whisper "illegitimate" with Alexander Whyte at His right hand? How can you? . . .

All these difficulties can be used for your own spiritual profit if you will come to them in the Spirit of God. There is a power with God, available to us all, that makes stumbling blocks into stepping stones. I'm old enough to have learned this: that the man who has every advantage is not the man to envy. The man who gets everything he wants, gets something he doesn't want, either an unsympathetic hardness of heart or a dangerous flaw in his will. Adversity is one of our greatest teachers. God polishes His jewels that way.

Why Jesus Never Wrote a Book
W. E. Sangster

May 4

WHEN WE CEASE TO BLEED
Isaiah 28:28

Many of us cannot be used as food for the world's hunger because we have yet to be broken in Christ's hands. "Grain must be ground to make bread," and being a blessing of His often requires sorrow on our part. Yet even sorrow is not too high a price to pay for the privilege of touching other lives with Christ's blessings. The things that are most precious to us today have come to us through tears and pain.

J. R. Miller

God has made me as bread for His chosen ones, and if it is necessary for me to "be ground" in the teeth of lions in order to feed His children, then blessed be the name of the Lord.

Ignatius

To burn brightly our lives must first experience the flame. In other words, we cease to bless others when we cease to bleed. Poverty, hardship and misfortune have propelled many a life to moral heroism and spiritual greatness. Difficulties challenge our energy and our perseverance but bring the strongest qualities of the soul to life. It is the weights on the old grandfather clock that keep it running. And many a sailor has faced a strong head wind, yet used it to make it to port. God has chosen opposition as a catalyst to our faith and holy service.

The most prominent characters of the Bible were broken, threshed and ground into bread for the hungry. Because he stood at the head of the class, enduring affliction while remaining obedient, Abraham's diploma is now inscribed with these words: "The Father of Faith."

Lettie Cowman

Job 42:3

GOD IS GOD
May 5

It's easy to thank God when He does what we want. But God doesn't always do what we want. Ask Job.

His empire collapsed, his children were killed, and what was a healthy body became a rage of boils. From whence came this torrent? From whence will come any help?

Job goes straight to God and pleads his case. His head hurts. His heart hurts. And God answers. Not with answers but with questions. An ocean of questions. . . . After several dozen questions . . . Job has gotten the point. What is it?

The point is this: God owes no one anything. No reasons. No explanations. Nothing. If he gave them, we couldn't understand them.

God is God. He knows what He is doing. When you can't trace His hand, trust His heart.

Grace for the Moment
Max Lucado

A fine story told of a professor of Harvard University effectively illustrates this higher mode of facing perplexity. The professor sought an interview with Philips Brooks upon a certain problem. He spent a radiant hour with the great preacher and came out a changed man whose life was transfigured. But presently it dawned upon him that during the interview he had quite forgotten to ask Phillips Brooks about his problem!

He says, however, "I did not care; I had found out that what I needed was not the solution of a special problem, but the contagion of a triumphant spirit."

The Quest of Serenity
G. H. Morling

May 6
PERSONAL ARMAGEDDONS
Matthew 11:29

We don't deliberately look for trouble in life. It comes. Suffering is a universal fact; no one can escape its claws. The rain falls upon the just and the unjust. We all face personal armageddons.

Some people have the mistaken idea that becoming a Christian will be a shelter from the personal storms of life. The story of many of our hymns will swiftly dispel this myth. A large number of our favorite hymns and spiritual songs were composed in the crucible of life.

Many illustrations could be given. Charlotte Elliott wrote "Just As I Am" when she was a helpless invalid. Frances Ridley Havergal, author of "Take My Life" and many other hymns, suffered much ill health. Fanny Crosby was blind, yet out of her suffering came such lovely songs as "Safe in the Arms of Jesus." The hymn "God Moves in a Mysterious Way" was composed by the poet William Cowper in an hour of great mental distress.

Billy Graham

I am thinking so much of you. My prayer for you is that the peace of God may enter into your heart so that you will spread peace all round.

The only way I know that leads to this is the way of Matthew 11:29. Verse 28 has a word for you, too, but verse 29 is all for you. You have borne a yoke—sometimes a heavy yoke—but His yoke is easy and His burden is light, because we do not bear it alone. It is a *double yoke*. We are fellow workers with Him in a new sense, when we give up making our own yoke and take His. It is a definite transaction between Him and our souls. "Take." He won't put it on us; He asks us to take. Then when we do, it is His yoke, not ours, thereafter.

Amy Carmichael

May 7
WHAT SUPPORTED ME?
Matthew 28:19-20

David Livingstone once addressed a group of students at Glasgow University. When he rose to speak, he bore on his body the marks of his African struggles. Severe illnesses on nearly 30 occasions had left him gaunt and haggard. His left arm, crushed by a lion, hung limp at his side. After describing his trials and tribulations, he said, "Would you like me to tell you what supported me through all the years of exile among people whose language I could not understand and whose attitude toward me was always uncertain and often hostile? It was this, 'Lo, I am with you always even unto the end of the world.' On those words I staked everything and they never failed."

Billy Graham

You can be a Christian, a saved man, without exerting a tremendous influence upon the lives of people around you, but it is impossible to live in intimate communion with Christ without leaving a mark on the life of every man with whom you associate.

Wilbur Chapman

Travelers tell us about a rain tree. It grows to be about 60 feet high and has a diameter of about 3 feet at the root. It imbibes and condenses moisture from the atmosphere as no other tree does and so it is called the rain tree. When all else is parched and dry, dying for water, this tree can draw from many sources the water of life. Its bark is usually dripping wet, not only in the moist season but also during the torrid heat of summer. So with the Christian who has learned to draw upon the resources of Christ.

Selected

FORCED TO RETURN TO THEE
Matthew 5:4

May 8

Behold what thou art, O my God, or at least what thou art in thy works, for no one can approach that source of glory which dazzles our eyes, to understand all that thou are in thyself. But at least I see clearly that thou makest use of the evils and the imperfections of creatures to create the good which thou hast resolved upon.

Thou hidest thyself behind the intruder, who annoys the faithful person who is impatient and jealous of his freedom to work, and who consequently needs to be interrupted to mortify his pleasure in being free and methodical in his good works.

It is thou, my God, who dost use slanderous tongues to destroy the reputation of the innocent, who need to add to their innocence the sacrifice of their reputation, which was too dear to them. It is thou who by the wicked schemes and mean tricks of the envious dost reverse the fortunes and the prosperity of thy servants, who still cling to this vain prosperity.

It is thou who dost suddenly hurry to the tomb people to whom life is a continual danger, and death a blessing which places them in safety. It is thou who makest of the death of these people a remedy, bitter indeed, but very healthy for those who clung to them in too intense and too tender a friendship.

Thus the same blow which takes away one person to save him, detaches another and prepares him for his death by the death of those who were the dearest to him. Thus in thy mercy, O my God, thou sheddest bitterness on all which is not thee, so that our hearts, formed to love them and to live by thy love, may be forced to return to thee, feeling that there is not support in all the rest.

Fenelon

May 9
EXCEPT THROUGH TRIALS
II Corinthians 7:5

Why is it that God leads us in this way, allowing such strong and constant pressure on us? One of His purposes is to show us His all-sufficient strength and grace more effectively than if we were free from difficulties and trials. "We have this treasure in jars of clay to show that this all-surpassing power is from God and not from us" (II Corinthians 4:7).

Another purpose is to bring us a greater awareness of independence upon Him. God is constantly trying to teach us how dependent we are on Him—that we are held completely by His hand and reliant on His care alone. This is exactly where Jesus Himself stood and where He desires us to stand. We must stand not with self-made strength but always leaning upon Him. And our stand must exhibit a trust that would never dare to take even one step alone. This will teach us to trust Him more. There is no way to learn of faith except through trials. They are God's school of faith, and it is much better for us to learn to trust Him than to live a life of enjoyment. And once the lesson of faith has been learned, it is an everlasting possession and an eternal fortune gained. Yet without trust in God, even great riches will leave us in poverty.

> Why must I weep when others sing?
>   "To test the deeps of suffering."
> Why must I work while others rest?
>   "To spend my strength at God's request."
> Why must I lose while others gain?
>   "To understand defeat's sharp pain."
>
> Why must this lot of life be mine
> When that which fairer seems is thine?
>   "Because God knows what plans for me
> Will blossom in eternity."

Days of Heaven Upon Earth
A. B. Simpson

May 10

READ THE LIVES OF THE SAINTS
II Timothy 4:10, 16

He who raises his head above the heads of others will sooner or later be decapitated. Or, in more Scriptural terms, "All that would live godly in Christ Jesus shall suffer persecution."

Watchman Nee

The Apostle Paul experienced this (trials) constantly. You remember how he says, "Demas hath forsaken me." That was not a light thing to Paul; he was troubled by it. He had to stand his trial absolutely alone; people on whom he thought he could rely suddenly ran away from him and there he was, alone. "No man stood with me." That is the kind of thing that grieves a Christian, and you have but to read the lives of the saints to find this kind of thing constantly. Read the journals of John Wesley and you will find he was frequently in this condition because of misunderstandings.

This, on a big scale, is to be found in the life of Charles Haddon Spurgeon in connection with the famous "Down Grade" controversy. Men who he had regarded as friends, and some of whom he had trained in his own college at his own expense, suddenly fell away from him. You have but to read his account of it to see how he was hurt and grieved. He was in heaviness because men whom he thought he could rely on suddenly failed him. It no doubt shortened his life.

I was reading in the journals of George Whitefield recently an account of this very thing. Whitefield had had a season of exceptional nearness to Christ and he was rejoicing in it, but he makes a note in his journal to remind himself of the fact that in some strange way such experiences were often followed by grievous trials, and "no doubt," he says, "I shall be subject to that again." He knew it, it was his experience; it is almost an inevitable law in the life of the man of God in a world of sin.

D. Martyn Lloyd-Jones

May 11

THE TROUBLE WITH TROUBLE
Job 5:7

The transatlantic connection was filled with static, but the sound of a broken heart on the other end of the line was all too clear. It was Craig's wife, Martha. As she spoke, everything inside me felt crushed. Craig and I grew up together. We attended the same college, played soccer together, and in fact looked so much alike that we were often mistaken for brothers. He married a pretty coed in college and after graduation enlisted in the Air Force. I hadn't seen Craig in years. Imagine my surprise when our paths crossed in the town where I began my first pastorate. Talk had it that Craig and Martha had been far from the Lord. When Martie and I heard that they had recommitted their lives to the Lord, we were overjoyed. It wasn't long before they became active in our little church. He taught our high school boys and Martha taught the girls. Before long, God led them to work with troubled teens on the island of Haiti.

They'd been in Haiti only a week, and now Martha was telling me that Craig had suffered a serious injury while diving into a pool. He didn't make it through the night. Martha was there alone. Less than 30 years old and already a widow. Her dreams and hopes dashed. How could this be? Job's comforters may not have had a lot right, but Eliphaz certainly had a point. "Man," he said, "is born to trouble as surely as sparks fly upward." Let's face it: trouble happens. In fact, as a friend of mine points out, if we really understood the depth of the Fall and the grip that sin has on this world, we would be surprised that anything good happens *at all*. The trouble with trouble is that is seems so indiscriminate. Good people suffer. Bad people prosper. Exploiters exploit with seeming impunity. Children are victimized by crack-addict parents, and elderly folks end up being neglected and marginalized.

Simply Jesus
Joseph M. Stowell

May 12
A PART OF HIS FATHER'S PLAN
John 19:30

After Craig's tragic death, questions plagued us all. Why, God? Why now? Why them? But God's grace was strengthening Martha's heart. In the midst of her hurt, she chose to see the suffering as a shared experience with Jesus. She wrote to me that she had decided to view her pain through His loss at the Cross. She marked the loneliness and despair in her heart, recalling the loneliness and despair Jesus had experienced for her. His words, "My God, why have You forsaken me?" echoed in her soul. She found solace in Jesus' confidence that His loss was not in vain but that His suffering was a part of His Father's wise and bigger plan. She chose to endure the pain for the joy that was set before her, just as Jesus did (Hebrews 12:2).

Martha found unusual supporting grace in meeting Jesus in her loss, and it opened the door of her heart to His strong and abiding presence. Recently she wrote in reflection: "During that time of emotional recovery, God revealed Himself in ways I could not imagine. Physical, financial, emotional, and spiritual needs were met in dramatic and supernatural ways."

Today Martha teaches a large women's Bible class, has a ministry to women in prison, and has a son who serves as a missionary. Had she not met Jesus in her sorrow, I wonder where lesser instincts might have taken her?

Simply Jesus
Joseph M. Stowell

May 13
"RIGHT IN THE MIDST OF YOUR PAIN"
Luke 9:23

If you are thinking here of the Cross, then you will struggle to meet Him in your sufferings. Most likely, none of us will be crucified—not literally. But the sufferings of Christ are far more extensive, more identifiable, than only the injustices of Golgotha.

Have you ever felt lonely, displaced, misrepresented, or misunderstood? Have you ever found yourself severely restricted? Denied of your rights and privileges? Betrayed by a close friend? Have you ever been left out of the power group and plotted against? Have you ever done right and suffered for it? Have you ever tasted the bitterness of injustice? Have you ever longed for your friends to stand with you in your moment of need, only to sense they're really too consumed with their own needs to pay much attention? Have you ever experienced unbearable pain? Have you ever felt abandoned by God? These, and many more, are the sufferings Jesus endured on our behalf. He bore them in love, patiently and willingly for us, so that "by His stripes, we are healed." If you found yourself nodding your head to any of those questions, you can identify with what He felt and suffered for you.

The question is not Are you willing to suffer? We have little choice about that. The real question is: Are you willing to meet Jesus there—right in the midst of your pain? Are you willing to make that choice? To experience Him in the midst of our pain requires that we stop whining about our trials. How often do we find our hearts complaining, *Why is He doing this to me? Does He really care? Does He truly feel the ache in my heart and the anguish in my spirit? Does He have any idea what He's putting me through?* Residual anger, revenge, bitterness, self-imposed depression, and despair are the rewards we reap from these attitudes.

Simply Jesus
Joseph M. Stowell

May 14

A MEANINGFUL COMPANION
I Peter 2:21

If we really desire to experience Him, we need to stop blaming God, reverse our self-centered demand for release, and realize for the first time in our lives that we are getting a firsthand experience of what He felt and experienced as He suffered for us. Stop and identify the type of trouble you feel. Think through Christ's suffering and identify where His pain meets yours. Ask Him to forgive you for feeling that you should be exempt. And as you feel His pain in yours, thank Him that He loved you enough to suffer like this for you. Stay there with Him. Refuse to let Satan draw you back into bitterness and self-pity, and you will find Jesus a meaningful companion in the midst of trouble.

We need to be deeply taken with the thought that in suffering we understand a little of what He went through for us. And maybe, just maybe, we will begin to grasp—sand particle by sand particle—the depth of His love for us. What words cannot express in trying to explain the marvelous love of Jesus, suffering servants feel in the deepest parts of their souls.

This is the fellowship of His sufferings. This is the intimacy of a shared experience with Jesus. This is where He waits to meet us. It's time to stop turning our back on Him in pain and flee to His embrace. But we are only free to do this when we have ceased to live to rejoice in ourselves. If we are intent to celebrate "me" in life, we will resist trials and quickly become embittered when they settle in for the long haul—to say nothing of the difficulty in meeting Jesus in pain when we have valued comfort and peace more than nearness to Him. If He is the supreme value in our lives, then we will be willing to meet Him in times of trouble.

Simply Jesus
Joseph M. Stowell

SHARED EXPERIENCES

May 15

I John 1:3

Moody Bible Institute has a policy that I do not travel alone. When our children were at home, I often traveled with a colleague from the Institute. After I returned home, I would reenter Martie's world of runny noses, school lunches, taxi runs, and bedtime stories. I'd try my best to brief her on the trip and tell her about all the things I had seen and the people I had met, but there really wasn't much connection. How could there be? For one thing, I'm a man. And most men like to cut to the bottom line, rather than share details. For another thing, she simply hadn't been there. After I would give my little spiel, she in turn would try to explain to me all that happened while I was gone—all the little trials and joys of caring for growing children. I did my best to enter into her experiences. But I really couldn't. I hadn't been there.

Now, however, our children are married and have homes of their own. Happily, Martie and I often travel together. We share the experiences of new places and new faces, of sometimes stressful meetings; we watch the Lord work through the ministry of His Word and experience the joy of His work together.... It's amazing how much closer we are today in our intimacy with one another. All because of shared experiences....

It's like that in our relationship with Jesus. You've got to capitalize on where your world merges with His. And suffering is one of the places where your world and His intersect. If you choose to see your season of suffering as a moment to capture a shared experience with God's Son, your intimacy with Him will become a deepening reality.... Yes, your pain will still be pain—sometimes extremely difficult to endure. But instead of focusing on the loss, the hardship, the obstacle, you will step through the door of a fellowship beyond words to describe.

Simply Jesus
Joseph M. Stowell

John 16:33   ## "I DON'T UNDERSTAND IT"   May 16

We have a wonderful neighbor in her eighties. Charmingly crusty, with an engaging personality, she seems to enjoy being a touch out-of-sorts about some things. It's her "gig," and we love her for it. She claims that her everyday consumption of gin and cigarettes "keeps her fresh." Her sister, on the other hand, is as proper as they come. She doesn't drink or smoke. She exercises faithfully at the local pool, and she complains about nothing. Last winter, while swimming her daily routine, she was taken ill and lay in a coma in the hospital for days, until she finally died. Our neighbor was stunned. Her sister was her only living relative. All she could say in the days following her sister's death was, "I don't understand it. *It should have been me! My sister was such a good person.*"

The truth, of course, is that none of us is exempt. Jesus stated very clearly, "In this world you will have trouble" and He was talking to His closest friends! Is there anyone left on the planet who actually feels that the world is gradually getting better and better? That we are more civilized? If you harbor such thoughts, consider the horrific events surrounding September 11, 2001—or just spend a few minutes with CNN on any given night. . . . Our instincts tell us to resist trouble. . . . We plot, manipulate, fret, seek revenge, doubt God and His goodness, threaten, harbor anger, flirt with bitterness, withdraw, and—if all else fails— throw a major pity party. And by the way, if you throw a pity party don't bother sending out invitations. Friends may try to cheer you up—and that would wreck everything. Thankfully, for those of us who seek the face of God in the midst of trouble, we discover that He is not surprised by the arrival of pain—and that He wants us to experience Him there.

Simply Jesus
Joseph M. Stowell

May 17

AN IMPORTANT TOOL
Romans 8:36-37

When I was eight years old, polio struck, causing a degeneration of my spine and developing what is called Spondyloisthesis grade IV. To make matters worse, when I was 23, I fell down a flight of concrete steps and was paralyzed for over 17 weeks before a spinal fusion. Later automobile accidents added to these injuries, resulting in a spinal disalignment and a fractured vertebrae. Orthopedic surgeons who reviewed my X-rays have agreed that, "It would be a miracle if this man could sit up, but it would be impossible for him to walk." But despite the miraculous part of my story, I am in constant excruciating pain that is beyond medical help. Therefore, what I want to share with you is that through the Spirit of God, pain doesn't have to separate you from God; instead it can serve a very powerful purpose in your life. In fact, it can be utilized as an important tool to take you TO God.

Today we hear a lot about the power of "self." There's self-realization, self-actualization, self-help, self this and self that. But the truth is, "self" cannot conquer pain. It can mesmerize the mind into thinking the pain doesn't matter, doesn't exist or is less than it is . . . but these are not real, lasting solutions to the ROOT of the problem. I found out the hard way that as long as our energies are concentrated on ourselves as we try to conquer suffering in our own power, the pain (whether it is physical, mental, emotional or spiritual) is more likely to become *amplified*. It can even bring you to a self-centered position where you think about little else. But there is a way to live life to the fullest in spite of the pain. That way is through Jesus Christ. For in His power you can go on to live a vibrant, satisfying life focused on loving God and serving others. When this happens, not only does the *experience* of the pain get smaller, but the number of things you think you need gets smaller too!

Selected

May 18

EXHAUSTED RESOURCES
Jeremiah 17:14

Please understand, I am not trying to deny that the pain exists. Neither am I trying to play down the severity of the pain some of you may be going through, pain which at times can drive you to utter distraction and seriously curtail your productivity. But I am saying that in my experience pain will begin to have less prominence in your thoughts and less power over ruling your life as you learn to pay less attention to it in the power of Christ. This does not mean that we are to eliminate our doctors or other health care practitioners. I sincerely believe that knowledge is given to these people by God. But what happens when medical care eventually comes to an end? What happens when the practitioner comes to the patient and says, "I've exhausted my resources. There's nothing more we can do."

I have found that when that day comes, that's when we turn willingly to the Great Physician. Through praise, worship, thanksgiving, and a new sense of hope, we receive. We receive healing in many areas, many of them being hidden areas of our hearts. We receive fresh life . . . and we are filled with His love. The more we receive the more we have to give . . . without anxiety, struggle or strain. As Christians, we don't have a monopoly on kindness or reaching out to people. But what we do have is a reason for doing these things, a purpose for reaching out and pushing past the self-centeredness that all pain can drive us to, and that reason is Jesus Christ Himself. I believe that God, in His love for us, does want us all healed. But we must remember that in His sovereignty it is He who will decide the details and timetable of our healing.

We might also want to note that until that great day when we meet Him face to face and exchange our corruptible bodies for our new, incorruptible ones, none of us have reached perfection.

Selected

FIRST, A TEARING DOWN
May 19

Hosea 6:1

Watchmen Nee puts first things first in saying, "The Lord does not set us here first of all to preach or to do any work for Him. The first thing for which He sets us here is to create hunger in others. No true work will ever begin without a sense of need being created. We cannot inject that into others; we cannot drive people to be hungry. That hunger is to be created, and that hunger can be created only through those who carry the impressions of God."

In preparation, there is a tearing down before there can be a building up. "Come and let us return unto the Lord; for he hath torn and he will heal us; he hath smitten, and he will bind us up" (Hosea 6:1). This applies to both growth and service J. C. Metcalfe faithfully writes: "It is more than comforting to realize that it is those who have plumbed the depths of failure to whom God invariably gives the call to shepherd others. This is not a call given to the gifted, the highly trained, or the polished as such. Without a bitter experience of their own inadequacy and poverty, they are quite unfitted to bear the burden of spiritual ministry. It takes a man who has discovered something of the measure of his own weakness to be patient with the foibles of others. Such a man also has a first-hand knowledge of the loving care of the Chief Shepherd, and His ability to heal one who has come humbly to trust in Him and Him alone. Therefore, he does not easily despair of others, but looks beyond sinfulness, willfulness and stupidity, to the might of unchanging love. The Lord Jesus does not give the charge, 'Be a shepherd to My lambs . . . to My sheep,' on hearing Peter's self-confident affirmation of undying loyalty, but He gives it after he has utterly failed to keep his vows and has wept bitterly in the streets of Jerusalem."

Principles of Spiritual Growth
Miles J. Stanford

May 20
WHEN YOU COME TO THE BOTTOM
Psalm 116:3

There is no doubt that sorrow has a value of its own, and that it has a place in life which nothing else can take. There is always something missing in life, until sorrow has entered into life. There is an Arab proverb which says: "All sunshine makes a desert." It is told that once Elgar, the great musician, was listening to a young girl singing. She had a beautiful voice and a well-nigh faultless technique, but she just missed greatness. "She will be great," said Elgar, "when something happens to break her heart." There are things which only sorrow can teach.

It might well be said that sorrow is the source of the great discoveries in life. It is in sorrow that a man discovers the things which matter and the things which do not matter. It is in sorrow that a man discovers the meaning of friendship and the meaning of love. It is in sorrow that a man discovers whether his faith is a merely superficial ornament of life or the essential foundation on which his whole life depends. It is in sorrow that a man discovers God. "When you come to the bottom," said Neville Talbot, "you find God." There is a deep sense in which it is literally true that sorrow has its own unique blessedness to give.

A Plain Man Looks at the Beatitudes
William Barclay

After the Great Plague in London, there came the Great Fire when a large portion of the city was devastated. Some time afterward, it was observed that strange and exotic flowers which had never before been seen, sprang up in the vacant lots. Seed which had long lain dormant in the cold soil suddenly sprang into life with the heat of the fire. The fire of God falling on a believer will achieve in ten minutes what he could not achieve in himself in ten years.

Spiritual Maturity
J. Oswald Sanders

NO BETTER WEAPON

May 21

Matthew 10:38

There are no better weapons than the cross. Although I have mentioned this on other occasions, yet I repeat it once more here. For it is at the beginning that one must not think of such things as spiritual favors. That is a very poor way of commencing to build such a noble and costly erection. If we should begin to build it upon such sand, it will all lapse and we shall always be having annoyances and temptations. It is not in these Mansions, but in those that are further on where manna comes down from heaven. Out there, the soul will have all that it longs to have, because it desires only what is the will of God and what is pleasing to God.

It is, indeed, very strange that, although we are full of a thousand imperfections and hindrances, and our virtues are so immature that we have scarcely learned how to walk, yet in spite of all this we find that we are not ashamed to desire the delights of prayer and to complain of periods of aridity. Never allow this to happen to you, my sisters. Instead, embrace the cross which your spouse has borne on His shoulders, and realize that this cross is also yours to carry. Let the one who is capable of the greatest suffering, suffer most for Him. And he will have the most perfect freedom. Indeed, all other things are of secondary importance. If our Lord would happen to grant them to you, then give Him heartfelt thanks for them.

St. Teresa of Avila

May 22

HALTING HALF WAY

Psalm 2:8

One of the lessons came through his failure to lead his loved flock with him in these new-found pastures. They had gloried in his evangelical preaching and had taken the unprecedented action of following him from their comfortable church home to a public hall in order to reach the unchurched masses. But they . . . ended in erecting a magnificent modern church loaded with debt, thus defeating his purpose. Nor had they any sympathy with his strong stand in declining to accept a salary as long as they refused to discharge the mortgage. It weighed upon his sensitive spirit, and this . . . resulted in a collapse so serious that for a time it seemed that his ministry was ended. Then it was that a larger ministry unfolded before him, and "the uttermost part of the earth" became his objective. Another great crisis to which he refers followed another collapse when he was so broken that the help of man was unavailing. Then he found that one of the provisions of redemption is "that the life also of Jesus might be made manifest in our body," and that by this same redemption right "we have the mind of Christ."

The Life of A. B. Simpson
A. E. Thompson

Think it not strange, if he who stedfast leaveth
  All that he loveth for the love of Me
Be as the prey of him who rendeth, rieveth
Breaketh and bruiseth, woundeth sore and grieveth,
And carefully a spray of sharp thorn weaveth
  To crown the man who chooseth Calvary.
Count it all joy, the blaming and the scorning,
  Ye who confess love's pure transcendent power;
Stay not for speech, heed not the wise world's warning,
  Thine is an incommunicable dower.
What will it be when sudden, in the morning
  From brown thorn budded purple Passion flower?

Amy Carmichael

Philippians 3:10   **WASTED SUFFERING**   **May 23**

Suffering is wasted if we suffer entirely alone. Those who do not know Christ, suffer alone. Their suffering is no communion. The awful solitude of suffering is not meant to seek communion in vain. But all communion is denied to it except that which unites our spirit with God in the Passion of Jesus Christ.

What can human sympathy offer us in the loneliness of death? Flowers are an indecency in a death without God. They only serve to cover the body. The thing that has died has become a thing to be decorated and rejected. May its hopeless loneliness be forgotten and not remind us of our own!

How sad a thing is human love that ends with death; sadder when it pitiably tries to reach out to some futile communication with the dead. The poor little rice cakes at a pagan tomb! Sad, too, is the love that has no communion with those we love when they suffer. How miserable it is to have to stand in mute sorrow with nothing to say to those we love, when they are in great pain.

No Man is an Island
Thomas Merton

May 24

USELESS SUFFERING

Job 5:17

When is suffering useless? When it only turns us in upon ourselves, when it only makes us sorry for ourselves, when it changes love into hatred, when it reduces all things to fear. Useless suffering cannot be consecrated to God because its fruitlessness is rooted in sin. Sin and useless suffering increase together. They encourage one another's growth, and the more suffering leads to sin, the more sin robs suffering of its capacity for fruitful consecration.

But the grace of Christ is constantly working miracles to turn useless suffering into something fruitful after all. How? By suddenly stanching the wound of sin. As soon as our life stops bleeding out of us in sin, suffering begins to have creative possibilities. But until we turn our wills to God, suffering leads nowhere, except to our own destruction.

No Man is an Island
Thomas Merton

You are willing to drink of the cup that I Drink of—the wine of sorrow and disappointment.
  You are Mine and will grow both of you more and more like Me, your Master.
  True it is today as it was in the days of Moses that no man can see My face and live.
  The self, the original Man, shrivels up and dies, and upon the soul becomes stamped My image.

God Calling
A. J. Russell

May 25
LEANING ON HER BELOVED
Song of Solomon 8:5

November 9, 1937, was her first Coming Day when it proved impossible for her to see anyone, but she treasured a note from Murray, "Peace be on every minute of your day, and love immeasurable from us all," and she gave God thanks "for May's and Godfrey's beautiful thought that instead of coming to my room, all should spend a little while in the House of Prayer for me." A few disconnected notes show how she learned more and more to lean on her Beloved as she climbed. January 25, 1936: This morning a thought came. Tara and I had been speaking of the excitement and joy of the children who have just gone up to the Forest, and I was longing to see their pleasure as they see it for the first time—such a foolish feeling—when suddenly I remembered that I shall see them when for the first time they look at the loveliness There. I shall be There to show them everything. October 27, 1938: Is it imagination, Lord, or Thine own word to me, that I shall come to Thee in sleep—no rending goodbyes—no distress to anyone? "I shall take thee in thy sleep"—is it Thy voice speaking, Lord? However it be, I ask that it may be the easiest way for my beloveds. November 2, 1938: "If so be that we suffer with Him." Lord Jesus, Thou hast made my prison so beautiful and my bonds so light that I greatly fear I do not "suffer with" Thee. . . . Do not let me miss the deepest thing Thou hast to give—the fellowship of Thy sufferings.

Once she had a vivid dream that she was healed. She walked three miles rejoicing in her strength, and then, when she began to tire a little, she saw a taxi pass. It stopped, but she hesitated, not sure if she had enough money for the fare. But the man said, "Don't spoil my joy," and so he drove her home. She told him how she had been healed by the touch of the Lord. "I had such a happy time with him." But she awoke, and it was a dream.

Amy Carmichael of Dohnavur
Frank Houghton

May 26

OUR LIGHT TRAGEDY

Hebrews 12:11

"For our light affliction which is but for a moment, is working for us a far more exceeding and eternal weight of glory."

Where are we to get our light in all this appalling tragedy? It is obvious nonsense to say that suffering makes saints; it makes some people devils. Hebrews 12:11 is referring to the suffering that comes to a person who is being exercised by the Spirit of God. We all know people who have been made much meaner and more irritable and more intolerable to live with by suffering; it is not right to say that all suffering perfects. It only perfects one type of person—the one who accepts the call of God in Christ Jesus.

"Therefore we do not lose heart. Even though our outward man is perishing, yet the inward man is being renewed day by day" (II Corinthians 4:16).

There is nothing, naturally speaking, that makes us lose heart quicker than decay—the decay of bodily beauty, of natural life, of friendship, of associations, all these things made a man lose heart; but Paul says when we are trusting in Jesus Christ these things do not find us discouraged, light comes through them. "For we do not preach ourselves, but Christ Jesus the Lord, and ourselves your servants for Jesus' sake." That is the rock on which Paul stands.

The Place of Help
Oswald Chambers

Even pain shows a new face when the glory-light beams upon it. Said Frances Ridley Havergal, the exultant singing spirit, with the frail, shaking, pain-ridden body, "Everybody is so sorry for me except myself." And then she uses the phrase, "I see my pain in the light of Calvary."

J. H. Jowett

May 27

SOMEONE WHO UNDERSTANDS
Matthew 27:45-46

Spurgeon once tells of how he was utterly depressed in spirit and soul, discouraged, and failing in health. Just before leaving for a recuperation, he preached on "My God, my God, why has thou forsaken me?" The experience was so sad that he wished it would never happen again.

Afterwards, a man came to see him. Spurgeon described him later as "one step away from the insane asylum," his head bulging, his hands nervous and his spirit totally depressed. The man told Spurgeon that after hearing his sermon, he felt that Spurgeon was the only one who could understand him and so he had come. Spurgeon comforted him as best he knew how from his own experience.

For five years, Spurgeon did not see the man. But "just last night" (he was delivering the above lecture to students at the College), "I saw him. It was like night and day. He was completely changed."

Spurgeon concluded that he was willing to undergo hundreds of such experiences now that he knew God permitted it to happen so that he could know and sympathize with people under similar predicaments.

Author Unknown

May 28
ANOTHER KIND OF SUFFERING
John 12:3

As long as we remain in the body, we shall be subject to a certain amount of that common suffering which we must share with all the sons of men. But there is another kind of suffering, known only to the Christian: it is voluntary suffering, deliberately and knowingly incurred for the sake of Christ. Such is a luxury, a treasure of fabulous value. And it is rare as well as precious, for there are few in this decadent age who will of their own choice go down into this dark mine looking for jewels. God will not force us into this kind of suffering. He will not lay this cross upon us nor embarrass us with riches we do not want. Such riches are reserved for those who apply to serve in the legion of the expendables, who love not their lives unto the death, who volunteer to suffer for Christ's sake and who follow up this application with lives that challenge the devil and invite the fury of hell. Such as these have said good-bye to the world's toys; they have accepted toil and suffering as their earthly portion. The marks of the cross are upon them and they are known in heaven and in hell. But where are they? Has this breed of Christian died out of the earth?

A. W. Tozer

By the breaking of that flask for the Lord's sake, the home in Bethany was pervaded with the sweetest fragrance. . . . Have you ever met someone who has suffered deeply, and whose experiences have compelled him to find satisfaction in the Lord alone? Then immediately you have become aware of something. Immediately your spiritual senses detect a fragrance—what Paul terms "a sweet savor of Christ." Something has been broken in that life in order to release what is there within of God Himself, and you cannot mistake it. Yes, the odor that filled the house that day in Bethany still fills the Church today. Mary's fragrance never passes.

Watchman Nee

May 29

THE SUFFERING OF GOD
Hosea 4:1-3

There is yet another dimension to the suffering of God, one seen clearly by the prophet Hosea. It was when this prophet's own wife had become a prostitute and his love has been viciously trampled time and time again that he began to understand that his own suffering was a microcosm of the suffering of God over Israel's sins.

"When Israel was a child, I loved him and out of Egypt I called my son. The more I called them, the more they went from me; they kept sacrificing to the Baals and burning incense to idols. Yet it was I who taught Ephraim to walk, I took them up in my arms; but they did not know that I healed them. I led them with cords of compassion, with the bands of love, and I became to them as one who eases the yoke on their jaws, and I bent down to them and fed them" (Hosea 11:1-4, RSV).

Think of it! God suffers in us, as a father suffers over his son and finally as a lover suffers whose devotion has been savagely spurned. God suffers this way over each human being—and suffers with a heart of infinite love, with an inconceivable sensitivity to all that we do in relation to Him.

Yet, God rejoices in His suffering—His suffering is transmuted into joy!—for He knows it is borne in order to destroy sin and death forever. It is not for Himself He suffers—it is for us. It is not for Himself He went to the cross—it is for us. It is not His own suffering that concerns Him—it is ours. One author put it this way:

> Those who think of the result of hastening or hindering the gospel think of it in relation to themselves and to the world. Few think of its relation to God. Few give thought to the suffering that sin has caused our Creator. . . . As the "whole creation groaneth and travaileth in pain together" (Romans

8:22), the heart of the infinite Father is pained in sympathy. Our world is a vast leprosarium house, a scene of misery that we dare not allow even our thoughts to dwell upon. Did we realize it as it is, the burden would be too terrible. Yet God feels it all.

Six months after the death of her husband, a friend of mine read this statement. She had been in deep depression, feeling no faith, no assurance. She told me that as she walked by the park benches in her little town and saw the drunks sitting there, she would think to herself about them, *If we wonder why He has allowed something to happen to us, we must also wonder why He allowed it to happen to Him.* "You're alive and he's dead." She saw how it was possible for a person to commit suicide. Mind you, these are the words of a very dedicated Christian.

It was when she read this statement that her mind was taken off her sufferings and focused on the sufferings of God and Christ. She told me that she was ashamed, ashamed that for so many months she had exhausted all her energies in self-pity, ignoring the anguish of the Son of God for the world—even for her own loss.

She said that her own suffering seemed unimportant in comparison. With tears in her eyes, she said that she now feels that she cannot add to that awesome burden in any way, especially not by letting her own troubles overwhelm her.

James Londis

May 30

A LETTER TO MRS. H.
II Corinthians 1:4

Long and often I have thought of writing to you; now the time has come. May the Lord help me to send a word in season! I know not how it may be with you, but he does, and to him I look to direct my thoughts accordingly.

I suppose you are still in the school of the cross, learning the happy art of extracting real good out of seeming evil, and to grow tall by stooping. The flesh is a sad dunce in this school; but grace makes the spirit willing to learn by suffering; yes, it cares not what it endures, so sin may be mortified, and a conformity to the image of Jesus be increased.

Surely when we see the most and the best of the Lord's children so often in heaviness, and when we consider how much he loves them, and what he has done and prepared for them, we may take it for granted that there is a reason for their sufferings. For it would be well within his power, and not a thousandth part of what his love intends to do for them, should he make their whole life here, from the hour of their conversion to their death, a continued course of satisfaction and comfort, without anything to distress them from within and without. But were it so, should we not miss many advantages?

In the first place, we should not be able to say: "As he was, so are we in this world." I think a believer would be ashamed to be so utterly unlike his Lord. What, the Master always a man of sorrows and acquainted with grief and the servant always happy and full of comfort! Jesus despised, reproached, neglected, opposed, and betrayed, and his people admired and caressed; he living in the want of all things, and they filled with abundance; he sweating blood for anguish, and they strangers to distress; how unsuitable would these things be!

Collected Letters
John Newton

May 31

A LETTER TO MRS. H.
II Corinthians 7:6

How much better to be called to the honor of filling up the measure of his sufferings! A cup of suffering was put into his hand on our account, and his love engaged him to drink it for us. The wrath which it contained he drank wholly himself, but he left us a little affliction to taste, that we might pledge him, and remember how he loved us, and how much more he endured for us than he will ever call us to endure for him.

Again, how could we, without suffering, manifest the nature and truth of Gospel grace? What place should we then have for patience, submission, meekness, forbearance, and a readiness to forgive, if we had nothing to try us either from the hand of the Lord, or from the hand of men. A Christian without trials would be like a mill without wind or water: the contrivance and design of the wheel-work inside would be unnoticed and unknown, without something to put it in motion from outside. Nor would our graces grow, unless they were called out to exercise; the difficulties we meet with not only prove but strengthen the graces of the Spirit. If a person was always to sit still, without making use of legs or arms, he would probably wholly lose the power of moving his limbs eventually; but by walking and working he becomes strong and active.

So, in a long course of ease, the powers of the new man would certainly languish; the soul would grow soft, indolent, cowardly, and faint; and therefore the Lord appoints his children such dispensations as make them strive and struggle, and pant. They must press through a crowd, swim against a stream, endure hardships, run, wrestle, and fight and their strength grows as they use it.

Collected Letters
John Newton

WHEN LIFE GETS HARD

Psalm 46:1-3

June 1

There comes a time in everyone's life when trouble and difficulties seem to gang up. When this happens—when life gets hard—what is the creative way to handle things?

FIRST: Don't try to do it all yourself. Do not struggle and fret. Do not strain and complain. Do all you can about things and then put everything into God's hands, trusting Him to bring it out right. You can depend upon God. He will not fail you. Let go and let God.

SECOND: Pray for guidance and believe that direction is *now* being given you. Believe this guidance can be trusted. Depend upon it, for it won't fail you.

THIRD: Pray for and practice a calm attitude. Disturbing things will remain disturbing as long as you are disturbed. But when you become peaceful, conditions will iron themselves out. You cannot think creatively when your mind is upset. Remember: upset minds upset; peaceful minds "peacefulize."

FOURTH: Saturate your consciousness with faith, the creative faith that things will turn out right. Say aloud every day several times: "Thou wilt keep him in perfect peace, whose mind is stayed on thee" (Isaiah 26:3, KJV); "In quietness and in confidence shall be your strength" (Isaiah 30:15, KJV); "Peace I give unto you; not as the world giveth, give I unto you. Let not your heart be troubled, neither let it be afraid" (John 14:27, KJV).

FIFTH: Remind yourself of one great truth: hard experiences *will* pass away. They *will* yield. They *can* be changed. So just hold on, with God's help.

SIXTH: There is always a light in the darkness. Believe that. Look for that light. The light is the love of God. "Thy word is a lamp unto my feet, and a light unto my path" (Psalm 119:105, KJV). Go ahead into the darkness unafraid.

SEVENTH: Ask the Lord to release your own creative ingenuity, your own strength and wisdom, which taken together can, for a fact, handle any problem successfully.

EIGHTH: Never forget that God cares for you, that He loves you. He wants to help you. Turn to Him, and gratefully accept His help.

NINTH: Remember that all human beings experience troubles similar to your own. Many years ago a graduating class gave a stone bench to their university on which were graven these words: "To those who sit here sorrowing or rejoicing, greetings. So also did we in our time."

TENTH: Finally, hold on to this great promise: "God is our refuge and strength, a very present help in trouble." And this is the truth. God will see you through, and a brighter day will dawn for you.

Source Unknown

James 4:7
TENDING THE LIGHT
June 2

In New York Harbor, between Manhattan Island and Staten Island, is a sunken shoal called Robbins Reef. A small lighthouse stands there, and for many years the keeper was an elderly widow, Mrs. Jacob Walker. One day she told her story to a reporter, who gave it to the world: "I was a young girl living at Sandy Hook, New Jersey," she said, "when I first met my husband. He was keeper of the Sandy Hook Light and took me there as his bride. I was happy there, for the lighthouse was on land and I could have a garden and raise flowers. Then one day we were transferred here—to Robbins Reef. As soon as we arrived I said to my husband, "I can't stay here! The sight of water wherever I look makes me too lonesome. I won't unpack." But somehow all the trunks and boxes got unpacked. Four years later my husband caught cold while tending the light. The cold turned to pneumonia, and they took him to the infirmary on Staten Island. I stayed behind to tend the light. A few nights later I saw a rowboat coming through the darkness. Something told me the message it was bringing. The man in the boat said, "We're sorry, Mrs. Walker, but your husband's worse." "You mean he's dead," I answered; and there was no reply. We buried my husband on a hillside on Staten Island. Every morning when the sun comes up, I stand at a porthole and look across the water toward his grave. Sometimes the hill is green, sometimes it is brown, sometimes it is white with snow. But it always brings a message from him—something I heard him say more often than anything else. Just three words: "Mind the light."

Facing a loss, accepting a loss, then reentering life and so moving through and beyond the loss—there is the first secret of managing bereavement. *A self-pitying life is a doomed life. Only the life which deliberately picks up and starts over again is victorious.*

Light From Many Lamps
Lillian Eichler Watson

ONLY OUR WILL

Romans 8:28-29

June 3

We do not want anything of all that he does not want. We attach our weak will to the all-powerful will which does all. Thus nothing can happen except what God wills. We are perfectly satisfied when his will is accomplished, and we find in God's good pleasure an inexhaustible source of peace and consolation. Our entire life is a beginning of the peace of the blessed, who say forever, "Amen, Amen." We worship, we praise, we bless God for all things. We see him constantly in everything, and in everything his paternal hand is the only thing with which we are concerned. There are no more evils, because everything, even the most terrible wrongs, "turn to good," as St. Paul said, "for those who love God." Can we call evil the suffering which God sends to purify and to make us worthy of him? That which does us so great a good cannot be an evil.

Then let us throw all our cares on the breast of so good a father. Let him do as he pleases. Let us be content to follow his will in all things and to place ours in his, so that we may disown it. It is not right that we should have anything for ourselves, we who do not belong to ourselves. The slave has nothing for himself. For how much stronger a reason the creature, who has at bottom only nothingness and sin, and in whom all is gift and pure grace, should not have anything of his own. God has only given him a free will, capable of possessing himself, in order to obligate him by this gift to strip himself more generously. We have nothing of our own but our will. All the rest does not belong to us. Disease takes away health and life. Riches are snatched away by violence. The talents of the mind depend on the condition of the body. The one thing truly ours is our will. And it is of this which God is jealous, because he has given it to us, not for us to keep, and to stay in charge of, but really to give it back wholly to him, just as we have received it, without holding back any of it.

Fenelon

June 4
THE MOST SUBLIME ACHIEVEMENT
Hebrews 11:27

To do and suffer God's will is still the highest form of faith, the most sublime Christian achievement. To have the bright aspirations of life forever blasted; to bear daily a burden and see no relief; to be fettered by some incurable disability—to be able to say in such a school of discipline, "It is the Lord. Let Him do what He will." This is faith at its highest and spiritual success at the crowning point. There are few more severe tests of character than pain, but while the suffering we cannot change, we can be conquerors.

Between the pages of the book he (Charles Cowman) was reading, a card was found bearing a few lines in his handwriting. It had the appearance of being well-worn and the words revealed what must have been uppermost in his mind. They were these: "He endured as seeing Him who is invisible. Endure when there is every external reason not to endure."

How often during those pain-filled nights, he would walk the floor softly singing:

> Shelter me, Lord! For the blast is strong.
> Shelter me, Lord! For the way is long;
> Cover me, Lord! For the night is cold
> Hush me to rest, in Thine arms enfold.

Missionary Warrior
Lettie Cowman

Romans 8:31-39 ## IMPOTENT ENEMIES **June 5**

Who can get between the love of Christ and Me? What sharp dividing force can cleave the two in twain and leave me like a dismembered and dying branch? Terrible experiences cannot do it. "Trouble, hardship, persecution, famine, nakedness, danger or sword!" All these may come about my house, but they cannot reach the inner sanctuary where my Lord and I are closeted in loving communion and peace. They may bruise my skin, they may even give my body to be burned, but no flame can destroy the love of Jesus which enswathes my soul with invisible defense.

And terrible forces cannot do it. "Angels, nor demons, nor any powers." These mysterious agents of darkness, for they must be the legions of the evil one, are unable to quench the light and fire of my Savior's love. The devil can never blow out the lamp of grace.

And terrible death itself cannot do it. Death does not separate me from Jesus. Death is the Lord's minister to lead me into deeper privilege and ripe experiences of grace and love. Therefore, "I will lay me down in peace and take my rest."

J. H. Jowett

O for a faith that will not shrink
Though pressed by many a foe,
That will not tremble on the brink of any earthly woe.
That will not murmur nor complain
Beneath the chast'ning rod,
But in the hour of grief or pain will lean upon its God.

William H. Bathurst

Psalm 25:16-17 ## SO TERRIBLY DARK **June 6**

After his traveling in the extreme heat, Hudson Taylor himself began to feel so ill that he told Jennie what to do if he became unable to help in the morning. An attack of pain had begun, the worst he had ever had, probably renal colic. Emily's journal for that awful night reads, "Things all looked so terribly dark. Would God forsake us and this infant Mission? No, I don't think I feared that, but it was so very hard to be there and hear poor Mr. Taylor moaning with pain, and little Gracie uttering incoherent words of raving." Mary Bell gave up her bed to Grace and did her share of nursing. Privacy was minimal in their circumstances. She too could hear Hudson Taylor's moans of pain and added, "He was so broken-hearted he cried most of the day." To talk privately with Maria he had had to take her out to a secluded rock-pool in a gulley where they sometimes bathed. There he had told her that there was no hope of Grace recovering. "There and then we put her into our Father's hands, pleading with him to do the best for her and for us." Grace died the next day.

The temple priests and Pengshan villagers, if they knew a death had taken place so near to them, could cause great difficulties from their superstitions about departed spirits. Idolatrous practices would be demanded. Refusal to comply could lead to violence. So secrecy must be preserved. Pillows were placed in the light tin bath tub, Grace's body laid on them, and more pillows and bedding piled over it. Traveling in the coolness of night was commonplace. Around midnight they started downhill. John McCarthy had been in Pengshan recuperating until August 4 and was in Hangzhou preparing to return to Yanzhou. His memory of how Maria and Hudson Taylor bore up through these experiences stayed with him for many years. He wrote: "They were sustained and helped to glorify God and be an example to those around of submission and joyful acquiescence in the will of God."

A J. Broomhall

June 7

FINAL PRECIOUS MOMENTS
Isaiah 43:2

It seems somehow incongruous that the days which irrevocably change one's life on earth should be filled with ordinary events: the rising of an ordinary February sun, an office filled with ordinary conversations, the sound of telephones ringing and car doors slamming and friendly *hellos* and dull rain and, "Leon, I know you really don't like it!"

No, looking back and reliving those final precious moments of earthly time, it still seems wrong that the valley should approach that way. There should be intimations and gentle cautions.

Half an hour later the doorbell summoned me to the front door to look wonderingly into the face of a blue-uniformed police officer.

"Are you Mrs. Steel?" he began slowly, as though groping for the right words. Or was this a speech he had given before, the words nearly memorized? I cannot be sure. "Yes, I'm Mrs. Steel." "Mrs. Steel, do you have a teenage boy about 18 and a girl a little younger?" "Well, yes, I do," I mumbled. "Mrs. Steel, it's getting colder. The rain is turning to ice. There has just been an accident on the 37 bypass. I'm sorry to have to tell you that your children and their friend have just been killed."

Suddenly I felt as if I had been pushed over a high cliff into a wild seething sea unable to swim. My mind was creating images: Leon and Lorna in their final moment, as the car spun out of control, and then the crunch of metal against their soft flesh. *It was too much.* The accident which had taken their lives would now surely take mine as well.

Thrice Through the Valley
Valetta Steel

Psalm 23:4 ## DOWN INTO THE BLACKNESS **June 8**

When the uniformed officer appeared at my door that cold February evening, the full impact of his words gradually penetrated my brain with a violent, paralyzing force. "Your children and their friend have just been killed." It was as though I were standing outside myself, a spectator to some gruesome drama. Certainly, in a moment, I would awaken from the nightmare.

With Danny and Henry, the valley had approached more gradually. I had had time to prepare, to brace myself for the dark finality of the loss; but this time the valley had come upon me suddenly, sucking me down, down into the blackness in one vicious gulp. And yet, even as my brain reeled under the impact, deep from within my being welled up the sweet, mysterious consciousness of the Presence, the everlasting arms: "Yea, though I walk through the valley of the shadow of death, I will fear no evil."

Thus, the words came almost unbidden to my lips, "Officer, I know where they are. They are with God." As I closed the door behind me a surge of comfort came from the realization, too, that God had prepared a spiritual family to stand with me in my hour of trial. I sensed at this time I was being supernaturally sustained by the Spirit of God and by the supporting, consoling love of my spiritual brothers and sisters. Still, a dark shadow would now and then flit across my mind. *Soon,* I thought, *I will come crashing down, crushed and wounded and helpless.* I felt I would be haunted, as though an old wound had been freshly opened; I would again experience the void left by the loss of my firstborn and the depression that came in the wake of Henry's death. Then God spoke a word of gentle rebuke: "If I can sustain you today," he said, "can't you trust me with tomorrow?"

Thrice Through the Valley
Valetta Steel

June 9

IN HIS STRONG EMBRACE

Isaiah 40:11

At that very moment, I felt myself in the strong embrace of the Spirit of God. I was being lifted upward, above the cold winter trees, sweetly, securely, into the warm presence of my Father. With a calm, which I instinctively knew had its source from beyond my own being, I heard myself saying, "Officer, I know where they are. They are with God."

Now there would be the phone calls, consoling friends, flowers, "arrangements," and at the last the long caravan of cars heading to the familiar plot of ground and newly spaded earth. Here I was walking the valley again—a painful scenario I knew too well. And yet concurrently, in the dark countenance of death, there kept coming sweet tokens from my mighty and loving heavenly Father. His love came in great billows, washing over my broken and bleeding heart, bringing again that refreshing comfort to me.

"Yea, though I walk through the valley of the shadow of death, I will fear no evil, for thou art with me" (Psalm 23:4). Yes, this was the valley again. I recognized it all right. It comes on you suddenly with a phone call, a knock at the door, the appearance of the messenger and the word.

Thrice Through the Valley
Valetta Steel

HE ESCORTS THEM

June 10

Isaiah 40:4

As news of the children's deaths was broadcast on TV and radio and conveyed by phone to friends all over the world, I sensed that I was being borne aloft on a surging tide of prayer and love. I have never known love like that. The world seemed literally to be dripping love, oozing at every pore. Was this the mysterious essence of Calvary—that love in all its sublime glory can in mortal minds only be understood when there is a cross? I wondered if others could discern the divine paradox the Spirit of God was enacting in the mortal life of Valetta Steel: that God never loves his children so dearly as when he lets them suffer. He never walks with them as closely as when he escorts them through the valley.

As I knew myself the special object of the love and prayers of God's people, I felt humbled as never before. What had I done to deserve this? Nothing, absolutely nothing. It was all of Him and suddenly I grasped the meaning of grace in a new way. The morning following the children's death, it was as though God had pulled back a curtain and let me peek into heaven. It was all joy. Leon and Lorna were there and saying, "Mother, won't you share our joy? Dad is here and our brother, too."

Thrice Through the Valley
Valetta Steel

Condition unchanged—no light, but to leave all with God. I am gaining a very little and I need to make up my mind not to allow self-pity to enter my heart, or it will be the undoing of me. I shall set my heart upon a certain work, keep it before me and *do* it.

Lettie Cowman Diary, 1924

June 11

I WILL NOT DOUBT
II Corinthians 1:7

I will not doubt, though all my ships at sea
  Come drifting home with broken masts and sails;
I will believe the Hand that never fails,
  From seeming evil works to good for me
And though I weep because those sails are tattered,
  Still will I cry, while my best hopes lie shattered;
"I trust in Thee."

I will not doubt, though all my prayers return
  Unanswered from the still, white realm above;
I will believe it is an all-wise love
  That has refused these things for which I yearn;
And though at times I cannot keep from grieving,
  Yet the pure passion of my fixed believing
Undimmed will burn.

I will not doubt, though sorrows fall like rain,
  And troubles swarm like bees about a hive.
I will believe the heights for which I strive
  Are only reached by anguish and by pain;
And though I groan and writhe beneath my crosses,
  Yet I will see through my severest losses
The greater gain.

An old seaman once said, "In fierce storms we must do one thing, for there is only one way to survive; we must put the ship in a certain position and keep her there." And this, dear Christian, is what you must do. You must anchor yourself steadfastly upon the Lord. And then, come what may—whether wind, waves, rough seas, thunder, lightning, jagged rocks, or roaring breakers—you must lash yourself to the helm, firmly holding your confidence in God's faithfulness, His covenant promises, and His everlasting love in Christ Jesus.

Richard Fuller

June 12

MENDER OF BROKEN HEARTS
Isaiah 57:15

Max I. Reich tells of passing a repair shop in the window of which was a sign reading: "We mend everything except broken hearts." Brother Reich stepped back and entered the store, and when a beautiful young Jewess came forward to serve him he said, "I saw your sign and want to ask what you do with people who have broken hearts." Oh!" she said, "We send them to the hospital."

"You are a Jewess, are you not? Did you ever read Isaiah 57:15? 'For thus saith the high and lofty One that inhabited eternity, whose name is Holy; I dwell in the high and holy place, with him also that is of a contrite and humble spirit, to revive the spirit of the humble, and I revive the heart of the contrite ones.' And," continued Mr. Reich, "there was also He who read Isaiah 61:1, in his hometown synagogue at Nazareth. The verse contains the words 'He hath sent me to bind up the brokenhearted.' And," said Mr. Reich, "the Messiah added, 'This day is the Scripture fulfilled in your eyes.'"

Author Unknown

GOD WANTS US TO REMEMBER
II Corinthians 11:30

June 13

The Christian often tries to forget his weakness; God wants us to remember it, to feel it deeply. The Christian wants to conquer his weakness and to be freed from it; God wants us to rest and even rejoice in it. The Christian mourns over his weakness; Christ teaches His servant to say, "I take pleasure in my infirmities; most gladly will I glory in my infirmities." The Christian thinks his weakness is his greatest hindrance in the life and service of God. God tells us that it is the secret of strength and success.

Andrew Murray

St. Teresa said, "God guides those He loves by the way of afflictions; the dearer they are to Him the more severe the trials."

Richard Baxter in Kidderminster seldom knew an hour free from pain.

St. Gerard: "His soul fattened on the strong meat of suffering."

St. Teresa of Lisieux: "Suffering became my treasure."

St. Gerard was placed under a foreman who was nothing less than a cruel brute. Saintliness draws persecution. There is that in a saint which unconsciously convicts sin and makes it savage. Through the fiery trial the saint-to-be never gave way to impatience or ill-humor. He would reel beneath the undeserved and unprovoked attacks of the tyrant and show no sign of anger. On one occasion, another apprentice saw St. Gerard actually smiling as he was being whipped, and dragged from him later the cause of gladness. As the blows fell, he had been thinking gratefully of what God might do of good by this means to his stubborn soul.

Selected

June 14

CONSTELLATIONS OF HOPE
Psalm 66:6

It is a profound statement that "through the water," the very place where we might have expected nothing but trembling, terror, anguish, and dismay, the children of Israel stopped to "rejoice in him"!

How many of us can relate to this experience? Who of us, right in the midst of our time of distress and sadness, have been able to triumph and rejoice, as the Israelites did? How close God is to us through His promises, and how brightly those promises shine! Yet during times of prosperity we lose sight of their brilliance. In the way the sun at noon hides the stars from sight, His promises become indiscernible. But when night falls—the deep, dark night of sorrow—a host of stars begin to shine, bringing forth God's blessed constellations of hope and promises of comfort from His Word.

Just as Jacob experienced at Jabbok, it is only once the sun sets that the Angel of the Lord comes, wrestles with us, and we can overcome. It was at night, "at twilight" (Exodus 30:8), that Aaron lit the sanctuary lamps. And it is often during nights of trouble that the brightest lamps of believers are set ablaze.

It was during a dark time of loneliness and exile that John had the glorious vision of his Redeemer. Many of us today have our "Isle of Patmos," which produces the brightest memories of God's enduring presence, uplifting grace, and love in spite of solitude and sadness. How many travelers today, still passing through their Red Seas and Jordan Rivers of earthly affliction, will be able to look back from eternity, filled with memories of God's great goodness and say, "We passed through the waters on foot. And yet, even in these dark experiences, with waves surging all around, we stopped and said, 'Let us rejoice in him!'"

J. R. Macduff

June 15

BLACK-EDGED ENVELOPES
Ecclesiastes 9:3

Our Lord's love letters often come to us in black-edged envelopes. His wagons rumble, but they are loaded with benefits. His rod blossoms with sweet flowers and nourishing fruits. Let us not worry about the clouds, but sing because May flowers are brought to us through the April clouds and showers.

C. H. Spurgeon

The David Lees of Calcutta did not try to explain why the landslide in Darjeeling buried all six of their children—they used it! Their lesser home broken up, they set up a bigger home, a home with 300 children in it, and had that many there continuously for 65 years. On the monument to commemorate these children, what do you think was written: "My God, Why?" No. These words: "Thanks be unto God which giveth us the victory through our Lord Jesus Christ." I heard Mrs. Lee say, "I've never had a sorrow in my life." Why? Her sorrows became songs. They were set to music.

When German missionaries in India lost their only daughter through leprosy, did they cry out in anguish, "My God, why?" No. Out of that bereavement they produced an achievement—they set up what has become the greatest leper home in India. Not what happens to you, but what you do with it after it happens determines the result.

E. Stanley Jones

Deeper and deeper grows the conviction that tragedy is the basis of things and redemption the way out, reason being but the human method of manipulating ideas; but if reason is projected into the "before" and "after" of human consciousness it becomes a misleading director.

Oswald Chambers

June 16

CLING AND WAIT

I John 4:18

It is a paradox that the Christ who died upon the cross should be able to bring such comfort to those who fear suffering and death, yet so it is. Professor Arnold Toynbee, the greatest living authority on world history, wrote ten large volumes on the history of mankind. In these books he traces the rise and fall of civilization after civilization. He analyses the reasons why they rose and fell, the outside pressure, the internal corruption. Naturally, we ask, will our civilization also crash to destruction? Toynbee's answer is "Not necessarily. It depends on the religious response we make to the dangerous situation in which we find ourselves." He then describes a dream he had years ago—a dream which obviously made a deep spiritual impression upon him at the time and which has been a source of comfort and inspiration ever since. In his dream he pictured himself in Ampleforth Abbey in Yorkshire. Above the altar is suspended from the ceiling a huge cross. In his dream Professor Toynbee saw himself clinging to the foot of the cross. He heard a voice saying, "Amplexus, expecta" (cling and wait). So Toynbee concludes his mighty study of history by giving this same message to mankind, afflicted as we are by all kinds of fears, "Cling to the cross and wait." The cross brings home to us the reality of the forgiving love of God and such "perfect love casteth out fear." Again the cross speaks to us of God's power to overcome—eventually—every kind of evil. In this faith let us learn the art of accepting the future.

Gordon Powell

When we set out on this quest, we found ourselves moving in the midst of a mighty host, but, as we have pressed forward, the marchers, company by company, have fallen out of the race. And now, as we stand and gaze with our eyes upon the farther shore, a single figure rises from the flood and straightway fills the whole horizon. There is the Savior.

A Study of History
Arnold J. Toynbee

June 17

HAPPY WAVES OF LIFE

John 10:10

One spring day when he (Tolstoy) was walking in the forest, his mind suddenly felt lighter and his whole body began to move more freely through the light-spattered dimness. Intrigued, he observed that he was always sad when he rejected God with his reason and always cheerful when he accepted him like a child. "At the thought of God, happy waves of life welled up inside me," he wrote. "Everything came alive, took on meaning. The moment I thought I knew God, I lived. But the moment I forgot Him, the moment I stopped believing, I also stopped living. . . . To know God and to live are the same thing. God is life."

With the same energy he had formerly applied to reviling the dogma of the Orthodox Church, Tolstoy now threw himself into piety. He who had even refused to attend the services in the house organized by Sonya for feast days now began to say his prayers morning and night without any prompting from anyone; he got up early for mass on Sunday, confessed and took communion, fasted on Wednesdays and Fridays. "I know what I am doing is right," he said, "if only because, in order to mortify the pride of the spirit, be united with my ancestors and follow men and continue my search for the meaning of life, I am sacrificing my physical comfort."

To tell the truth, his mortification of the spirit was greatly attenuated by the feeling that he was being united, not only with the people, but with his own youth. He was not prospecting new ground, he was turning back into an old familiar path. The appeal of religion was heightened by the appeal of his childhood memories. . . . "It was a strange thing," he admitted, "but the life force I rediscovered then was it not the oldest of all, that of the very beginning of my life."

Henri Troyat

Job 42:5   **"I WAS SCOURGED INTO IT"**   **June 18**

Job's experience was of trouble, dreadful, heartbreaking trouble. And mark this well. It was not only his health and his home and his happiness that had crashed in one all-engulfing cataclysm—though that was true. But something else as well had gone with the wind of the frightful hurricane: his philosophy of life, his conventional code which had never faced up to the depth and tragedy of existence, his conscious rectitude and religiosity—that too had crashed in ruin. And the man looked up from the wreckage. "I had heard of Thee with the hearing of the ear; but now—now out of the depths—mine eye seeth Thee!"

Now we all know there are many different ways of encountering God. Other men have met God along quite different roads—Wordsworth in nature, Haydn in music, Teilhard de Chardin in science, and so on. But here is one of the classic ways—the way of trouble, the way of the wind and the whirlwind. When a man faces the night and the tempest, when civilization finds the old secure foundations shaking and tottering beneath it, when a nation looks out over a final abyss, as we did after Dunkirk, or as all the nations do today, poised on the precipice of this nuclear age, when the great inexorable questions about the meaning of life and the purpose of it all hit our souls like a tornado—it can be then, in the mercy of providence, that the hour of vision comes.

The Covenanters, hunted and harried over the moors, declared that never had they experienced such fellowship with Christ as when the enemy dragoons were after them. "I was not persuaded into religion," wrote Cowper the poet, "I was scourged into it." And anything that crashes violently through the defenses of our common days can be a potential preparation for a new coming of the Lord.

                                                           James S. Stewart

June 19

"GOD, HOW CAN YOU STAND IT?"
Isaiah 63:9

Suffering is not a new phenomenon in human experience. Ancient Jews, as well as Christians, wrestled with the problem of pain. And even patient Job is disturbed by God's ominous silence over his own suffering.

But there is one dimension of God's relationship to suffering that is missing in most discussions of suffering. That is the extent to which God participates in human agony. If God knows everything, after all, He must suffer even more profoundly than we do. When a doctor sees a leper, for instance, he or she is touched and genuinely sympathetic, feeling some pain. But then the doctor can leave, removing the leper from conscious experience. That doctor cannot suffer as the leper does, feeling not only some physical sensations but also the loneliness and ostracism, the loss of dignity and self-assurance. The doctor cannot, but God can and does!

When I worked in New York, just off 46th Street and Broadway, I used to watch the thousands—even millions—of people who would go to lunch each day. "God, how do You stand it?" I wondered. Each person's face seemed etched with lines of care and suffering. In many cases, as one of my friends said after the accidental death of her teenage daughter in an auto collision, they endure a "sorrow that knows no bottom." "God, how do You stand it?" When we wonder why it happens to us, we must remember that it happens to Him.

If God did not intervene to spare His Son and Himself the tragedy, it helps me accept the fact He did not intervene to spare me or my loved one. In other words, God must have a very good reason for allowing human anguish to continue when He Himself is involved in it.

James Londis

THE LAST CHALLENGE
Romans 8:38-39

June 20

Now Paul comes to the last challenge in which he considers the possibility that *we* might fail. All these other challenges have been in terms of God's attitude toward us—any weakening of God's power, any lessening of God's love, and the attitude of the Lord Jesus Christ Himself as judgment has been committed to Him. They have all been from that side. But now he takes up an argument from our side, What if *we* should fail? What if we as the result of trials and troubles and tribulations, should somehow or other fail and thereby be separated from the love of Christ? He takes this up and answers it. Note again his method. He gives a list of the possible things that may come to try us. Then to make it complete, he gives us a quotation from the Old Testament; "For thy sake we are killed all the day long, we are accounted as sheep for the slaughter" (Psalm 44:22).

He means that these trials and troubles and tribulations will come, and do come, and particularly because we are Christians. The New Testament, far from promising us a life of ease and a life in which there will be no difficulties and problems, rather does the opposite. It says that because we are Christians we are likely to meet additional troubles. The early Christians were severely persecuted because they were Christians. They were told that they must renounce their Christianity and say "Caesar is Lord." But this involved the denial of Christ, and for long years and for His sake they were "killed all the day long," being "destitute, afflicted, tormented." Christians must expect tribulations. The ancient Romans used to thresh their corn by means of what they called a "tribulum," a kind of sledge or wooden platform studded underneath with sharp pieces of flint or with iron teeth; and the impression given here is of a man being beaten, and beaten down, because of his loyalty to Christ. It may include death itself. "We are accounted as sheep for the slaughter" is a way of describing the possibility of death.

D. Martin Lloyd-Jones

June 21
HE ALLOWED SUCH A TERRIBLE THING
Romans 8:18

A woman came with anger in her heart against God. "How can I teach my children that God will take care of them as He promised after He has allowed such a terrible thing?"

I realized this would be one of the main questions in everyone's mind. As she continued her complaint against God, I remembered a time when I heard a Sunday School teacher end her story by having the children repeat after her, "If I love God, He will protect me and nothing bad will ever happen to me." Chills were going over me as I heard the same principle voiced. Could she not recall how God's people, all through the ages, had been killed? I sent an arrow prayer heavenward, "Help me, Lord, for I don't know the right words to say." I began, "I can only tell you what I believe, for it seems your belief is different than mine. Evil has been present in the world since Satan made his move to take control of the world from God, and evil will be with us until we reach the deadline God has set for us. During this period of time, He never promised Christians they would be free from the effects of evil—in fact, quite the opposite. As long as we are not isolated from other people, we will be hurt by the sin spill-over. Now, He has promised to be with us in evil and always show us a way out of it when it is more than we can bear. This He did for Dana. He shared everything with her and then took her home to Himself since her innocence could not accept the evil lashed out at her. We even believe she was unconscious at the time and did not experience what went on with her body but Paul writes in Romans 8:18: 'For I reckon that the sufferings of this present time are not worthy to be compared with the glory which shall be revealed in us!'"

Night of Anguish, Morning of Hope
Jean Mize

June 22

PRICELESS WORDS

Matthew 6:34

A man was visiting his beloved wife who had spent considerable time in the hospital during the past year. The situation did not seem hopeful. On his way home, he fell, breaking his hip, and now both were hospitalized. As I thought of these persons and of their fine courage and faith, I wondered how they would react to this new adversity. When I visited the husband my fears proved to be without foundation. He quoted a line he remembered from a sermon he had heard while in Boston on vacation:

> Life is hard by the yard,
> But it is a cinch by the inch.

These words may not go down in history as great literature, but from a practical point of view, they are priceless, because they are the basis of a good philosophy for living. My friend did not merely quote these words—he was living by them. When life seems hard and you grow so weary that you wonder if you can take another step, just remember—"It is a cinch by the inch."

Too many people break down with the burdens of life because they try to carry too much at a time—yesterday's, today's, and tomorrow's burdens. "Life by the yard is hard!"

Call to mind these words: "Therefore do not be anxious about tomorrow, for tomorrow will be anxious for itself. Let the day's own trouble be sufficient for the day."

Behind the Clouds
L. H. Mayfield

June 23

SORROW UNMASKED
Job 6:8-10

Then a woman said, Speak to us of Joy and Sorrow.
And he answered: Your joy is your sorrow unmasked.
And the selfsame well from which your laughter rises was oftentimes filled with your tears.
And how else can it be?
The deeper that sorrow carves into your being, the more joy you can contain.
Is not the cup that holds your wine the very cup that was burned in the potter's oven?
And is not the lute that soothes your spirit, the very wood that was hollowed with knives?
When you are joyous, look deep into your heart and you shall find it is only that which has given you sorrow that is giving you joy.

Kahlil Gibran

I am amazed to find that pain and grief
By some strange alchemy, if bravely borne,
Become a power, vital beyond belief,
To bless and comfort other hearts that mourn.
I did not dream through those far lonely days,
Those bitter hours when pleading for release,
That God would move in His mysterious ways
To make those hours a means to others' peace.

That one's own darkness may become a light
For hurt, bewildered ones—'tis strange to me;
Yet out of pain is often born a white
Undying flame of love and sympathy;
The power that comes to dry another's tears
Was generated through long bitter years.

Grace Noll Crowell

SUFFERING SOWERS

John 4:37-38
June 24

The Lord of the Harvest knows that the glowing reports of success in his work have been preceded many times by the anonymous faithfulness of suffering sowers. As the Lord himself said to the twelve, "That is how the saying comes true: 'One sows and another reaps.' I sent you to reap a crop for which you have not toiled. Others toiled and you have come in for the harvest of their toil" (John 4:37-38).

This does not mean that we are looking for suffering or that we have a kind of evangelical masochism. As Peter says, there is suffering that may come because we have "done wrong." That is not the suffering associated with the lordship of Christ. It could be suffering that comes simply because we do not obey his Word or because we do not take reality seriously. I am speaking of that other kind of suffering where the cause is obedience to the Lord and faithfulness to him.

I have a friend, a pastor who spent some years in jail in Cuba. No reason was given in his case other than his refusal to submit unconditionally to the regime there. He is now free; he ministers in a difficult situation in the same country, isolated, confined to his city, carefully watched. But he has been told by local authorities that to them he is more dangerous than a thousand soldiers fighting against the regime. And around the world under every type of regime we have brethren whose faithfulness to the Lord means suffering with him. Never let the fear of suffering rob you of the joy of obedience to the Lord's call.

Even when we cannot see immediately the way in which our suffering is used by God, we can rejoice because Christ is a pioneer of any suffering we may go through.

David M. Howard

June 25
THE HAMMER, FILE AND FURNACE
Malachi 3:2

The devil, things and people being what they are, it is necessary for God to use the hammer, the file and the furnace in His holy work of preparing a saint for true sainthood. It is doubtful whether God can bless a man greatly until He has hurt him deeply. Without doubt we of this generation have become too soft to scale great spiritual heights. Salvation has come to mean deliverance from unpleasant things. Our hymns and sermons create for us a religion of consolation and pleasantness. We overlook the place of the thorns, the cross and the blood. We ignore the function of the hammer and the file.

The Root of Righteousness
A. W. Tozer

A study was done in 1977 on the impact of an abnormal child upon the parents. In summary, 30 families with a newborn mongoloid were followed for 18 months to 2 years and interviewed 6 times. Few differences could be found in the mental or physical health of the parents in the two groups. Interestingly enough, a low rate of broken homes was found among the families of mongoloid children living at home. There was an increased incidence of divorce and separation in families of similar children in institutions. Author Ann Gath reports, "Despite their grief, the parents of almost half the Mongol children in the study felt drawn closer together and their marriage rather strengthened than weakened by their shared tragedy, a view similar to that expressed by parents of older Mongol children in a survey of school age siblings of Mongol children (done earlier)." A study by Burton in 1975 revealed that 64 percent of mothers and 53 percent of father of children with fibrocystic disease also believed that their problems and distress had brought them closer to their spouses.

Whatever Happened to the Human Race?
Francis A. Schaeffer

June 26

CONFORMITY TO THE CROSS
Micah 7:8

Thomas 'a Kempis wrote that sometimes "he is so comforted with desire for tribulation and adversity for love of conformity to the cross of Christ, that he would not wish to be without grief and tribulation; because he believes that he shall be unto God so much the more acceptable, the more and heavier things he can suffer for him."

There is something about an absolute demand for comfort, even in the littlest things, that wrecks our communion with God. My natural man tells me I have a right to live in total comfort, so whenever this comfort is threatened because the climate control malfunctions or life circumstances push back a meal for an hour or two, I get a true picture of the demandingness of my heart and the bitterness and anger that cause my spirit to growl, like an untamed beast, at the slightest discomfort or inconvenience.

I am learning the need to benefit from discomfort, to allow myself at times to go hungry or be cold and learn from the experience, rather than crying for deliverance. Dietrich Bonhoeffer wrote that if we do not have some of the ascetic in us we will find it hard to follow Christ. Difficulty—or to use spiritual language, the cross—has always been a part of Christian spirituality and always will be. Being full and comfortable rarely leads me to remember God, but it is amazing how hard it is to forget Him when I am fasting.

In the history of the church the desire for suffering at times became unbalanced, but today we have gone too far the other way. Fenelon provides a healthy balance by reminding us that we are not to seek difficulties, but when they come, we should "never let them go by without result."

Seeking the Face of God
Gary L. Thomas

June 27

THE HARVEST OF SUFFERING
Psalm 116:3

Was it not Erskine of Linlathen who said that of all the waste in the world nothing was so wasteful as a wasted sorrow? Fancy going through some great grief and not learning the lesson that tears had to teach! Fancy entertaining Sorrow in the home and not finding the gift she always brings in her hand! The saints believe that no sorrow met in God is sterile of good. Suffering buys something, they believe, worthy of the price which pain has paid. Woe never need be wasted. Their thought of God will not allow the saints to trifle with the idea that His tender heart is indifferent to their longsuffering. Good will come of it. Love will find a way.

And there is more courage in that faith than the inexperienced know. One of the sternest tests God allows to fall upon His saints is to permit them to suffer apparently for nothing; not to see the fruits of their pains. His Son passed out of sight of men unvindicated. The sun set in blood and there was darkness over all the earth. Many a saint endures and sees no fruit to it. . . . One discerning writer says "God has a further step that He must ask of saints of George Herbert's calibre. There comes in the lives of most saints a strange hiatus, when it seems as if the sacrifice that they have made is of no value and leads nowhere; a pause that looks like complete frustration." Endure that! See your sacrifice in the eyes of the world, not as the splendid deed of a noble soul but as the quixotic aberration of a fool. In the dark, these brave souls hold still to the skirts of God. . . . With this longsuffering, they confidently believe that He will purchase something worthy of the price which pain has paid.

The Pure of Heart
W. E. Sangster

June 28

GENTLENESS WITH FAILURE
I Corinthians 4:21

Some years previously he (Walker) had written after a tour among the scattered churches: "I was distressed about the state of many of the Christian congregations. They have not had a thorough overhauling for years. Bishop Sargent had neither time nor strength for visiting all the little congregations; and X has rather been going in for grand new plans than for investigating the condition of our native church. So it remains for us to try and prune the vine, by lopping off dead and useless branches and rendering the conditions of growth more favorable." Wider and more intimate knowledge confirmed the early impressions, and the time was full of keen distress: "The Lord guide us aright" is the prayer at the end of a journal entry of special sorrow in this connection; and again: "Heard of revival in Uganda. When shall we have wave of blessing in Tennevelly?" There is still the same strict self-judgment wherever he touches upon himself in these notes: "I spoke unadvisedly with my lips; Lord, set a watch. Oh for a heart sensitive towards Christ" closes the record of a busy day.

Among the duties of life from this year onward was that of examining fellow-missionaries in Tamil; and the different records, as his press letter-book shows them, suggest an examiner as interested as any examinee could be in the result. This is how a failure is dealt with: "Health has been against him, as you know. We are more than sorry not to be able to pass him in all his subjects. He is a conscientious man, and will, I am sure, remedy his defects. . . ." Those who did not know the private story of his own great disappointment at Cambridge wondered sometimes at his gentleness with failure; but those who knew it wondered more at the gracious ways of God, Who does not shrink from allowing such things to shadow the lives of His beloved.

Walker of Tinnevelly
Amy Carmichael

Matthew 6:14   **A SMOLDERING FIRE**   **June 29**

Unforgiveness is like fire that smolders in the belly, like smoke that smothers the soul. It is destructive because it is insidious. Occasionally it flares up in the form of bitter denunciation and explosions of rage. But most of the time it is content to stay low to the ground, where it goes unnoticed, quietly doing its deadly work.

Unforgiveness should not be confused with healthy responses to loss. The quest for justice, for example, reflects our belief in the moral nature of the universe. When wrong is done, we believe the wrongdoer should be punished. Anger, in turn, is a legitimate emotional response to suffering. When someone has done something hurtful to us, we want to strike back and hurt them. And grief is a natural condition that follows on the heels of loss. When we feel the absence of someone or something we lost, our soul cries out in anguish. These responses indicate that a normal person has just suffered loss and has begun the healthy but painful process of healing.

Unforgiveness is different from anger, grief, or the desire for justice. It is as ruinous as a plague. More destruction has been done from unforgiveness than from all the wrongdoing in the world that created the conditions for it. This destruction can occur on a large scale, as we see in Northern Ireland or in the Middle East. It can also occur on a small scale, as we observe in gang warfare, family feuds, and conflicts between former friends. In the name of unforgiveness people can do terrible things.

A Grace Disguised
Jerry Sittser

June 30

FORGIVENESS IS COSTLY
Matthew 18:21-35

Forgiveness is costly. Forgiving people must give up the right to get even, a right that is not so easy to relinquish. They must show mercy when their human sensibilities tell them to punish. Not that a desire for justice is wrong. A person can both forgive and strive for justice. Wrong that is forgiven is still wrong done and must be punished. Mercy does not abrogate justice; it transcends it. However difficult, forgiveness in the end brings freedom to the one who gives it. Forgiving people let God run the universe. They let God punish wrongdoers as he wills, and they let God show mercy as he wills, too. That is what Job and Joseph came to. . . . That is also what Jesus decided, as demonstrated by the pardon he granted his accusers and executioners while dying on the cross.

I think that I was spared excessive preoccupation with revenge because I believe that God is just, even though the judicial system is not. Ultimately every human being will have to stand before God, and God will judge every person with wisdom and impartiality. Human systems may fail; God's justice does not. I also believe that God is merciful, in ways that far exceed what we could imagine or muster ourselves. It is the tension between God's justice and mercy that makes God so capable of dealing with wrongdoers. God is able to punish people without destroying them, and to forgive people without indulging them. Forgiving people, therefore, define the role they play in life modestly. They simply let God be God so that they can be normal and happy human beings who learn to forgive. Rather than think that they must even all scores, make sure justice prevails, and punish all wrongs, they simply choose to live as responsibly and humbly as they can. . . . and they try to do what is right in the face of so much wrong.

A Grace Disguised
Jerry Sittser

July 1
THE MANY ILLS THE FLESH IS HEIR TO
Hebrews 4:15-16

I think that there is also another kind of suffering. . . . It comes neither from the rod nor from the cross, not being imposed as a moral corrective nor suffered as a result of our Christian life and testimony. It comes in the course of nature and arises from the many ills the flesh is heir to. It visits all alike in a greater or lesser degree and would appear to have no clear spiritual significance. Its source may be fire, flood, bereavement, injuries, accidents, illness, old age, weariness, or the upset conditions of the world generally.

A. W. Tozer

God gets down on His knees among us. Gets on our level and shares Himself with us. He does not reside afar off and send us diplomatic messages. He kneels among us. The posture is characteristic of God.

The discovery and realization of this, what defines what we know of God, is Good news. God shares Himself generously and graciously. Whichever form the blessing takes, it implies an exchange of the contents of the soul. God enters into our need. He anticipates our goal. He gets into our skin and understands us better than we do ourselves.

Everything we learn about God through Scripture and in Christ tells us that He knows what it is like to change a diaper for the 13th time in the day, have a report, over which we have worked long and carefully, gather dust on somebody's desk for weeks and weeks; find our teaching treated with scorn and indifference by children and youth; discover that the integrity and excellence of our work has been overlooked, and the shoddy duplicity of another's rewarded with a promotion.

Eugene H. Peterson

July 2

THIS THING IS FROM ME
Zechariah 2:8

My child, I have a message for you today. Let me whisper it in your ear, that it may gild with glory any storm clouds which may arise and smooth the tough places upon which you may have to tread. It is short—only five words—but let them sink into your innermost soul; use them as a pillow upon which to rest your weary head: "This thing is from Me." Have you ever thought of it, that all that concerns you, concerns Me too, "For he that toucheth you toucheth the apple of His eye." I would have you learn, when temptations assail you and the "enemy comes in like a flood," that this thing is from Me; that your weakness needs My might, and your safety lies in letting Me fight for you. You are very "precious in my sight" (Isaiah 43:4), therefore it is My special delight to educate you.

Are you in money difficulties? Is it hard to make both ends meet? This thing is from Me, for I am your pursebearer and would have you draw from and depend upon Me. My supplies are limitless (Philippians 4:19). I would have you prove My promises. Let it not be said of you, "In this thing ye did not believe the Lord your God" (Deuteronomy 1:32). Are you in difficult circumstances, surrounded by people who do not understand you, who never consult your taste, who put you in the background? This thing is from Me, I am the God of circumstances: "Thou camest not to this place by accident; it is the very place God meant for thee." Have you not asked to be made humble? See then, I have placed you in the very school where this lesson is taught; your surroundings and companions are only working out My will. Are you passing through a night of sorrow? This thing is from Me. I am the "Man of sorrows and acquainted with grief" (Isaiah 53:3). I have let earthly comforters fail you that, by turning to Me, you may obtain everlasting consolation (see II Thessalonians 2:16-17).

Laura A. Bartner Snow

July 3
PASSING THROUGH A NIGHT OF SORROW
II Thessalonians 2:16-17

Has some friend disappointed you, one to whom you opened your heart? This thing is from Me. I have allowed this disappointment to come, that you may learn that I want to be your Confidant. Has someone repeated things about you that are untrue? Leave them to Me and draw closer to Me, thy shelter out of the reach of "The strife of tongues," for I will "bring forth thy righteousness as the light, and thy judgment as the noon day" (Psalms 37:6). Have your plans been upset? This thing is from Me. You made your plans, then came asking Me to bless them. But I would have you let Me plan for you, and then I take the responsibility for "This thing is too heavy for thee; thou are not able to perform it thyself alone" (Exodus 18:18).

Have you longed to do some great work for Me, and instead been laid aside on a bed of pain and weakness? This thing is from Me. I could not get your attention in your busy day, and I want to teach you some of my deepest lessons. "They also serve who only stand and wait." Are you suddenly called upon to occupy a difficult and responsible position? Launch out on Me, I am trusting you with "the possession of difficulties," and "for this thing the Lord thy God shall bless thee in all thy works, and in all thou puttest thine hand unto" (Deuteronomy 15:10).

This day I place in your hands this pot of holy oil; make use of it freely, My child. Let every circumstance, as it arises, every word that pains you, every interruption that would make you impatient, every revelation of your own weakness, be anointed with it! Remember, "Interruptions are divine instructions." Therefore, "Set your hearts unto all the words which I testify among you this day . . . for it is not a vain thing for you because it is your life and through this thing ye shall prolong your days in the land" (Deuteronomy 32:46-47).

Laura A. Bartner Snow

July 4

NOT IN SOME CHARMED CIRCLE
Romans 8:24-25

We do not live in some magic or charmed circle because we are Christians. We are never promised exemption from the troubles that flesh and blood are heir to in a fallen, sinful world such as this. So we must not be surprised when evils befall us; we must not be disappointed and become dejected. Still less must we begin to query the truth of the Christian gospel. The devil will tempt us to do so. "Ah," he says, "you believed in Christ, and you thought everything was going to be trouble-free but look at your position. Your gospel is not true." The best reply to such a challenge is to understand and grasp this argument that "hope that is seen is not hope; for what a man seeth, why doth he yet hope for?" We are now living by faith and in hope. So get hold of this negative argument and it will save you from ever being surprised or disappointed, and ultimately from being dejected.

D. Martyn Lloyd-Jones

If God has made your cup sweet, drink it with grace; if He has made it bitter, drink it in communion with Him.

Oswald Chambers

It is more than comforting to realize that it is those who have plumbed the depth of failure to whom invariably God gives the call to shepherd others. This is not a call given to the gifted, the highly trained or the polished, as such. Without a bitter experience of their own inadequacy and poverty, they are quite unfitted to bear the burden of spiritual ministry. It takes a man who has discovered something of the measures of his own weakness to be patient with the foibles of others. Such a man also has a firsthand knowledge of the loving care of the Chief Shepherd, and His ability to heal one who has come humbly to trust in Him and Him alone.

J. C. Metcalfe

July 5

APPOINTMENTS OF LOVE
I Kings 12:24

The disappointments of life are simply the hidden appointments of love.

C. A. Fox

"This is from Me," the Savior said,
  As bending low He kissed my brow,
"For One who loves you thus has led.
  Just rest in Me, be patient now.
Your Father knows you have need of this,
  Though, why perhaps you cannot see—
Grieve not for things you've seemed to miss.
  The thing I send is best for thee."

Then, looking through my tears, I plead,
  "Dear Lord, forgive, I did not know,
It will not be hard since You do tread,
  Each path before me here below."
And for my good this thing must be,
  His grace sufficient for each test.
So still I'll sing, "Whatever be
  God's way for me is always best."

Author Unknown

July 6

YOUR HEAVENLY FATHER KNOWS
Matthew 11:26

A visitor at a school for the deaf was writing questions on the board for the children. Soon he wrote this sentence: "Why has God made me able to hear and speak and made you deaf?" The shocking sentence hit the children like a cruel slap on the face. They sat paralyzed, pondering the dreadful word "Why?" And then a little girl arose. With her lip trembling and her eyes swimming with tears, she walked straight to the board. Picking up the chalk, she wrote with a steady hand these precious words: "Yes, Father, for this was your good pleasure" (Matthew 11:26). What a reply! It reaches up and claims an eternal truth upon which the most mature believer, and even the youngest child of God, may securely rest—the truth that God is your Father. Can you state that truth with full assurance and faith? Once you do, your dove of faith will no longer wander the skies in restless flight but will settle forever in its eternal resting place of peace: your Father!

I still believe that a day of understanding will come for each of us, however far away it may be. We will understand as we see the tragedies that today darken and dampen the presence of heaven for us take their proper place in God's great plan— a plan so overwhelming, magnificent, and joyful, we will laugh with wonder and delight.

Arthur Christopher Bacon

> Chance has not brought this ill to me;
> It's God's own hand, so let it be,
> For He sees what I cannot see.
> There is a purpose for each pain,
> And He one day will make it plain
> That earthly loss is heavenly gain.

Selected

Luke 8:25   **BRAZEN HEAVENS (I)**   **July 7**

For about a year now I have been witness to a drama that is all too familiar to us mortal men. Someone finds he has cancer; the medical treadmill begins, with its implacable log of defeat; hope is marshaled, begins the march, is rebuffed at every juncture, is finally quietly mustered out. And meanwhile, because the people in the drama are Christian believers, everyone is dragged into the maelstrom that marks the place where our experience eddies into the sea of the Divine Will. The whole question of prayer gapes open.

The promises are raked over. And over and over. "Is there enough faith on our part?" "We must scour our own hearts to see that there is no stoppage there—of sin or of unbelief." "We must stand on the promise." "We must *claim* thus and such." "We must resist the Devil and his weapons of doubt." And we leap at and pursue any and all reports and records of healings. "Look at what happened to so-and-so!" "Listen to this!" "I've just read this wonderful pamphlet." We know the Gospel accounts by heart. We agree that this work of healing did not cease with the apostolic age. We greet gladly the tales of healing that pour in from all quarters in the Church—no longer only from those groups that have traditionally "specialized" in healing, but from the big, old, classic bodies in Christendom—Rome, Anglicanism, Lutheranism, Presbyterianism, and so forth. "God is doing something in our day," we hear, and we grasp at it eagerly.

And meanwhile the surgery goes on its horrific way, and the radiation burns on, week after grim week; and suffering sets in, and the doctors hedge and dodge into the labyrinthine linoleum and stainless-steel bureaucracy of the hospital world, and our hearts sicken. . . . And the question comes stealing over us: "Where is now their God?"

                                                               Thomas Howard

July 8

BRAZEN HEAVENS (II)
II Corinthians 12:8

We look for some light. We look for some help. Our prayers seem to be vanishing, like so many wisps, into the serene ether of the cosmos (or worse, into the plaster of the ceiling). We strain our ears for some word from the Mount of God. A whisper will do, we tell ourselves, since clearly no bolts or thunderings have been activated by our importunity (yes, we have tried that tactic, too: the "nonfaith" approach).

But only dead silence. Blank. Nothing. "But Lord, how are we supposed to know if we're on the right track at all if we don't get some confirmation from you—some corroboration—in *any* form, Lord—inner peace maybe, or some verse springing to life for us, or some token. Please let us have some recognizable attestation to what you have said in your Book." Nothing. Silence. Blank.

Perhaps at this point we try to think back over the experience of the people of God through the millennia. There has been a whole spectrum of experience for them: glorious deliverances, great victories, kingdoms toppled, widows receiving their dead back, men wandering about in sheepskins and goatskins—

"Men wandering about in sheepskins and goatskins? What went wrong there?" "That's in the record of faith." "But then surely something went wrong." "No. It is part of the log of the faithful. That is a list of what happened to the people of faith. It is about how they proved God."

The whole spectrum of experience is there. The widow of Nain got her son back and other mothers didn't. Peter got out of prison and John the Baptist didn't. Elijah whirled up to heaven with fiery horses and Joseph ended in a coffin in Egypt. Paul healed other people but was turned down on his own request for healing for himself.

Thomas Howard

July 9

GOD, DID YOU FORGET?
Isaiah 49:15

Christmas and New Year's over, I was tired. On the evening of January 4, I carried my lively infant son, four days shy of his first birthday, to his room and tucked him into his crib. He cried a few times, as he often did, but there was nothing in the sound of his cry to cause alarm. I . . . went to bed, never dreaming that I had seen my son alive for the last time.

The next morning I bent over Dickie's crib to awaken him, but there was no movement. He was dead. The doctor would pronounce it a crib death, a defect of the thymus gland which can choke an infant to death in an instant. At the moment of the horrifying discovery, I was alone in the house with Kathleen, Rolland having gone to speak at the high school. I fell into a chair, sobbing uncontrollably. Kathleen, five years old, turned to me half annoyed, "Oh, Mother," she said, "God will give you another baby." Those childish words came as a reminder that both of my children had been cesarean and it was commonly thought that a third cesarean delivery posed an unreasonable hazard. No doubt, I reflected bitterly, I will never have another child. The weeks and months that followed were the darkest of my life. From the mountaintop . . . and the almost tangible sense of God's presence, I was plunged into a dark night of despair. Dark suspicions preyed on my mind. "God," I accused, "did you forget I am a Christian, your child? Did you forget that I have sacrificed to become a missionary? Why didn't you tell me that my little boy needed me?" I thought of the children I had seen thronging the streets of China. At one time I had felt sorry for them, prayed for them. But now while those children—ragged and undernourished as they might be—lived, laughed and played, my son was gone never to return. On the wall beside the stairway in our home, I had hung a plaque bearing a familiar motto, "Jesus Never Fails." Now I couldn't stand to look at those words. They seemed to mock my faith. Never fail? "But, Jesus," I protested, "You did fail." I felt my soul shriveling. The sun no longer arose over the horizon in my world. All the laughter and joy had been squeezed out of my life, leaving it a hollow shell. Prayer did not seem to help. Even the Word, always my solace, did not speak in those long night hours.

When my spirits were lowest, God sent me a special friend, Viola Sewell. Viola attended our church, although she was not a member. She came to me, not with scripture verses or advice or judgments or exhortations to get on with the business of living. Rather she just brought her gentle presence. She made herself available to talk with me, just to be there every day if I needed her. She is still a treasured friend, and I'll always remember her kindness.

The Key Goose
Mildred Rice

July 10
OUT OF THE SLOUGH OF DESPOND
Psalm 40:2

About this time our missionary friends in China, Orville and Aileen French, felt impressed to pray for us. Late one night Orville woke up, wrote a poem and sent it to us. It ended with these lines: "I'll place my whys beneath the cross and reap some fruit for Thee." That message was, indeed, God's word to me and expressed a truth I needed to get a hold of. The whys of Dickie Dean's death would probably never be answered in this life. It was time now to stop struggling with them and just lay them at the foot of the Cross. Steadily I began to climb out of the slough of despond, but it was months before I could sit down to a meal without looking at Dickie's empty place and find my eyes blurring with hot tears. In spite of my fears, the doctor approved my having another child and by cesarean. Edward was born on February 19, 1944, in the hospital in Angola, Indiana. All went well. Edward, too, had a defective thymus gland, but a simple procedure—a series of X-ray treatments—corrected the problem. Still, after losing Dickie, I couldn't relax with my new son. Continually anxious and fretful, I found myself watching his every move. Again and again, I would hurry into his room half expecting to find that he, too, had slipped away, just as Dickie had.

We were traveling in Canada one summer when Ed came down with a cold, touching off the now familiar cycle of panic. Too upset to go to church, I fell on my knees to pray. The Lord began talking to me. "You know," He said, "you are not treating this baby as a normal mother would. You are obsessed with the fear that he will die. That is not normal and that is not living by faith. A normal mother thinks her baby is going to live, not die. That is what I want you to be, a normal mother." That morning a great burden rolled off of me. When the others came home from church, I was walking on air. God had delivered me from fear.

The Key Goose
Mildred Rice

July 11

IS GOD? DOES GOD?
II Corinthians 1:18-22

Annie determined that there was to be "no moaning of the bar when (she) put out to sea." The last years of her life brought her no ease from her affliction, no lessening of pain and suffering. Yet, we think that those closing years she really exemplified more than ever some of the sweetness of her earlier verses. In Annie's own notes from which this sketch of her life is written, her affliction receives little notice. She would have it so. Although crippled, she did not consider herself helpless and that she could do nothing but bemoan her lot. She believed that God had laid her aside for a purpose, even though that purpose was obscure to her at times, but she also believed that He had work for her to do and she put her very best into the writing of her poems, rendering this ministry unto Him. . . . She wrote, and out of the crucible of suffering she was able to administer that comfort to others wherewith she herself had been comforted of God. No one but God and she knew what suffering she endured as the disease became worse with the passing of the years, and new complications developed. But through it all her faith in the goodness and mercy of God never wavered. For more than 40 years there was scarcely a day when she did not suffer pain. For 37 years she became increasingly helpless. Her joints had become rigid, although she was able to turn her head, and in great pain write a few lines on paper. But long before these years of helplessness, she had received her one great affirmation from God which settled all her doubts. Perhaps the shortest stanza which she wrote was upon the words, "For all the promises of God in him are yea, and in him Amen." From this verse she wrote:

> Man's "Why?" and "How?"
> In ceaseless iteration storm the sky.
> "I am"; "I will"; "I do"—sure Word of God,
> Yea and Amen, Christ answers each cry;
> To all our anguished questionings and doubts
> Eternal affirmation and reply.

Life of Annie Johnson Flint

July 12
HOW I TREAT MY FRIENDS
Psalm 51:17

Once when Teresa was complaining to God of her pains, she said he told her "But this is how I treat My friends," to which she readily replied: "Yes, my Lord, and that is why Thou hast so few of them." Finally, Teresa's great concern about the danger of seeking favors in prayer underscores her humility in trusting in God. Once again she emphasized that God chooses to give Himself only to the humble—only to those who have earned nothing. . . . On her deathbed her last words, repeated over and over again, were the lines from a Psalm of David: "A sacrifice to God is an afflicted spirit; a contrite and humbled heart, O God, Thou wilt not despise."

Life of St. Teresa

Carey was startled at the woe in Marshman's face, when he broke in upon him in Calcutta so unexpectedly that Thursday morning, March 12, 1812. What great fresh sorrow could have befallen the Mission? They had recently been "smitten with breach upon breach,"—five burials at Serampore since Christmas: Sister Mardon on Christmas Day, leaving three children; a woman-servant of Mrs. Marshman's, of 11 years' faithfulness; Herbert, a boarder of Marshman's, dear almost as a son; Ward's darling Mary, of 6 years; and only a week back an infant of Marshman's own, named William Ward Marshman, for love of the colleague. Of what more distressful bereavement was Carey to hear? Of what "rough wind" in those days of the "east wind"?

When he learned that the Mission printing works were a shell of burnt and naked walls, with only a few business documents rescued, he was "dumb with silence," his heart frozen within him. . . . overwhelmed by the blow of God's hand.

Life of William Carey
S. Pearce Carey

Psalm 4:1   A LIVING DEAD MAN   **July 13**

I remember the first time I realized I had no fight left. It began on the one-year anniversary of the accident. I felt a nervous agitation come on, a brooding anxiety. I sensed that something was wrong, but apprehension of it eluded me—as if I had misplaced something important and had forgotten not only where I had misplaced it but what I had misplaced in the first place. Over the next month I became increasingly restless. Eventually I started to feel a tremor inside myself, not only in my body but also deep down in my soul. I sensed that I was close to a breakdown.

I learned later that I had become profoundly depressed. Only then did I discover a language to describe my own clinical state. That language came from William Styron's book *Darkness Visible*, which tells the story of his own descent into depression. Unlike physical pain, which usually points to some concrete abnormality like a broken leg, the pain of depression reflects an abnormality that cannot be so easily observed or explained. . . . But willing an end of depression is as difficult as healing a broken heart. Human strength alone is insufficient for the task. Like Styron, I found depression completely debilitating. It took Herculean strength for me to get out of bed in the morning. I was fatigued all day long, yet at night I was sleepless. I would lie awake by the hour, feeling the torment of a darkness that no one could see but me. I had trouble concentrating. I was apathetic and desireless. I could not taste food, see beauty, or touch anything with pleasure. I exacerbated the problem by telling virtually no one about the struggle. Friends and colleagues marveled at how well I was doing. But inside I was a living dead man. I finally became desperate enough to see a counselor, and for two months I took an anti-depressant so that I could function normally without losing my mind.

A Grace Disguised
Jerry Sittser

July 14

A VICTIM OF DISTRACTION
Exodus 13:17-14:4

I need His leadership in the daytime. Sometimes the daylight is my foe. It tempts me into carelessness. I become the victim of distraction. The "garish day" can entice me into ways of trespass, and I am robbed of my spiritual health. Many a man has been faithful in the twilight and night who has lost himself in the sunshine. He went astray in his prosperity; success was his ruin. And so in the daytime I need the shadow of God's presence, the cooling, subduing, calming influence of a friendly cloud.

"And by night in a pillar of fire." And I need God's leadership in the night. Sometimes the night fills me with fears and I am confused. The darkness chills me, sorrow and adversity make me cold and I shiver in uncertain going. But my God will lead me as a presence of fire. He will keep my heart warm even in the midnight, and He will guide me by the kindlings of His love. There shall be "nothing hidden from its heat." And my bewildering fears shall flee away, and I will sing "songs in the night."

J. H. Jowett

July 15

UTTERLY WEARY

Isaiah 45:3

"I am utterly weary of life. I pray the Lord will come forthwith and carry me hence. Let Him come above all with His last judgment. I will stretch out my neck, the thunder will burst forth and I shall be at rest." And having a necklace of white agates in his hand at the time, he added: "O God, grant that it may come without delay. I would readily eat up this necklace today for the judgment to come tomorrow." The Electress Dowager one day, when Luther was dining with her, said to him, "Doctor, I wish you may live 40 years to come." "Madame," replied he, "rather than live 40 years more, I would give up my chance of Paradise."

Life of Martin Luther

It is the glory of God to conceal His treasures in embarrassments, i.e., in things that involve us in difficulty. "I will give thee the treasures of darkness." We would never have suspected that treasures were hidden there, and in order to get them we have to go through things that involve us in perplexity. There is nothing more wearying to the eye than perpetual sunshine, and the same is true spiritually. The valley of the shadow gives us time to reflect, and we learn to praise God for the valley because in it our soul was restored in its communion with God. God gives us a new revelation of His kindness in the valley of the shadow. What are the days and the experiences that have furthered us most? The days of green pastures, of absolute ease? No, they have their value; but the days that have furthered us most in character are the days of stress and cloud.

Oswald Chambers

July 16

ENDLESS TROUBLES

II Corinthians 8:1-2

On August 2 Hudson Taylor went out to hire canal and river boats to take all the household except Lae-djun and James Williamson to the foot of Pengshan mountain. Marie was so prostrate, "I feared she was not likely to last long," so often did her cough and fever reduce her to helplessness. Grace had been off her food . . . but he was not anxious about her as he was for Herbert, aged six and febrile. Any hint of hydrophobia since his dog bite on the cheek alarmed them all. Four-year-old Howard (Freddie) had been hot and drowsy recently, but not really ill until Hudson Taylor came home from hiring the boats, to find him in convulsions. By the time he had recovered in a tepid bath, it was late in the day. And then by the time boats reached the water gate through the city wall, it was closed. Grace was tired and irritable so the McCarthys took her into their larger boat with more space to lie down. After a sweltering night and day, they reach Pengshan on August 5 and on the cool hilltop, living a gypsy life for a few days in the derelict temple, three tumbledown sheds and an open pavilion, all quickly improved. Maria had had to be carried up. She and the two boys "were really ill," Jennie thought.

Grace complained of headache the next day and by the 8th had a high fever. Now Hudson Taylor was more worried about her. . . . A message from Shaoxing came that Jane McLean's dysentery had relapsed and Mrs. Stevenson and her child were both ill. Would he please come? He hurried to Shaoxing by fast footboat, dosed Jane McLean and brought her back with Emily to look after her. . . . Friday had been distressing for Maria. Freddie had had more fever and convulsions, but Grace, lying in the fresh air on Rudland's camp bed, was incoherent when Maria struggled from her own bed to go and see her.

Hudson Taylor and China's Open Century
A. J. Broomhall

Psalm 42:5-7 ## GOD TAKES AWAY ALL **July 17**

God abandons our whole entire being—flesh, blood, sensibility, intelligence, love—to the pitiless necessity of matter and the cruelty of the devil, except for the eternal and supernatural part of the soul.

Gateway to God
Simone Weil

Everything loses its flavor. God takes away all and the enjoyment of friendships as well as all the rest. Need we be surprised? He even takes away our joy in his love and his law. We no longer know where we are. The heart is blighted and nearly extinguished. It would not know how to love anything. The bitterness of having lost God, whom we had felt so sweetly with such fervor, is wormwood spread over everything which we have loved among his creatures. We are like an invalid who feels his weakness from lack of nourishment.

Then do not speak of friendship. The very name hurts and would bring tears to our eyes. Everything overcomes us. We do not know what we want. We have affections and griefs as a child does. We cannot tell the reason, and they vanish like a dream the moment that we speak of them. Whatever we say of our condition seems always a lie, because it stops being true when we begin to speak of it. Nothing lasts in us. We cannot respond to anything, nor promise ourselves anything, nor even describe ourselves. . . . Everything changes. Nothing is left to us and our hearts least of all. . . . To speak of natural goodness, of tenderness, generosity, constancy, gratitude for our friends to a sick and suffering soul is like talking of dancing and music to a person who is dying. The heart is like a tree withered to the root.

Fenelon

July 18

WHATEVER HE WANTS TO ACCOMPLISH
Colossians 3:15

I realized Satan was working on my subconscious mind in order to weaken my faith and give me doubts concerning Dana's death. I took the problem to the Lord several times but the dream kept returning. I knew that sometimes there is within a person an unconscious refusal to accept the death of a loved one, and it would manifest itself in this way. I was ashamed to find this weakness in me after all the beautiful things God had done. I could not talk about it for a time. Then one day I shared it with the family, only to find some of them were having a similar problem. We began praying for each other and sharing this part of our lives with others who had lost loved ones. The dreams left and we rejoice in the peace that has replaced them.

As I sit here in retrospection upon this memorable year, I can see God's hand even more. Truly His thoughts were not our thoughts, neither were His ways our ways, for His ways were higher than our ways and His thoughts higher than our thoughts. One of my favorite sayings is: "Peace and joy are twin blessings of the gospel. Peace is joy resting and joy is peace dancing."

I have experienced both this year, according to His promise in Isaiah, even when there did not appear to be anything to be joyful about. He has allowed us the privilege, not only of seeing spiritual growth in our own family but also of seeing other lives change. I commit this writing to Him knowing that everything we do in His will will accomplish whatever He wants it to accomplish and will not return void. I hope you can see the sufficiency of my Lord and Savior and if you do not know Him personally, that you would choose to do that today.

Night of Anguish, Morning of Hope
Jean Mize

STABBED WIDE AWAKE

Isaiah 53:4-5

July 19

The majority of people who have never been touched by affliction see Jesus Christ's death as irrelevant. When a man gets to his wits' end and things go hard with him, his thick hide is pierced and he is stabbed wide awake. Then for the first time he begins to see something else—"At last I see. I thought that He was stricken, smitten *of God* and afflicted; but now I see He was wounded for *my* transgressions."

The great fundamental revelation regarding the human race is that God has redeemed us; and Redemption enters into our lives when we are upset enough to see we need it. There is too much common sense used, "pills to cure an earthquake" given; and "the gospel of temperament" preached. It is an insult today to tell some men and women to cheer up. One of the most shallow, petty things that can be said is that "every cloud has a silver lining." There are some clouds that are black all through. At the wall of the world stands God with His arms outstretched; and when a man or woman is driven there, the consolations of Jesus Christ are given. Through the agonies in human life, we do not make redemption, but we see why it was necessary for God to make it. It is not necessary for every man to go through these agonies, but it takes a time of agony to get the shallow skepticism knocked out of us. It is a good thing to be reverent with what we do not understand. A moral agony gives a man "a second wind," and he runs better after it and is a good deal more likely to win.

The Shadow of an Agony
Oswald Chambers

July 20

THE LONG PROCESS IN FIRES
Isaiah 54:11

Along with the gold in both Eden and Paradise, we find precious stones (Genesis 2:12; Revelation 21:19). Gemstones are not produced in a day. Time is a vital factor in their formation. They are wrought by long process in the fires of earth, and their beauties are displayed by skillful cutting. In spiritual terms this implies values that are inwardly wrought by the divine patience in you and me. Such values are costly. Those unwilling to pay will never come by them. Grace is free; but only a high price buys precious stones. Many a time we shall want to cry out, "This is costing too much!" Yet the lessons we learn as we pass with Him "through fire and water"—these are the really worthwhile things. In the light of God some things perish of themselves; there is no need to wait for the fire. It is in what has stood God's test of time that true worth lies.

Watchman Nee

I needed the quiet so He drew me aside.
Into the shadows where we could confide.
Away from the bustle where all the day long
I hurried and worried when active and strong.

I needed the quiet tho at first I rebelled
But gently, so gently, my cross He upheld
And whispered so sweetly of spiritual things
Tho weakened in body, my spirit took wings
To heights never dreamed of when active and gay,
He loved me so greatly He drew me away.

I needed the quiet. No prison my bed,
But a beautiful valley of blessings instead—
A place to grow richer in Jesus to hide.
I needed the quiet so He drew me aside.

Alice Hansche Mortenson

July 21

NO CONVENIENT TIME
II Corinthians 8:3-7

What has all this to do with affliction? A great deal. There is a refining process going on, and one of the ways of recognizing that something is taking place is that, in the midst of trials, these Christians in Macedonia are sharing their very meager goods with others. In other words, they are thinking more about other people's needs than their own, giving evidence of a work of the Holy Spirit taking place within themselves, as natural selfishness in the time of suffering is turned to generosity.

The polishing process is not a glamorous happening that needs a rarified, spiritual atmosphere in which to take place, an "ivory tower" in which to take a monk's vow in some ethereal way, but refining which is the very warp and woof of everyday life—right down to the grass-roots level of taking half of your apple pie to an invalid neighbor, making a batch of rolls for the family whose mother is in the hospital having a new baby, or sharing your garden produce with an apartment dweller. Malachi talks about a sharing of money, needful if God is to bless even in this life, but there is far more; and a portion consists of a concrete sharing of things that are not just "extra," but an actual part of your own Sunday-dinner preparation or your Saturday picnic fare.

All this is not to be just when everything is going well for us, and the neighbor is in the hospital, but when we have a twisted knee or have just had sad news on the phone or a crushing telegram. Is there no time for pushing aside others for our private sorrow? No, there is always a mixture. There is never a time when it is "convenient" to care for someone else. There is always what could be considered a "conflict," and sensitivity as to what to do first is part of the polishing process.

Affliction
Edith Schaeffer

II Kings 4:24-28 ## TAKING AWAY THE GIFT **July 22**

God takes away what he has given. But he does not take it away to deprive us of it forever. He takes it away so that he can better give it, so that he can give it back without the impurity of this evil sense of ownership which we mingle with it without noticing it in ourselves. The loss of the gift takes away our ownership, and the sense of possession being taken away, the gift is given back a hundredfold. Then the gift is no longer the gift of God. It is God himself in the soul. It is no more a gift of God because we consider it no longer as something apart from him.

God's most usual way with souls then is first to attract them to him in order to detach them from the world and from gross desires, by making them taste . . . sweetness. In the first sensitive attraction, the whole soul is turned to mortification and prayer. It fights itself constantly in all things. It does away with all external consolations, and those of friendship are also curtailed because it is conscious of the impurity of self-love. There remain only the friends to whom we are bound by similarity of feeling, or those whom we cultivate for charity or for duty's sake. . . .

There are plenty of souls which never pass this state of fervor and spiritual abundance. But there are others which God leads farther and which he divests jealously after having clothed and adorned them. These last fall into a state of distaste, dryness and languor, in which everything is a burden to them. Far from being responsive to friendship, the friendship of the people whom they formerly enjoyed the most becomes irritating to them. A soul in this state feels that God and all his gifts are withdrawing from it. It is a time of agony and a kind of despair.

Fenelon

July 23
HIDDEN SECRETS
Exodus 20:21

God has still His hidden secrets, hidden from the wise and prudent. Do not fear them. Be content to accept things that you cannot understand. Wait patiently. Presently He will reveal to you the treasures of darkness. The riches of the glory of the mystery. Mystery is only the veil of God's face. Do not be afraid to enter into the cloud that is settling down on your life. God is in it. The other side is radiant with His glory. "Think it not strange concerning the fiery trial which is to try you as though a strange thing happened unto you, but rejoice in as much as ye are partakers of Christ's suffering." When you seem loneliest and most forsaken, God is nigh. He is in the dark cloud. Plunge into the blackness of its darkness without flinching. Under the shrouding curtain of His pavilion you will find God awaiting you.

"As a man stood on a high peak of the Rocky Mountains watching a storm raging below, an eagle came up through the clouds and soared away toward the sun, and the water upon him glistened like diamonds. Had it not been for the storm he might have remained in the valley. The sound and light caused him to rise towards God."

What the precious Lord is doing I do not know, but He makes me know it is all right. Mrs. Clark and Corneal said, "God is so present that they could not really pray and were resting in Him." Charlie asked about 6 a.m. for some grape juice, the first he has asked for anything in nearly a week. In the evening he wanted me to sing and asked for some songs. He could hardly remember just how it went, but it was something about "when all hope is gone keep hoping on." I knew it was our old battle hymn, "When obstacles and trials seem like prison walls to me and hope finds its strength in helplessness and calmly waits for Thee."

Lettie Cowman Diary, 1924

John 15:13   **A HARMONY ABOUT LIFE**   **July 24**

The most graphic story written in recent years is Ernest Gordon's *Through the Valley of the Kwai*. It is the struggle of prisoners of war to survive in the face of almost impossible circumstances. It abounds with inspired persons who refused to quit. From the utter despair of the Death Camp came a spiritual triumph time and time again.

One such case was a man who was quite young, yet aged because of the suffering he had endured. He was exposed to the miracle that had been taking place in the Death Camp. He reflected for a moment—"Do you know what I've come to think? There's harmony about life. When you put yourself in tune with that harmony, you sense a rightness about things. You know a peace in your heart." Here was a lad who had in a very real sense brought life out of death.

There is a harmony about life. When one begins to realize this, nothing can really bring about a discord. Through faith he sees that whatever may be happening *around* him need not be happening *to* him. Even the storms cannot put him out of tune, for he has an anchor.

There is harmony in life, but one must put himself in tune with this harmony. The miracle of the Kwai took place when those suffering souls began to forget their own miseries in ministering to others whose miseries were even greater. "Greater love has not man than this."

Behind the Clouds
L. H. Mayfield

Job 13:15   **IT DOESN'T MAKE SENSE**   **July 25**

As I share my testimony in churches, homes, and at women's retreats, the question I am most often asked is: "After all you've been through—losing a child to leukemia, a husband to Hodgkin's disease, the sudden death of your two remaining children in an automobile accident—after all that, how can you retain your faith in a loving God? How can you go on smiling, praising the Lord, talking about his goodness? It doesn't make sense."

I answer that nowhere in Scripture are we told that because we are God's children we will be spared the harsh realities of human life. The Bible says, "Yet man is born unto trouble, as the sparks fly upward" (Job 5:7). Though God showers blessings and goodness upon us without measure, it is also true that his very Son, the one he loves most, is the one he allowed to suffer the most.

God wants us to share in the character of his Son. So, even though suffering offends our shallow, human view of a loving God, the Christian who has passed through the fire learns with Pascal a high logic: "The heart has its reasons which reason cannot understand." In the business of spiritual heart surgery, God's keenest instrument is suffering. Why? Because only in dying do we learn to live and only in relinquishing everything do we know what true gain is.

Since God loves us and only allows good, we can only understand suffering in the light of the resurrection. Resurrection power means that something positive will arise from all suffering for the Christian, just as Christ arose from the dead.

Thrice Through the Valley
Valetta Steel

HOW TO MEET YOUR TROUBLES (I)
II Corinthians 4:17

July 26

1. *Determine to profit by your trouble* in every way possible and ask God to make it work for your good. Paul Hutchens in his book *How to Meet Your Troubles* says, "Let God put your troubles to work in your behalf. This can be done. They can become His servants to accomplish in you some very blessed things. . . ." A. S. London says that suffering rightly met always develops lovely character traits such as sympathy, understanding, charity, forbearance, fortitude, courage, and other desirable traits. "Suffering is necessary for soul growth. . . . Adversity and sorrow uncover the real man or woman."

2. *Take the long viewpoint.* Remember that trouble does not always last. If it does not end on earth, it will at least end in heaven. The Apostle Paul wrote of his trouble being but for a moment. Dr. London tells of a minister who was going through a great trial. He went to the Bible for consolation and help. His eyes fell on these words, "And it came to pass." He said, "All right, it will not be with me long; it came to pass."

3. *Do not try to explain life.* "Sooner or later all of us encounter disasters, restrictions, and disappointments which we are unable to explain. We must regard life not as a problem to be solved but as a succession of concrete situations to be met—met bravely, confidently, hopefully."

E. Stanley Jones says, "Jesus accepts the fact of human suffering. He does not deny it, nor explain it away. Yet he met pain and injustice and transformed them into something higher." Arthur Wentworth Hewitt in his book *The Bridge* says, "More and more I believe it is better just to relax in unquestioning trust. We do not know the answer to the problem of human suffering, but God does."

Vivian Ahrendt

July 27
HOW TO MEET YOUR TROUBLES (II)
Matthew 26:39

4. *Help others.* A wise editor of a newspaper column often advised those in trouble, "When you feel that you can't stand your trouble, do something for someone else quick."

Lloyd Ellis Foster says, "Either suffering will drive your emotional energies inward so that they are wasted in self-pity, or it will express itself in a ministering outreach to human need. Bury your hurt, cover it, conceal it, and it will destroy your inner life. Project it, use it, apply it as God in Christ did, and it will save your life." Louis A. Banks says, "There is no greater health-lift for the soul than to stretch out a helping hand to a brother who is weaker than ourselves and save him from fainting."

5. *Submit to God's will.* Do not rebel and become bitter. Guy Edward Mark tells about a woman who had been sick a long time. Finally she had a critical operation. God heard prayer, and she improved rapidly and was home in a remarkably short time. Then she became ill again, this time with a bad case of pleurisy. The pain was so bad that for three weeks she was kept under the influence of an anesthetic. The doctor was unable to account for this condition.

After the woman recovered, she gave her testimony in a church service. She said that when the pleurisy came she rebelled against God. She felt she had had enough sickness. It was not fair to have this new trouble. She lay in bed day after day with rebellion in her heart and got sicker and sicker. Then one day she said simply and earnestly, "Lord, thy will be done." Soon everything was different. The presence of Christ overwhelmed her and gave her peace.

Vivian Ahrendt

July 28
THE BOLTS AND BUFFETS OF THE ENEMY
Psalm 91:5

Even the stings and arrows of tortuous fortune, even the bolts and buffets of the enemy, are welcome: since God has sent them for your good and that He, when you have done all and still stood, shall be glorified by your brave endeavor and endurance. "According to the will of God." Ah, that is *the gleam that lightens every gloom*; that is the sunshine which makes it daylight, even in the darkest night. It is Thy will, my Father and I can only say, "Amen. Thy will, not mine, be done." The apostle Peter, however, is very practical; and whereas he is more than willing to give this sympathetic word, he follows it by instruction which would serve his hearers in the evil day. I believe that this instruction is equally applicable to those who are in any sort of sorrow, to those who are enduring any sort of trial. . . . All who suffer "according to the will of God" in mind or body or estate, in things temporal or in things spiritual, are included here. And this is the advice: "Let them commit the keeping of their soul to him in well doing, as unto a faithful Creator."

Now . . . let me say that it is evident that *the chief danger* . . . is of a spiritual sort. Those who suffer are charged to commit the keeping of their souls to Him. Remember to whom the apostle spoke, to those who were suffering, persecuted, for the name and cause of Jesus Christ. They were in constant peril. They died daily. . . . Peter comes to them and says, "What you have to do is to commit your souls to Him." I think I can imagine some of them saying to Peter, "Oh, but Peter, it is our bodies we are most concerned about. See these gaping, aching wounds; see these emaciated frames". . . . Peter's advice remains the same, "Commit your souls to Him" because souls are more than bodies and because the danger to the soul is more to be dreaded than the danger to the outward frame.

Listening to the Giants
Warren Wiersbe

July 29

FOR YOUR SAKE
Revelation 22:20

She and I have prayed together many times. On one occasion she prayed, "O Father, may Jesus come soon and receive the reward He so richly deserves. He has suffered enough, and so have You. You have waited long enough. Come soon—for Your sake."

Now I had never heard anyone pray that way before. But I immediately recognized it as the utterance of a Christian with profound understanding into the nature of God's love. Even as Jesus stands before the Father and prays that His people may be kept from the evil one, His people should pray that Jesus may come soon and receive His reward, outlined in Scripture with these words: "They shall be his people, and God himself shall be with them, and be their God. And God shall wipe away all tears from their eyes."

This is the faith that modern man has lost. Wiesel is correct when he says that "God is there, hanging on the gallows" not because God is dead but because He endured that hanging and bore even Wiesel's burden of losing his faith as Job did for a time.

So as we look to Jesus by faith in the hour of trial, we will see the Lamb slain, slain in every funeral procession, slain in every bloated belly on our evening news programs, slain in every nervous breakdown, slain in every unkind and insulting word that passes between husband and wife, slain in every jealous look or racial slur, slain in every act of cheating, in every vile thought.

God's word is clear: "Behold the (slain) Lamb of God, which taketh away the sin of the world" (John 1:29).

James Londis

LETTER TO MR. C (I)

July 30

II Peter 1:4

Dear Sir,　　　　　　　　　　　　January 16, 1775

The death of a near relative called me from home in December, and a fortnight's absence threw me so far behindhand in my course, that I deferred acknowledging your letter much longer than I intended. I now thank you for it.

I can sympathize with you in your troubles; yet knowing the nature of our calling that, by an unalterable appointment, the way to the kingdom lies through many tribulations, I ought to rejoice rather than otherwise, that to you it is given, "not only to believe, but also to suffer." If you escaped these things, whereof all the Lord's children are partakers, might you not question your adoption into his family? How could the power of grace be manifest, either to you, in you, or by you, without afflictions? How could the corruptions and devastations of the heart be checked without a cross? How could you acquire a tenderness and skill in speaking to those who are weary, without a taste of such trials as they also meet with? You could only be a hearsay witness to the truth, power, and sweetness of the precious promises, unless you have been in such a situation as to need them, and to find their suitableness and sufficiency.

The Lord has given you a good desire to serve him in the Gospel, and he is now training you for that service. Many things, yes, the most important things, belonging to the Gospel ministry, are not to be learned from books and study, but by painful experience. You must expect a variety of exercise; but two things he has promised you—that you shall not be tried above what he will enable you to bear and that all shall work together for your good.

　　　　　　　　　　　　　　　　　　　　John Newton

II Peter 2:9   **LETTER TO MR. C (II)**   **July 31**

We read somewhere of a conceited orator who declaimed upon the management of war in the presence of Hannibal, and of the contempt with which Hannibal treated his performance. He deserved it; for how should a man who had never seen a field of battle be a competent judge on such a subject? Just so, were we to acquire no other knowledge of the Christian warfare than what we could derive from cool and undisturbed study, instead of coming forth as able ministers of the New Testament and competently acquainted with the devices, the deep-laid counsels and stratagems of Satan, we should prove but mere declaimers. But the Lord will take better care of those whom he loves and designs to honor. He will try, and permit them to be tried in various ways—he will make them feel much in themselves, that they may know how to feel much for others.

And as this previous discipline is necessary to enable us to take the field in a public capacity with courage, wisdom, and success that we may lead and animate others in the fight, it is equally necessary, for our own sakes, that we may obtain and preserve the grace of humility, which I perceive he has taught you to set a high value upon. Indeed, we cannot value it too highly; for we can be neither comfortable, safe, nor habitually useful without it. The root of pride lies deep in our fallen nature and where the Lord has given natural and acquired abilities, it would grow apace, if he did not mercifully watch over us and suit his dispensations to keep it down. Therefore, I trust he will make you willing to endure hardships as a good soldier of Jesus Christ. May he enable you to behold him with faith holding out the prize, and saying to you: "Fear none of these things that thou shalt suffer, be thou faithful unto death and I will give thee a crown of life."

John Newton

August 1
WHEN DELIVERANCE DOES NOT COME (I)
John 11:17-21

A couple of items in the Gospels seem to me to suggest something for the particular situation where deliverance did not, in fact, come and where apparently the juggernaut of sheer nature went on its grim way with no intervention from Heaven.

One is the story of Lazarus and the other is the Emmaus account. You object immediately: "Ah, but in both those cases it turned out that the dead *were* raised." Well, perhaps there is something there for us nonetheless.

For a start, the people involved in those incidents were followers of Jesus, and they had seen him, presumably, heal dozens of people. Then these followers experienced the utter dashing of all their expectations and hopes by death. God did not, it seemed, act. He who had been declared the Living One and the Giver of Life seemed to have turned his back in this case. What went wrong? What did the household at Bethany *not* do that the Widow of Nain had done? How shall we align it all? Who rates and who doesn't? Whatever it is that we might have chosen to say to them in the days following their experience of death, we would have had to come to terms somehow with the bleak fact that God had done something for others that he had not done for them.

From the vantage point of 2,000 years, we later believers can, of course, see that there was something wonderful in prospect, and that it emerged within a very few days in both cases. The stories make sense. They are almost better than they would have been if the deaths had not occurred. But, of course, this line would have been frosty comfort for Mary and Martha, or for the two en route to Emmaus, if we had insisted to them, "Well, surely God is up to something. We'll just have to wait."

Thomas Howard

August 2
WHEN DELIVERANCE DOES NOT COME (II)
John 11:17-21

The point is that for x number of days, their experience was of defeat. For us, alas, the "x number of days" may be greatly multiplied. And it is small comfort to us to be told that the difference then between us and, say, Mary and Martha's experience of Lazarus' death or of the two on the road to Emmaus, is only a quantitative difference. "They had to wait four days. You have to wait one, or five, or seventy years. What's the real difference?" That is like telling someone on the rack that his pain is only quantitatively different from mine with my hangnail. The quantity *is* the difference. But there is, perhaps, at least this much of help for us whose experience is that of Mary and Martha and the others, and not that of the widow of Nain and Jairus and that set: the experience of the faithful *has* in fact included the experience of utter death. That seems to be part of the pattern, and it would be hard indeed to insist that the death was attributable to some failure of faith on somebody's part.

There is also this to be observed: that it sometimes seems that those on the higher reaches of faith are asked to experience this "absence" of God. For instance, Jesus seemed ready enough to show his authority to chance bystanders and to the multitudes; but look at his own circle. John the Baptist wasn't let off—he had his head chopped off. James was killed in prison. And the Virgin herself had to go through the horror seeing her son tortured. No legions of angels intervened there. There was also Job, of course. And St. Paul—he had some sort of healing ministry himself, so that handkerchiefs were sent out from him with apparently healing efficacy for *others*, but, irony of ironies, his own prayer for *himself* was "unanswered." He had to slog through life with whatever his "thorn" was.

Thomas Howard

August 3
WHEN DELIVERANCE DOES NOT COME (III)
Luke 24:19-24

And so we begin to think about all our prayers and vigils and fastings and abstinences, and the offices and sacraments of the Church, that have gone up to the throne in behalf of the sufferer. They have vanished, as no sparrow, no hair, has ever done. Hey, what about that? And we know that this is false. It is nonsense. All right then—we prayed, with much faith or with little; we searched ourselves; we fasted; we anointed and laid on hands; we kept vigil. And nothing happened. . . .

Was it not the case with Lazarus' household at Bethany and with the two en route to Emmaus? And is it not the case with the Whole Story, actually—that it must be allowed to finish, and that this is precisely what the faithful have been watching for since the beginning of time? In the face of suffering and endurance and loss and waiting and death, what is it that has kept the spirits of the faithful from flagging utterly down through the millennia? Is it not the hope of Redemption? Is it not the great Finish to the Story. . . . Does it not entail what amounts to a redoing of all that has gone wrong, and a remaking of all that is ruined, and a finding of all that has been lost in the shuffle, and an unfolding of it all in a blaze of joy and splendor? A finding of all that is lost? All sorrow and all petitions and tears and vigils and fastings? Yes, all petitions and tears and vigils and fastings.

"But where *are* they? The thing is over and done with. He is dead. They had no effect." Hadn't they? How do you know what is piling up in the great treasury kept by the Divine Love to be opened in that Day? How do you know that this death *and* your prayers and tears and fasts will not *together* be suddenly and breathtakingly displayed before all the faithful and before angels and archangels and before kings and widows and prophets, as gems in that display?

Thomas Howard

August 4

WAIT TO SEE THE UNFOLDING
I Kings 17:7

Week after week, with an unwavering and steadfast spirit, Elijah watched the brook dwindle and finally dry up. Often tempted to stumble in unbelief, he nevertheless refused to allow his circumstances to come between himself and God. Unbelief looks at God through the circumstances, just as we often see the sun dimmed by clouds or smoke. But faith puts God between itself and its circumstances and looks at them through Him.

Elijah's brook dwindled to only a silver thread, which formed pools at the base of the largest rocks. Then the pools evaporated, the birds flew away, and the wild animals of the fields and forests no longer came to drink, for the brook became completely dry. And only then, to Elijah's patient and faithful spirit did the word of the Lord come and say, "Go at once to Zarephath" (verse 9).

Most of us would have become anxious and tired and would have made other plans long before God spoke. Our singing would have stopped as soon as the stream flowed less musically over its rocky bed. We would have hung our harps on the willows nearby and begun pacing back and forth on the withering grass, worrying about our predicament. And probably, long before the brook actually dried up, we would have devised some plan, asked God to bless it, and headed elsewhere.

God will often extricate us from the mess we have made because "his love endures forever" (I Chronicles 16:34). Yet if we had only been patient and waited to see the unfolding of His plan, we would never have found ourselves in such an impossible maze, seeing no way out. We would also never have had to turn back and retrace our way, with wasted steps and so many tears of shame. "Wait for the Lord" (Psalm 27:14). Patiently wait!

F. B. Meyer

DURING THE STORMS
Matthew 7:25-27

August 5

Faith grows during storms. These are just four little words, but what significance they have to someone who has endured life-threatening storms! Faith is that God-given ability that, when exercised, brings the unseen into plain view. It deals with the supernatural and makes impossible things possible. And yes, *it grows during storms*—that is through disturbances in the spiritual atmosphere. Storms are caused by conflicts between the physical elements, and the storms of the spiritual world are conflicts with supernatural, hostile elements. And it is in this atmosphere of conflict that faith finds its most fertile soil and grows most rapidly to maturity.

The strongest trees are found not in the thick shelter of the forest but out in the open, where winds from every direction bear down upon them. The fierce winds bend and twist them until they become giants in stature. These are the trees that toolmakers seek for handles for their tools because of the wood's great strength. It is the same in the spiritual world. Remember, when you see a person of great spiritual stature, the road you must travel to walk with him is not one where the sun always shines and wildflowers always bloom. Instead, the way is a steep, rocky and narrow path, where the winds of hell will try to knock you off your feet and where sharp rocks will cut you, prickly thorns will scratch your face, and poisonous snakes will slither and hiss all around you.

The path of faith is one of sorrow and joy, suffering and healing comfort, tears and smiles, trials and victories, conflicts and triumphs, and also hardships, dangers, beatings, persecutions, misunderstanding, trouble, and distress. Yet "In all these things we are more than conquerors through him who loved us" (Romans 8:37).

E. A. Kilbourne

August 6

"DOCTOR, HOW LONG?"

Isaiah 63:9

He (William Carey) had never known days so dark as when early in mid-January Thomas, the keeper of the purse, reported that their first year's income was exhausted, with no more to be looked for from England till the next autumn's "venture." He had pitiably miscalculated their first year's expenses; their resources had been hopelessly inadequate. Who can gauge Carey's woe with his family of seven; his wife in grave dysentery; Felix's recovery still in anxious doubt; his only home the comfortless garden house . . . 12 per cent, the lowest rate for borrowed money, and no help possible from England for at least ten months?

How could he be other than "much dejected," and again "very much dejected," "full of perplexity about temporal things," his "mind much hurt," and again "much grieved and dejected," and again "very weary"? The "city of sunshine and palaces" was bleak and lonely. The mental disorder and distress, which harrowed Mrs. Carey and her home for the next 13 years, dates from this misery. Ill with dysentery, her first-born son still worse, unable to afford even bread, appalled at their destitution in the strange and friendless city—her brain began to give way, her kindly nature suffered change. Who shall lay the melancholy to her charge? Nothing was here for reviling; everything for compassion and tears. Missionaries' wives paid dearly in these pioneer years, Carey's wife soonest and heaviest.

William Carey
S. Pearce Carey

A doctor once asked by a patient who had met with a serious accident, "Doctor, how long shall I have to live here?" The answer, "Only one day at a time" taught the patient a precious lesson. It was the same lesson God had recorded for His people of all ages long before. The day's portion in its day.

Andrew Murray

August 7
TESTINGS WITHOUT, TEMPTATIONS WITHIN
James 1:12

The mature person is patient in trials. Sometimes the trials are testings on the outside, and sometimes they are temptations on the inside. Trials may be tests sent by God, or they may be temptations sent by Satan and encouraged by our own fallen nature. We may ask, "Why did James connect the two? What is the relationship between testings without and temptations within?"

Simply this: if we are not careful, the testings on the outside may become temptations on the inside. When our circumstances are difficult, we may find ourselves complaining against God, questioning His love, and resisting His will. At this point, Satan provides us with an opportunity to escape the difficulty. This opportunity is a temptation.

There are many illustrations of this truth found in the Bible. Abraham arrived in Canaan and discovered a famine there. He was not able to care for his flocks and herds. This trial was an opportunity to prove God; but Abraham turned it into a temptation and went down to Egypt. God had to chasten Abraham to bring him back to the place of obedience and blessings. When Israel was wandering in the wilderness, the nation often turned testings into temptations and tempted the Lord. No sooner had they been delivered from Egypt than their water supply vanished, and they had to march for three days without water. When they did find water, it was so bitter they could not drink it. Immediately they began to murmur and blame God. They turned their testing into a temptation, and they failed.

Certainly, God does not want us to yield to temptation, yet neither can He spare us the experience of temptation. We are not God's sheltered people; we are God's scattered people. If we are to mature, we must face testings and temptations.

Warren W. Wiersbe

August 8
FULL OF PEACE AS WELL AS PAIN
Acts 21:14

Sufferings arising from anxiety, in which the soul adds to the cross imposed by the hand of God an agitated resistance and a sort of unwillingness to suffer—such troubles arise only because we live to ourselves. A cross, wholly inflicted by God and fully accepted without any uneasy hesitation, is full of peace as well as of pain. On the contrary, a cross not fully and simply accepted but resisted by the love of self, even slightly, is a double cross; it is even more a cross, owing to this useless resistance, than through the pain it necessarily entails.

Fenelon

If you say, "But life is so uncertain and all my calculable security so precarious; and time runs so fast and opportunities vanish never to return; and health snaps and plans fail and dear ones die, and never morning wears to evening but some heart must break; and even for me, at any moment some sudden crashing dispensation of trouble may break in to wreck and ruin the whole pattern and structure of my hopes"—if you feel inclined to argue thus, do stop and think! Is there any point in your past experience of which you can say, "God failed me there?" Be honest about this. Call to mind, if you will, the darkest and most shattering sorrow you have ever had.

I challenge you to look up into the face of heaven and say, "Lord God, You failed me there!" You know you cannot do that. For was it not precisely there in the darkest valley that you proved how all sufficient is His grace? St. Augustine said a marvelous thing about the love of God in Christ. *Non amat et deserit:* He does not love and desert. Has He not promised to be with you right on to the judgment seat and beyond? Expect great things from God!

James S. Stewart

August 9

A MATTER OF PRIVILEGE
Philippians 1:29

Let it be remembered that our suffering with Christ is not a yoke of bondage, but a matter of privilege; not an iron rule, but a gracious gift; not constrained servitude, but voluntary devotedness. "Unto you it is given, in the behalf of Christ, not only to believe in Him, but also to suffer for His sake." Moreover, there can be little doubt but that the real secret of suffering for Christ is to have the heart's affections centered in Him. The more I love Jesus, the closer I shall walk with Him, and the closer I walk with Him and the more faithfully I imitate Him, the more I shall suffer with Him. Thus it all flows from love to Christ; and then it is a fundamental truth that "we love Him because He first loved us."

C. H. Mackintosh

Our hearts are continually prone to wander from Him; prosperity and enjoyment all too easily satisfy us, dull our spiritual perception, and unfit us for full communion with Himself. It is an unspeakable mercy that the Father comes with chastisement, makes the world round us all dark and unattractive, leads us to feel more deeply our sinfulness, and for a time lose our joy in what was becoming so dangerous.

Andrew Murray

The more I saw my own misery, incapacity and nothingness, the plainer it appeared that they rendered me fitter for the designs of God, whatever they might be. "Oh, my Lord," said I, "take the weak and the wretched to do thy works, that thou mayest have all the glory of them and that man may attribute nothing of them to himself. If thou shouldst take a person of eminence and great talents, one might attribute to him something thereof; but if thou take me, it will be manifest that thou alone art the author of whatever good shall be done."

Madame Guyon

August 10
NOT IN VAIN THE TEDIOUS TOIL
Job 23:10

Not in vain, the tedious toil
On an unresponsive soil;
Travail, tears in secret shed
Over hopes that lay as dead.
All in vain, thy lord replies;
Nothing is too good to be:
O believe, believe to see.

Did thy endeavor turn to dust?
Suffering—did it eat like rust,
Till the blade that once was keen
As a blunted tool is seen?
Dust and rust thy life's reward?
Slay the thought, believe the Lord.
When thy soul is in distress
Think upon His faithfulness.
What if love unrecognized,
Whitening heavenly fields, surprised.

Amy Carmichael

It is a tremendous moment when first one is called upon to join the great army of those who suffer. The vast world of love and pain opens suddenly to admit us one by one within its fortress. We are afraid to enter into the land, yet you will, I know, feel how high is the call. It is as a trumpet speaking to us, that cries aloud, "It is your turn—endure." Play your part. As they endured before you, so now, close up the ranks—be patient and strong as they were. Since Christ, this world of pain is no accident untoward or sinister, but a lawful department of life, with experiences, interests, adventures, hopes, delights, secrets of its own. These are all thrown open to us as we pass within the gates—things that we could never learn or know or see, so long as we were well. God help you to walk through this world now opened to you, as through a kingdom, royal and wide and glorious.

Henry Scott Holland

August 11

BEREFT OF THE TOWER
II Corinthians 5:6-9

Later that year our deputation schedule took us to meetings in Plymouth, Indiana. There, on a Saturday morning, Rolland was stricken with a massive heart attack. An emergency prayer bulletin was sent to friends throughout the U.S.A. and the world. God wonderfully answered prayer and spared Rolland's life for two more years. But one April morning in Los Angeles, the home call came. Just the day before, for no apparent reason, Rolland had called me aside to give full details for his funeral arrangements. As we talked together, he reminded me that, "To be absent from the body is to be present with the Lord." Two days later he suffered a final heart attack. We had been married 38 years. God wonderfully sustained me in that the greatest loss of my life, saving me from the kind of depression which immobilized me after the death of my second child, Dickie Dean. I'll speak more about that later. Now I found myself suddenly bereft of the tower that had been my support through most of my adult life. Decisions I had always left to my husband, I now had to make alone. In the wake of this sorrow appeared a gruesome intruder, cancer.

In November 1973, I was in meetings in the East when I was taken sick. I had had minor stomach problems most of my life, but this was different. I checked into the hospital at my next stop in Indiana. The results seemed reassuring, "Everything seems to be normal," was the doctor's diagnosis. "But," he added, "call me in a week for the final report." The following week, while I was at a ski lodge in Ohio, dutifully I called the hospital for a report. "Mildred Rice," came the voice on the other end of the line, "I am glad you called. You have cancer. Plan to return home to Los Angeles immediately and prepare for surgery." That night Norma and Renee Palmer, in whose home I was staying, called their pastor, asking him to anoint me with oil and pray for me.

The Key Goose
Mildred Rice

August 12

HIS BANNER OVER ME
Song of Solomon 2:4

When the pastor walked in, I liked him immediately. After anointing me and praying he said, "God gave me a verse for you." He opened his Bible and read, "His banner over me is love." "Now," he announced, "there is a song in Sunday school we sing based on this text and we're going to sing it, all five verses, with the motions, and claim it for you." I felt like a dope trying to sing that song. I was not too familiar with the words and felt awkward going through the motions like a child in Sunday school. In the middle of this embarrassing charade, the Lord spoke. "You know what's the matter with you," He said, "you're letting this verse go right in one ear and out the other, and it's not going down into your heart at all. You'd better pay attention to what you are singing. It's my Word and it's My Word for you."

In L.A., when I checked into the hospital, Kathleen was with me. "Mother," Kathleen said, "you're going to be fine in the morning." "That may be," I told her, "but I can't be sure. The Lord took your father to heaven this year, and how do I know it isn't my turn in the morning? So don't promise me that I will be well. If you want to help me, just remind me that His banner over me is love and I'll be fine." She reached into her handbag and took out a notebook and wrote, "His banner over me is love, Song of Solomon 2:4." She tore out the page and placed it under my pillow. That night I slept perfectly. The surgery the next day was a success, exceeding my greatest expectations. Fifteen years have passed and there has been no recurrence of the cancer. I recently had a complete physical exam and came out with a clear bill of health. I am 75 and have recently traveled to New Zealand, Australia and South Africa on strenuous missionary tours that had me speaking once or twice a day. How faithful God has been!

The Key Goose
Mildred Rice

August 13

IF GOD IS IN CONTROL
Isaiah 55:12-13

If God is in control, though we feel the pain and shed the tears, there is an indescribable peace that God will work everything out. A grace principle is also a determining factor of what our actions will be. This principle states that those most closely involved are given the most grace, or ability, or understanding to accept the situation.

God is a God of purpose and this purpose also influences our actions. In Isaiah 55:12-13 God promises to bring good out of bad and give us such joy and peace that it should be an everlasting sign. He had a purpose to accomplish, and when we plugged into that purpose by asking Him to take over our lives, His emotions became ours to accomplish that purpose. This purpose and the accompanying grace are subject to His divine will, and we are not to question Him.

The last thing is the spiritual gifts God gives you when you take Him as Savior. One of my gifts is faith. This is an elusive word that really just means believing every word of God. Having been a student of His Word to some extent all my life, when my world seemed depopulated because one person was missing, I took His words and leaned on them. The faith He gave me was what directed me in my actions.

All of these things sway our actions concerning grief. We can show sorrow, shed tears, and mourn our loss. This is good and healthy, bringing healing. We can also become angry, bitter, and feel sorry for ourselves in our loss, and God is not pleased. But even then, if we go to God and tell Him what we feel, ask His forgiveness, accept His cleansing and determine to seek Him, He will forgive us and wrap us in His comforting love, and we will be healed.

Night of Anguish, Morning of Hope
Jean Mize

August 14
MISERABLE, CALAMITOUS SPECTACLE
Job 14:1

"In London," wrote Pepys (August 31, 1665), "died 7,496 and of them 6,102 of the plague." Gravediggers carried away in carts those who died in the streets and buried them in common ditches. Altogether some 70,000 Londoners, a seventh of the population, died of the plague in 1665. By December the pestilence abated. People dribbled back to work. In February, 1666, the court returned to the capital.

The survivors had hardly time to reconcile themselves to their losses when another disaster struck the city. It was bad enough that in June, 1666, the Dutch sailed boldly into the Thames and there destroyed English vessels with broadsides heard in London. But at three o'clock on the morning of Sunday, September 2, in a baker's shop in Pudding Lane, a fire began which in three days burned down most of London north of the river. Again circumstances conspired: a dry summer, the houses nearly all of wood and close together; many homes left vacant by families spending the weekend in the country; stores full of oil, pitch, hemp, flax, wine and other readily combustible wares; a strong wind that carried the fire from roof to roof and from street to street; and the lack of organization and equipment to deal with such a fire at such a time of night. Evelyn, fortunate in Southwark, ran up to the riverbank:

> Where we beheld . . . the whole city in dreadful flames near the waterside; all the houses from the (London) Bridge, all Thames street and upwards towards Cheapside. . . . The conflagration was so universal and the people so astonished that from the beginning, I know not by what despondency or fate, they hardly stirred to quench it; so that there was nothing heard or seen but crying out and lamentation, running about like distracted creatures. . . . So it burned the churches, public halls, exchange, hospitals, monuments, and ornaments . . . houses,

furniture, and everything. Here we saw the Thames covered with goods floating, all the barges and boats laden with what some had time and courage to save, as, on the other side, the carts, etc., carrying out to the fields, which for many miles were strewn with movables of all sorts, and tents erected to shelter both people and what goods they could get away. Oh, the miserable and calamitous spectacle, such as haply the world had not seen since the foundation of it. . . . All the sky was of a fiery aspect, like the top of a burning oven. . . . God grant my eyes may never behold the like who now saw about 10,000 homes all in one flame! The noise and crackling and thunder of the impetuous flames, the shrieking of women and children, the hurry of people, the fall of towers, houses, and churches was like a hideous storm; and the air all about so hot . . . that they were forced to stand still, and let the flames burn on, which they did for nearly two miles in length and one in breadth.

The Story of Civilization
Will and Ariel Durant

August 15

A VULNERABLE HUMAN BEING
Hebrews 2:14-18

The incarnation means that God came into the world as a vulnerable human being. God was born to a woman, Mary. He was given a name, Jesus. He learned to walk and talk, read and write, swing a hammer and wash dishes. God embraced human experience and lived with all the ambiguities and struggles that characterize life on earth. In the end he became a victim of injustice and hatred, suffered horribly on the cross, and died an ignominious death. The sovereign God came in Jesus Christ to suffer with us and to suffer for us. He descended deeper into the pit than we will ever know. His sovereignty did not protect him from loss. If anything, it led him to suffer loss for our sake. God is therefore not simply some distant being who controls the world by a mysterious power. God came all the way to us and lived among us. The icy cliff became a pile of sand at our feet.

The God I know has experienced pain and therefore understands my pain. In Jesus I have felt God's tears, trembled before his death on the cross, and witnessed the redemptive power of his suffering. The Incarnation means that God cares so much that he chose to become human and suffer loss, though he never had to. I have grieved long and hard and intensely. But I have found comfort knowing that the sovereign God, who is in control of everything, is the same God who has experienced the pain I live with every day. No matter how deep the pit into which I descend, I keep finding God there. He is not aloof from my suffering but draws near to me when I suffer. He is vulnerable to pain, quick to shed tears and acquainted with grief. God is a suffering Sovereign who feels the sorrow of the world.

A Grace Disguised
Jerry Sittser

August 16
CARING FOR THE LORD
James 1:26-27

We who are "earthen vessels" get sick, we who are "one of the least of these my brethren" are the people of the King, the sheep of His pasture, the brothers and sisters of Christ. We are meant to visit each other, take care of the poor, visit people in nursing homes and hospitals, in tumbledown cottages, palaces, tents, caves—wherever are the sick who are His brethren. We are to have no other opportunity of visiting Christ when He is sick! Does this hit us with a hard shock? He is not saying, "Heal the sick." He is talking about visiting with the idea of bringing comfort and love. This is coupled with the reality that there will always exist physically hungry children of the Living God who need money or a lovely meal—piping hot and beautifully arranged and carried into a hut or a run-down apartment house—served as if we were serving the Lord Himself.

Visiting the sick means that there will always be those who are sick. Feeding the hungry implies a personal involvement with someone who needs human and individual loving care, not just campaigning for a change of the political setup. Taking a stranger into one's home is quite different from giving money to keep a flophouse open. Going to a prison and visiting the people who are there is the only way we can visit the Lord in prison. The picture is powerful in its force. . . . We cannot miss the striking fact that Jesus says that the sick are to be cared for in some very personal way. We should check up on ourselves sometime: "Have I sent the Lord a card or a letter or a bunch of flowers in His sickness this week?" Day after day, week after week, instead of being tempted to say, "They shouldn't be so sick. What's wrong with their lives or their faith?" We are instead to be asking ourselves, "Have I failed to care for the Lord in some person's need when offered that opportunity?"

Affliction
Edith Schaeffer

August 17

A SHRINKING BACK
Matthew 26:39

Jesus in the Garden experienced a shrinking back from suffering and made a request: "If it be possible, remove this 'cup,' this terrible affliction and suffering ahead of Me. Please take it away." And Jesus knew what it felt like to get a negative answer which pointed Him to the necessity of keeping on. He did this that we might go to heaven, have eternal life, be forgiven of our sins, but also so that we might be given victory through having access to His strength in our weakness when troubles assail us. He did this so that the answer to our cries could be: "My strength is made perfect in weakness.... My grace is sufficient for thee."

Think for a moment of the fact that Jesus not only had to continue on the path of agony and suffering without relief, but that in the middle of it He was accused of not being truly the Son of God because He did not come down from the cross. Those "If you are the Son of God, then prove it" tauntings were the worst kind of temptation we can imagine. Satan repeats himself constantly when he brings that kind of mocking in haunting forms with jeering faces or sarcastic voices, as human beings say to us: "How can a Christian have that kind of trouble? If you were really a child of God, you wouldn't have such a succession of difficulties!"—"But you can't be a Christian mother if you have twins born so deformed at birth. You'd better find some way of proving you are a Christian. These sons should be healed!"—"Prove it! Prove it! Prove it!" say all kind of voices in all sorts of forms. Had Jesus "proved it" that day by coming down from the cross and calling upon legions of angels to appear immediately, the men would have been thrown off their feet—true. But the result would have been the most gigantic defeat in all of history, affecting every single believer from Old Testament times until the end. The "proof" would have destroyed salvation and the final victory over all death.

Affliction/ Edith Schaeffer

REFUSING TO BE DISILLUSIONED
Matthew 26:73-75

August 18

A certain type of innocence is culpable. Innocence is the characteristic of a child, but innocence in a man or woman is culpable and wrong. It means that their own whiteness is so guarded that they are unfit for life. Men and women must be pure and virtuous, and virtue is always the outcome of conflict.

Most of the suffering in human life comes because we refuse to be disillusioned. For instance, if I love a human being and do not love God, I demand of that man or woman an infinite satisfaction which they cannot give. I demand of them every perfection and every rectitude, and when I do not get it, I become cruel and vindictive and jealous. Think of the average married life after, say, five or ten years; too often it sinks down into the most commonplace drudgery. The reason is that the husband and wife have not known God rightly, they have not gone through the transfiguration of love, not entered through the discipline of disillusionment into satisfaction in God, and consequently they have begun to endure one another instead of having one another for enjoyment in God. The human heart must have satisfaction, but there is only one being who can satisfy the last aching abyss of the human heart, and that is our Lord Jesus Christ. That is why He is apparently so severe in regard to every human relationship. He says if we are going to be His disciples, occasion may arise when we must hate both father and mother, and every closest tie there is. Our Lord has no illusions about men, and He knows that every relationship in life that is not based on loyalty to Him will end in disaster.

The Place of Help
Oswald Chambers

August 19

CONSECRATED GRIEFS
Revelation 12:11

There is such a thing as consecrated griefs, sorrows that may be common to everyone but which take on a special character for the Christian when accepted intelligently and offered to God in loving submission. We should be watchful lest we lose any blessing which such suffering might bring.

But there is another kind of suffering, known only to the Christian: it is voluntary suffering deliberately and knowingly incurred for the sake of Christ. Such is a luxury, a treasure of fabulous value, a source of riches beyond the power of the mind to conceive. And it is rare as well as precious, for there are few in this decadent age who will of their own choice go down into this dark mine looking for jewels. But of our own choice it must be, for there is no other way to get down. God will not force us into this kind of suffering; He will not lay this cross upon us nor embarrass us with riches we do not want. Such riches are reserved for those who apply to serve in the legion of the expendables, who love not their lives unto the death, who volunteer to suffer for Christ's sake and who follow up their application with lives that challenge the devil and invite the fury of hell. Such as these have said good-bye to the world's toys; they have chosen to suffer affliction with the people of God; they have accepted toil and suffering as their earthly portion. The marks of the cross are upon them and they are known in heaven and in hell.

But where are they? Has this breed of Christian died out of the earth? Have the saints of God joined the mad scramble for security? Has the cross become no more than a symbol, a bloodless and sterile relic of nobler times? Are we now afraid to suffer and unwilling to die? I hope not, but I wonder. And only God has the answer.

The Root of the Righteous
A. W. Tozer

August 20
THE BREAD OF THE STRONG
Philippians 3:8

Nearly all of those who serve God, think of serving him for themselves. They think of gain and not of loss; of being comforted and not of suffering; of possessing and not of being deprived; of increase and never of decrease. On the contrary, all work within consists in losing, sacrificing, lessening, belittling oneself, and even divesting oneself of the gifts of God, so as to cling to him alone. We are constantly like invalids obsessed with their own health, who feel their pulse 30 times a day, and who need a doctor to reassure them by ordering frequent remedies, and telling them that they are getting better. That is nearly all the use we made of a director. We only revolve in a small circle of common virtues and never go wholeheartedly beyond that.

The director, like the doctor, flatters, comforts, encourages, keeps up our fussiness and sensitiveness over ourselves. He only orders mild little remedies, which become a habit. As soon as we find ourselves deprived of sensible blessings, which are only milk for babies, we believe that all is lost. This is a clear proof that we cling too much to the means, which are not the ends, and that we always want everything for ourselves. Privations are the bread of the strong. It is they which make the soul robust, which take it away from itself, which offer it purely to God. But we are desolate when they commence. We believe that all is in reverse, when all is beginning to be established firmly and to be purified. We want very much to have God make what he wishes of us, provided that he always makes something great and perfect. But unless we want to be destroyed and annihilated, we will never be the victims of a destruction from which nothing remains, which the divine fire consumes. We would like to enter into pure faith, and always to keep our own wisdom; to be a child, and to be great in our own eyes. What a fantasy of spirituality!

Fenelon

August 21

TENDERNESS TOWARDS ALL
Matthew 10:29

Even the misery of the sailors did not prevent John Woolman from feeling for the poor cocks and hens taken on board for a sea store. "I observed the cocks crow while we were near the land, but afterwards I did not hear one of them crow till we came near the English coast. In observing their dull appearance and the pining sickness of some of them, I often remembered the Fountain of goodness, who gave being to all creatures, and whose love extends to caring for the sparrows. I believe where the love of God is verily perfected, and the true spirit of government watchfully attended to, a tenderness towards all creatures made subject to us will be experienced and a care felt in us that we do not lessen that sweetness of life in the animal creation which the great Creator intends for them under our government."

In England, too, he was concerned for the horses driven to death in the stage coaches. "So great is the hurry in the spirit of this world, that in aiming to do business quickly and to gain wealth, the creation at this day doth loudly groan." At great inconvenience to himself he refused to travel in these coaches, journeying mostly on foot, nor would he send or receive letters by them.

The hardships he endured in his journeyings ended his life while on this English visit.

The Life of John Woolman
E. A. Blackburn

August 22

PAIN AS A GIFT
II Corinthians 1:4-5

Bear one another's burdens, the Bible says. It is a lesson about pain that we all can agree to. Some of us will not see pain as a gift; some will always accuse God of being unfair for allowing it. But, the fact is, pain and suffering are here among us, and we need to respond. The response Jesus showed was to bear the burdens of those He touched. To live in the world as His body, His emotional incarnation, we must follow His example.

"What a wonderful God we have," Paul says. "He . . . wonderfully comforts and strengthens us in our hardships and trials. And why does He do this? So that when others are troubled, needing our sympathy and encouragement, we can pass on to them this same help and comfort God has given us. You can be sure that the more we undergo sufferings for Christ, the more He will shower us with his comfort and encouragement" (II Corinthians 1:3-5 LB).

This plan of the body meshes with the way God is working in the world. Sometimes He does enter in, occasionally performing miracles, often giving supernatural strength to those in need. But mainly He relies on us, His agents, to do His work in the world.

Where Is God When It Hurts?
Philip Yancey

August 23

MY DOWRY, ONLY CROSSES
Colossians 2:15

From henceforth crosses were not spared me, and though I have had abundance of them hitherto, yet they were only the shadows of those which I have been since obliged to pass through, pursuant to a marriage contract, which I had lately entered into with our Lord Jesus Christ. In this spiritual marriage I claimed for my dowry only crosses, scourges, persecutions, ignominies, lowliness, and nothingness of self, which in his great goodness, and for wise ends, as I have seen, he has been pleased to grant and confer upon me.

One day, being in great distress on account of the redoubling of outward and inward crosses, I went into my closet to give vent to my grief. M. Bertot was brought into my mind, with this wish, "Oh, that he was sensible of what I suffer!" Though he wrote but very seldom, and with great difficulty, yet he wrote me a letter dated the same day about the cross, the finest and most consolatory he ever wrote me on that subject. Sometimes my spirit was so oppressed with continual crosses, which scarcely gave me any relaxation, that when alone my eyes turned every way, to see if they could find anything to give some relief. A word, a sigh, a trifle, or to know that anyone took part in my grief, would have been some comfort; but that was not granted me, not even to look toward heaven, or make any complaint. Love held me then so closely, that it would have this miserable nature to perish, without giving it any support or nourishment.

Oh, my dearest Lord! Thou yet gave my soul a victorious support, which made it triumph over all the weaknesses of nature, and seized thy knife to sacrifice it without sparing.

Life of Madame Guyon

August 24

TRIUMPHANT SUFFERS
Galatians 3:11

As I read the stories of triumphant sufferers, I find that, by faith they do three things that enable them to rise superior to their pain. In faith, they accept their trial. They do not exhaust their energies in futile questions, nor do they become resentful. They take, instead, an attitude of positive acceptance. It is the positiveness that makes the difference. They go even beyond resignation in regarding their trouble as being in some way, they know not how, within the scope of God's plan and, as such, something to be accepted, not merely endured.

In that brave attitude of faith, the noble Dr. Edward Wilson sank into his last sleep amid the snows of Antarctica. Before he died he wrote to his wife words which are a sublime expression of the faith which accepts positively its trial as from the hand of God. We read with reverence these two extracts from his last letters: "I shall simply fall and go to sleep in the snow, and I have your little books with me in my breast-pocket. . . . Don't be unhappy—all is for the best. We are playing a good part in a great scheme arranged by God himself, and all is well. . . ."

"I leave this life in absolute faith and happy belief that if God wishes you to wait long without me it will be to some good purpose."

The Quest for Serenity
G. H. Morling

THE VOICE OF THE DEAD
August 25
Hebrews 11:1-6

With what voice shall we speak when we are dead? What will men hear when they turn their thoughts towards us? What part of us will remain alive, singing or jarring in men's remembrance? It is the biggest part of us that retains its voice. In some of us it is wealth, in others it is goodness; some go on speaking in their cruelty, others in their gentleness. Cain still speaks in his jealous passion. Abel speaks in his faith. Dorcas speaks in her "doing good and helping the poor." Judas Iscariot speaks in his betrayal. Yes, something goes on speaking. What shall it be?

But these biggest things not only continue to speak in the ears of memory, they persist as actual forces in the common life of man. Our faith is not buried with our bones, nor is our avarice or pride. Our characters do not die when our hearts cease to beat. "The evil that men do lives after them," and so does the good. But deeper than our deeds, our dominant dispositions persist and mingle as friends or enemies in the lives of others. By them we, being dead, still speak, and we speak in subtle forces which aid or hinder other pilgrims who are fighting their way to God and heaven.

J. H. Jowett

August 26

SHUT IN WITH HIM

II Timothy 1:12

My pen utterly fails in describing the six shut-in years, as it was an experience when all the powers of darkness seemed bent on destroying faith in God's love. Charles Cowman seemed to be in the center of a furnace seven times heated, but thanks be unto God, "even there, God held his hand and kept that which had been committed to Him." The refining fires never raged beyond His control. The billows, which in their approach, threatened to submerge him as they came on, lifted him up to the heaven he was bound for. All the waves were crested with God's benediction.

One of the things for which he prayed more than another was that he might be "rich in faith," and God sent him to the school where the lesson is taught. He answered his prayer in His own way, permitting him to be shut-in with Himself that he might find the treasure of darkness, delivering him with such a mighty Hand that he was glad that the tempest arose, for the furious winds and tumbling seas revealed to him "what manner of Man this is."

Every morning was a miracle of resurrection and the beginning of a new day was like rising up out of death. To dare that sense of death and to launch forth morning after morning with what seemed an impossible effort, needed a faith that the reader can scarcely realize. He had never a night of whole, unbroken sleep throughout the six years, and added to it, unutterable agony when the heart attacks would seize him. It was a great furnace for a great soul, walking with death always in sight, yet his pain-lined face was aglow with the Master's joy all the time. Blood marks stain the steps that lead to the throne and scars are the price of scepters. Grief has always been the lot of greatness. It is an open secret.

Missionary Warrior
Lettie Cowman

August 27

WE MUST TELL JESUS
Matthew 14:12

Few of us are so isolated that we can live without ever having some of our friends involved in tragic accidents In our modern society there are many ways in which our loved ones may face death. When tragedy does strike, what should we as God's children do?

I was helped recently through meditating upon a verse from Matthew 14. The story concerns the execution of John the Baptist by order of Herod the king. How did John's disciples and friends react to the death of their leader? Verse 12 simply states: "And his disciples came, and took up the body and buried it, and went and told Jesus." When tragedy struck, they told Jesus all about it.

Some may feel that such a reaction is too simple, and that to offer it as an example is too simplistic. But work it out in terms of what we now know about the Lord Jesus. We must tell Jesus because He understands the entire circumstance involving our loved one or friend. The stark fact about ourselves is that we do not know. We simply cannot understand why a father is cut down in the prime of life, or why a mother is taken from her home. We do not know why the promising young man or young woman is smashed to death in some automobile accident. But Jesus understands. He is Lord of life and death. . . . I was recently in a church where a little Christian lad went home to be with Jesus after almost a year of suffering. I was deeply impressed by the way in which all involved—his parents, his pastor, his friends—were strengthened by the Lord to face the trial. Their secret lay in this: they had told Jesus about it.

    Have we trials and temptations?
    Is there trouble anywhere?
    We should never be discouraged,
    Take it to the Lord in Prayer.

                                                        Selected

August 28
A NEW BILLY GRAHAM (I)
II Timothy 3:16

Several hundred students had assembled at Forest Home Conference Center, 5,280 feet above sea level. . . . Among the chief speakers were Edwin Orr and Billy Graham. Graham was delivering a course of addresses in the mornings and Orr in the evenings. Of the latter, Billy Graham said: "The messages Dr. Orr gave as one of the others speakers were of tremendous blessing in my own life. His logical development of the whole subject of full surrender and the outpouring of the Spirit stirred the whole conference, evening by evening." Seven years later, Billy Graham wrote in an issue of *Christianity Today:*

"In 1949, I had been having a great many doubts concerning the Bible. I thought I saw apparent contradictions in Scripture. Some things I could not reconcile with my restricted concept of God. When I stood up to preach, the authoritative note so characteristic of all great preachers of the past was lacking. Like hundreds of young seminary students, I was waging the intellectual battle of my life."

At one o'clock in the morning, Billy Graham sat down with Edwin Orr beside the fish pond outside Orr's cabin. Seventeen simultaneous after-meetings had just concluded, and Graham was deeply moved. Orr's book, *Good News in Bad Times*, tells how the conversation began with the subject of surrender and how he felt led to suggest that perhaps his need was in the realm of the mind and not heart or will. When Edwin Orr talked to him, he did not know that Billy Graham's intellectual problem involved the question of the authority of Scripture. After half an hour of conversation, Graham walked off into the woods to pray. "Out of that sacred hour," wrote F. W. Hoffman in his volume *Revival Times in America*, "came a new Billy Graham."

Write the Vision!
A. J. Appasamy

II Peter 1:20 ## A NEW BILLY GRAHAM (II) **August 29**

Billy Graham wrote of that experience: "I remember walking down a trail, tramping into the woods, almost wrestling with God; I dueled with my doubts, and my soul seemed to be caught in the crossfire. Finally, in desperation, I surrendered to the Living God as revealed in Scripture. I knelt before the open Bible and said, 'Lord, many things in this book I do not understand. But Thou hast said, *The just shall live by faith.* Here and now, by faith, I accept the Bible as Thy Word. I take it all, I take it without reservations. Where there are things that I cannot understand, I will reserve judgment until I receive more light. If this pleases Thee, give me authority as I proclaim Thy Word and through that authority convict men of sin and turn sinners to the Savior.'" Orr was still awake when Graham returned to say that he had been filled afresh with the Spirit of God, adding that God had given him a vision of what was going to happen down the mountain in Los Angeles. Within six weeks, Billy Graham started his Los Angeles Crusade and during that crusade he applied the secret that changed his ministry. He had never before seen such crowds of people in his meetings. There were sensational cases of outright conversion. The newspapers began to splash with headlines the doings of the crusade. At first, the evangelist was alarmed by the publicity and told Orr that some of his advisers thought that the publicity might be "the kiss of death" to the whole movement. The evangelists were sitting in a parked car in the darkness, for privacy's sake. On Orr's lap was a copy of his recently-published Oxford thesis on the Awakening of 1858-9. He held it to the light and showed Graham a paragraph dealing with the '58 Revival. "The press, which speaks in the ear of millions, is taken possession of by the Spirit, willing or unwilling, to proclaim His wonders and go everywhere preaching the Word in its most impressive, its living forms."

Write the Vision!
A. J. Appasamy

Matthew 14:13   **DURING THE RESTS**   **August 30**

There is no music during a musical rest, but the rest is part of the making of the music. In the melody of our life, the music is separated here and there by rests. During those rests, we foolishly believe we have come to the end of the song. God sends us times of forced leisure by allowing sickness, disappointed plans, and frustrated efforts. He brings a sudden pause in the choral hymn of our lives, and we lament that our voices must be silent. We grieve that our part is missing in the music that continually rises to the ear of our Creator. Yet how does a musician read the rest? He counts the break with unwavering precision and plays his next note with confidence, as if no pause were ever there.

God does not write the music of our lives without a plan. Our part is to learn the tune and not be discouraged during the rests. They are not to be slurred over or omitted, not used to destroy the melody or to change the key. If we will only look up, God Himself will count the time for us. With our eyes on Him, our next note will be full and clear. If we sorrowfully say to ourselves, "There is no music in a rest," let us not forget that the rest is part of the making of the music. The process is often slow and painful in this life, yet how patiently God works to teach! And how long He waits for us to learn the lesson!

                                                                               John Ruskin

August 31
PRAYER AND THE LIFE OF LOVE
I Peter 4:7-8

In our text, watching unto prayer and fervent love are closely linked. This is true, too, in the spiritual life. The man who prays only for himself will not find it easy to be in the right attitude towards God. But where the heart is filled with fervent love to others, prayer will continually rise to God for those whom we love, and even for those with whom we do not agree.

There would be a great defect in this little book on brotherly love if we neglected to indicate what an important place prayer holds in the life of love. These two fruits of the Spirit are inseparably connected. If you wish your love to grow and increase, forget yourself, and pray, pray earnestly, for God's children and His Church. And if you would *increase in prayerfulness*, give yourself in fervent love to the service of those around you, helping to bear their burdens. What a great need there is, at this time, of earnest, powerful intercessors! Let those who complain that there is so little love among Christians, acknowledge that one of the chief signs of love is lacking in themselves, if they do not *pray much and often for their brethren.* I am deeply convinced that God desires His children, as members of one body, to present themselves each day before the Throne of grace to pray down the power of the Spirit upon all believers. Union is strength. This is true in regard to the Kingdom of Heaven. Real spiritual unity will help us to forget ourselves, to live unselfishly, wholly for God and our fellowmen. And the word of Peter will be applied to our lives—"Watching in prayer . . . fervent in love."

Andrew Murray

September 1
IN THE FACE OF DIFFICULTY
Psalm 119:67

Fine artistic things seem always to be done in the face of difficulties, and the rocky soil, which seems to give the finest flower, is contempt. Don't fool yourself, George, appreciation doesn't make artists. It ruins them. A man's best work is done when he is fighting to make himself heard, not when swooning audiences wait for his paragraphs.

A Life in Letters
John Steinbeck

God has His own ways of deepening the shallow soil. Sometimes He drives a ploughshare of grief right through it. Sometimes He digs and delves with the instruments of discipline and affliction. The shallow soil, said Jesus, "lacked moisture." Sometimes the moisture God supplies is moisture of bitter tears. Yet, even so, must we not pray, like Maesfield's Saul Kane watching the ploughman in the field in the grey light of morning—"O God, do that for me! Whatever the cost, deepen Thou my spiritual life"?

    O wet red swathe of earth laid bare,
    O truth, O strength, O gleaming share
    O patient eyes that watch the goal,
    O ploughman of the sinner's soul,
    O Jesus, drive the coulter deep
    To plough my living man from sleep.

James S. Stewart

God whispers to us in our pleasures, speaks in our conscience, but shouts in our pain; it is His megaphone to rouse a deaf world.

C. S. Lewis

ESSENTIAL TRIALS

September 2

I Peter 1:7

Let me then put it in a final general principle in this form. These trials are essential, says Peter, in order to show the genuineness of our faith. His actual phrase is—"that the trial of your faith." Now "trial" there means "the attestation of it." The picture he has in his mind is of a test being applied to something, and then after it has been tested, a certificate is given.

For instance, the report on a ring might be, "Yes, it is 18 carat gold." That is what is meant by trial. He is not interested in the process as such; trial is the certification of attestation, declaring the genuineness of our faith. The approved character of our faith is thus manifested. That is why these things happen to us.

D. Martyn Lloyd-Jones

Now the combat is going to begin: now God and the blessed angels are observing what constancy, what fortitude there is in my soul, and how far the Divine authority and the remembrance of my own prayers and resolutions will weigh with me, when it comes to a trial.

Philip Doddridge

There is a great want about all Christians who have not suffered. All the wounds of Christ send out sweetness—all the sorrows of Christians do the same. Commend me to a bruised brother, a broken reed—one like the Son of Man. The Man of Sorrows is never far from him. To me there is something sacred and sweet in all suffering; it is so much akin to the Man of Sorrows.

Robert Murray McCheyne

September 3
WHEN THEY CANNOT EXPLAIN
II Corinthians 4:17

Unexpected light falls for them (Christians) on the mysteries of life. When they cannot explain why dark things happen, they are still serene because they are sure that the God behind all things is deeply wise and deeply loving. They stand up to the severe testings of life with courage and confidence. When the doctor shakes his head over them, when they feel a grim disease creeping up their body, when a dear one is certified insane, when their dearest has inoperable cancer, when the coffin is standing beside the bed . . . they are never more sure of the nearness of God.

W. E. Sangster

I am thinking of a little woman long afflicted but who had marvelous faith in the eternal verities of religion. Oh, how pitiful was her condition. One day, realizing her serious affliction and with ever deepening sympathy, her aunt who cared for her said to her, "My dear niece, if the Lord Jesus were to ask you today to choose whether you would go to heaven and be taken out of this world of suffering, or whether you would stay here a while longer, you would have no trouble on making choice, would you, dear?" She waited a moment and said, "I would ask Jesus to decide it for me, for I would not know which was the better for me."

And that is exactly the thing for us to say. I would ask Him to decide it for me, whether I should get out of all this tribulation and suffering and pain, and go to the House of Life and Light and Love with all the limitations of earth left behind me forever, or whether I should learn some more lessons and get more discipline—some more of walking by faith and not by sight. We are not to be afraid to pray this prayer.

George W. Truett

THINGS THAT HINDER

September 4

I John 5:15

Amy Carmichael could be severely practical in reminding colleagues of the things that hinder united prayer. Once she noted down "three facts that if remembered save time and energy in a prayer meeting:"
  1. We don't need to explain to our Father things that are known to Him.
  2. We don't need to press Him, as if we had to deal with an unwilling God.
  3. We don't need to suggest to Him what to do, for He Himself knows what to do.

This early morning I looked up about our special prayer for X, a light fell on the words, "We know *that we have* the petitions that we desired of Him." We pray from the ground of that certainty, not towards certainty but from it. (Is that why we have the words, "In everything by prayer and supplication *with thanksgiving*"? We give thanks before we see.) Then the thought came, "What is it that we *have* in this sense already received? Surely just this: that the glory of the Lord will be manifested (for is not this what we desired of Him?), and that the very best will be done from His eternal point of view, for the work committed to us." Once in the Forest in October, 1933, a prayer meeting was held in her room. Yesterday (she wrote to Godfrey) we had the prayer meeting in my room, and the one thing we prayed about was Prayer. I know we have all, for some time back, felt the need of something more in our prayer life. I have, personally, and I know others have, and there are many in our Family who come to prayer meetings because it is the custom to do so, but who are not urged by a great desire. It is the lack of prayer-hunger that often makes a big united meeting difficult. The one thing we seem to need most is a revived prayer life in our own souls—then the wave will flow out to the others.

Something To Die For
Elizabeth Elliot

September 5
THEY EMBRACED MY GRIEF
Isaiah 59:1

A pastor in the Midwest wrote me about an experience he had several years ago, a "nervous breakdown" the doctors called it.

"The most painful part of it was the seeming silence of God. I prayed, I thought, to a silent darkness. I have thought a lot about this. He only seemed silent. The problem was partly my depression and partly the Christian community. For most Christians, I was an embarrassment. Nothing they said dealt with what I endured. One pastor prayed for me in generalities and pieties that were utterly unrelated to the situation. They would not feel my pain. Other people just avoided me. Ironically, Job's friends were probably a help to him, psychologically. At least they forced out feelings, even if angry ones. Their pronouncements were useless, but they did deal with the questions and gave Job the impression that maybe God was around somewhere. No one in the Christian community, except my wife, helped me even to that degree."

Years later the same pastor, with renewed mental health, was reading Psalm 145 from the pulpit. He tried to concentrate, but something was plaguing him: his week-old grandson had just died, grieving the whole family. He couldn't continue reading the words about God's goodness and fairness. His voice choked, he stopped reading, and he told the tense congregation what had happened. "As people left the church," he remembers, "they said two important and helpful things: 1. 'Thank you for sharing your pain with us.' 2. 'I grieve with you.' This simple statement was the most helpful thing said. I did not feel alone. Unlike during the time of depression before, I was not abandoned by God and His people. They embraced my grief."

Philip Yancey

September 6
AGE THAT OPPOSES MEDITATION
Psalm 19:14

Most of us would agree with these words of Jacques Ellul even when applied to ourselves:

> The man of our time does not know how to pray; but much more than that, he has neither the desire nor the need to do so. He does not find the deep source of prayer within himself. I am acquainted with this man. I know him well. It is I myself.
>
> *Prayer and Modern Man*

We live in an age that opposes meditation, contemplation and prayer. The cultural values of our society have unduly permeated the worship, life and service of the church. To a great extent, all of us are faced with a mindset characterized by the success syndrome, pragmatic functionalism (if it works, it's good), the myth of self-fulfillment, materialism, a fragmentation and impersonality of life, a frenetic pursuit of pleasure, and tyranny of timepieces—schedules, computers, jet flights, and telephones.

Coupled with this spirit of the times is a marked confusion among many Christians concerning the great framework of God's grace in our spirituality and prayer life. A major problem we have is our failure to recognize that our God and heavenly Father is waiting, ready, and able to help us in our prayers to Him. All too often we fail to trust God and fail to realize the enabling power of His Spirit in and among us. The life and writing of Teresa of Avila can help us greatly in this vital dimension of *prayer in life*. Her thoughts and example are significant indeed for the church of Jesus Christ these four centuries later. . . . Prayer for Teresa is much more than just "saying our prayers." It is God giving Himself and we receiving Him.

Preface to a Life of Prayer
Clayton Berg, Jr.

Mark 8:34-35   **AN AWFUL TOLL**   **September 7**

The earliest to go forth were five young men who sailed for the Congo, Africa, in November, 1884, three years before the Christian and Missionary Alliance was regularly organized. Within a few months of their arrival on the field their leader, John Condit, died of fever. Indeed, the opening of both the Congo and Sudan field proved a painfully costly undertaking. Those deadly climates exacted such an awful toll of lives that for years the missionary graves in both fields outnumbered the living missionaries.

The pioneer Alliance missionary to China, Revered William Cassidy, was never permitted to reach that land, but died of smallpox contracted on the Pacific voyage and was buried in Japan. Those who followed after him faced a China that was then seething with bitter anti-foreign feeling; and especially in the totally unevangelized provinces of Kuangsi and Hunan, where they were among the early pioneer forces, were they called upon to endure no little hardship and danger. Others pressed on westward to the remote borders of Tibet and knocked at the doors of that hostile and devil-possessed land, to enter which had been one of the main objectives in mind when the Alliance was organized. A little later a band of 45 workers from Sweden penetrated the far north, and amid many vicissitudes planted stations beyond China's Great Wall on the borders of Mongolia. The Boxer uprising of 1900 brought this mission to a tragic end. Twenty-one of its foreign workers and fourteen of their precious children were brutally murdered, and the rest made a hazardous escape across the desert into Siberia and after harrowing experiences reached their European homes.

The Life of A. B. Simpson
A. E. Thompson

September 8
GOD'S TOOL IN YOUR LIFE
Hebrews 12:15

One of the greatest barriers that prevents us from experiencing God's unsurpassed peace is a root of bitterness. Planted as a seed of anger, rejection, or resentment, bitterness grows into a poisonous emotion that chokes out the peace of God in our lives and defiles the lives of family members and friends.

If you are or have been embittered against someone because of an unjust circumstance, you know the emotional price you pay. It affects you physically and spiritually, releasing its hostile toxins at the slightest upset. You cannot hide a bitter spirit. It spills over into all that you do.

But the good news of the gospel is freedom from every form of bondage, including a bitter spirit. You do not have to be its slave or allow it to fester a day longer. In honest prayer before God, admit your bitterness. Be specific. Acknowledge it as sin and repent, changing your mind and heart about its corrosive influence. This attacks the problem at its root—sin against God—and creates the right climate for healing and restoration.

Next comes one of the most difficult steps toward dislodging the stronghold of bitterness. You must choose to view the offending party or circumstance as God's tool in your life. That is fundamental to a long-term freedom. Everything that comes into your life is filtered through the will of God. God has allowed this person or event, as painful as it may be, to touch your life for your personal spiritual growth. This is the extraordinary biblical view that will excavate the root of bitterness from your spirit.

Charles Stanley

September 9
BROKEN-WORLD EXPERIENCES
Genesis 50:20

We searched out the biblical biographies of every man and woman whose world had broken for one reason or another. As I've noted elsewhere, we discovered that almost everyone in the Bible was conversant with some kind of broken-world experience. And we came to understand that in almost every case the broken-world moments were the turning points to great spiritual insight, development, and godly performance. That was both a comfort and a marvelous promise.

We also turned to the spiritual classics. Here, our friends became women and men such as Amy Carmichael whose personal world broke through no fault of her own when she suffered a series of accidents and spent the last 20 years of life bedridden; Oswald Chambers whose life was probably shortened through his enormous intensity and physical exertion in serving the Lord during the World War I period; William and Catherine Booth who plowed through powerful ridicule and discouragement to establish the work of the Salvation Army. . . . Mrs. Charles Cowman's *Streams in the Desert* and Chambers' *My Utmost for His Highest* became a daily spiritual feeding, never failing to provide a word from God to nourish our hearts. The prayers of Quoist, Baillie, and Francois Fenelon, the words of Tozer and the liturgical worship of the Book of Common Prayer became our spiritual lines to the deep. And out of them all, words came from heaven itself each day to help in the rebuilding process.

Because we had more time here at Peace Ledge, we read more. And both of us came to a similar conclusion as we discussed the books we were reading. Books written by people who had sustained some sort of a broken-world experience—debilitating illness, humiliating failure, intense persecution, conflict with evil, numbing disappointment—were powerful in their ability to reach into our inner spirit.

Gordon MacDonald

September 10
ALL SUFFERING EXCLUDED
I Peter 2:20

Suppose, contrary to fact, that this world were a paradise from which all possibility of pain and suffering were excluded. The consequences would be very far reaching. For example, no one could ever injure anyone else; the murderer's knife would turn to paper or his bullets to thin air; the bank safe, robbed of a million dollars, would miraculously become filled with another million dollars . . . ; fraud, deceit, conspiracy, and treason would somehow always leave the fabric of society undamaged. Again, no one would ever be injured by accident: the mountain-climber, steeplejack, or playing child falling from a height would float unharmed to the ground; the reckless driver would never meet with disaster. There would be no need to work; there would be no call to be concerned for others in time of need or danger, for in such a world there could be no real needs or dangers. To make possible this continual series of individual adjustments, nature would have to work "special providences" instead of running according to general laws which men must learn to respect on penalty of pain or death. The laws of nature would have to be extremely flexible. . . . One can at least begin to imagine such a world. It is evident that our present ethical concepts would have no meaning in it. If, for example, the notion of harming someone is an essential element in the concept of wrong action, in our hedonistic paradise there could be no wrong actions—nor any right actions in distinction from wrong. Courage and fortitude would have no point in an environment in which there is, by definition, no danger of difficulty. Generosity, kindness, the agape aspect of love, prudence, unselfishness, and all other ethical notions which presuppose life in a stable environment, could not even be formed. Consequently, such a world, however well it might promote pleasure, would be very ill adapted for the development of the moral qualities of human personality. In relation to this purpose it would be the worst of all possible worlds.

John Hick

September 11
THE INFLUENCE OF THE BIBLE
Proverbs 13:13

The influence of the Bible has benefited humanity more than any book that has ever been written. In 1852 American patriot and statesman Robert C. Winthrop said these profound words: "Diffuse the knowledge of the Bible and the hungry will be fed and the naked clothed. Diffuse the knowledge of the Bible, and the stranger will be sheltered, the prisoner visited, and the sick ministered unto. Diffuse the knowledge of the Bible, and Temperance will rest upon a surer basis than any mere private pledge or public statute. Diffuse the knowledge of the Bible, and the peace of the world will be secured. . . ." The Scripture has accomplished these and much more in the lives of countless millions of people. How much is the Bible influencing *your* life? Are *you* reading it regularly? Is its influence daily making an impact in your heart? Are you part of those 27,000,000 who read it day by day or the millions of others who read it only occasionally—or who read it not at all. . . . The benefits of the Bible in your life and in the lives of millions of others are absolutely incalculable. As one has said:

It is God's highway to Paradise.
It crowns womanhood with beauty and manhood with strength.
It furnishes adequate motives for self sacrifice.
Children grow in character under its influence.
Youth is vitalized by its teaching.
The commonest work of life is glorified by it. . . .
It is light on the pathway in the darkest night.
It is the sun that never sets and shines for all. . . .
It leads . . . men to integrity and uprightness.
It drives clouds from the sky and shelters from the storm.
It breaks the chains of the prisoner.
It awakens men and women opiated by sin.
It warms the heart refrigerated by a cold and heartless world.

D. James Kennedy

September 12

IT KNOWS ALL ABOUT US
Psalm 119:105

No reader of the New Testament can miss the fact that it knows all about our human problems—fear, moral cowardice, illness of body and mind, loneliness, insecurity, hopelessness, despair, cruelty, abuse of power, and the rest—but equally no reader of the New Testament can miss the fact that it resolves all of these problems, one way or the other, into fundamental problems of sin against God. By sin, the New Testament means, not social error or failure in the first instance, but rebellion against, defiance of, retreat from a consequent guilt before God, the creator; and sin, says the New Testament, is the basic evil from which we need deliverance and from which Christ died to save us. All that has gone wrong in human life between man and man is ultimately due to sin, and our present state of being in the wrong with our selves and our fellows can't be cured as long as we remain wrong with God. . . .

If you want to judge how well a person understands Christianity, find out how much he makes of the thought of being God's child and having God as his Father.

Pitfalls and perplexities regarding the ministry of the Spirit abound among Christians today. The problem isn't in finding the correct verbal labels, but in knowing what it is in experience that corresponds to the work of God to which the labels refer. Thus, we are all aware that the Spirit teaches the mind of God and glorifies the Son of God.

Knowing God
J. I Packer

Psalm 119:25 ## GET INTO THE WORD **September 13**

"If we confess our sins, he is faithful and just and will forgive us our sins and purify us from all unrighteousness" (I John 1:9). Continually confess your need of him. Never think you can go it alone. You can't. But you can do it through Christ. Remember Paul's statement: "I can do everything through him who gives me strength" (Philippians 4:13). That is true for you as well. Isn't that tremendous! Pray for the enlightenment of the Spirit of God upon his word. Ask him to infuse his word with his Spirit and to breathe life into your soul through that word. As the psalmist wrote, "I am laid low in the dust; renew my life according to your word" (Psalm 119:25).

Get into the word. Take notes on your pastor's sermons and pray over them, asking the Lord to help you apply them to your life. Find a simple reading program that keeps you on a daily schedule throughout the year. Start a good Bible study—one that makes you dig into the word of God for yourself. Find a Christ-centered Bible study discussion group that you can join that has the word of God as the only base and source of discussion.

And don't forget to memorize the Scriptures systematically. This is the key. Through Scripture memory, the blessed Holy Spirit has constant access to your life. He can bring a verse to mind that will encourage you or enable you to help another. Soon, through God's word and prayer, God will transform your life into that of a vibrant, rugged soldier of the cross with an eye single to his glory.

Disciples in Action
Leroy Eims

Psalm 23 ## GOD'S PSYCHIATRY **September 14**

"If People would repeat Psalm 23 seven times before going to sleep each night, we would rarely see an emotional breakdown," said one thoughtful psychiatrist. Charles Allen, approaching it from the standpoint of a Bible scholar, simply calls this magnificent piece of poetry "God's psychiatry." What magic lies in these 115 words? Their very familiarity may be their greatest handicap.

A legend from India talks of the time when the gods first made the earth. "Where shall we hide the secrets that will help people understand the world they live in?" they asked. "If they are too easily found, no one will discover them. Are the mountains high enough or are the oceans deep enough? Or are they too high or too deep?"

Maurice Berquist

The Spirit-filled walk demands, for instance, that we live in the Word of God as a fish lives in the sea. By this I do not mean that we study the Bible merely, nor that we take a "course" in Bible doctrine. I mean that we should "meditate day and night" in the sacred Word, that we should love it and feast upon it and digest it every hour of the day and night. When the business of life compels our attention we may yet, by a kind of blessed mental reflex, keep the Word of Truth ever before our minds.

A. W. Tozer

September 15

PRACTICING PRAYER
Philippians 4:6

The best instruction I can give you as helpful or preparatory to the Spirit of Prayer is already fully given where we have set forth the original perfection, the miserable fall and the glorious redemption of man. It is the true knowledge of these great things which can do all for you which human instruction can do. These things must fill you with a dislike of your present estate, drive all earthly desires out of your soul, and create an honest longing after your first perfection. For prayer can only be taught you by awakening in you a true sense and knowledge of what you are, and what you should be, and filling you with a continual longing desire of the heart after God, His life and Holy Spirit. When you begin to pray, ask your heart what it wants and have nothing in your prayer but what the state of your heart puts upon you demanding, saying, or offering to God.

The one and only infallible way to go safely through all the difficulties, trials, dryness or opposition of our evil tempers is this: *to expect nothing from ourselves,* but in everything expect and depend upon God for relief. Keep fast hold of this thread, and then let your way be what it will, temptation or the rebellion of nature, you will be led through all to a union with God. *For nothing hurts us in any state but an expectation of something in it and from it, which we should only expect from God.* And thus it will be till the whole turn of our minds is so changed, that we as fully see and know *our inability to have any goodness of our own, as to have a life of our own.* When we are happily brought to this conviction, the whole spirit of our mind becomes a true faith and hope and trust in the sole operation of God's Spirit, looking no more to any other power to be formed in Christ new creatures, than we look to any other power for the resurrection of our bodies at the last day.

What a universal confession there is that we pray too little. How strange that our highest privilege, holding fellowship with God in prayer, is to so many a burden and a failure, and to so many more a matter of form without the power. Let us learn the lesson that to expect nothing from ourselves is the first step. And then truly with the heart to expect everything from God. These two thoughts lie at the root of all true prayer. Instead of our thoughts being centered on man, on ourselves and our needs, let them become centered on God in His glory and His love, and prayer will become a joy and a power, and our trials will become our greatest blessings, because they compel us to wait upon God.

God's Best Secrets
Andrew Murray

THE ANTIDOTE

September 16

II Corinthians 12:8-9

After Dickie's death, it was long months before I managed to climb out of the pit. However, amazingly, following Rolland's death, not only was I spared depression, but also that kind of bereavement that many widows experience.

It is true, of course, that a long interval of time separated those two deaths. During those intervening years, I learned a good deal about walking with God and the all-sufficiency of my Savior. But there was something else I discovered, almost by accident. The week before Rolland's fatal heart attack he had written a letter inviting our Taiwan workers, John and Gloria Su, to California for meetings. When I returned from the hospital, newly widowed, my eyes fell on that letter atop the radio. It was addressed and stamped but Rolland had never mailed it. I picked it up intending to throw it in the wastebasket. Hostessing John and Gloria was now out of the question, I told myself. With Rolland gone, I was sure to be devastated by grief, incapacitated. I would need lots of time to be alone. I would need time to reflect, time to mourn, time to recover, time to put my life in order. But try as I would, I could not throw away that letter. I recognized this as a check of the Holy Spirit—the sort of inner prompting I had gradually, through the years, come to acknowledge (often reluctantly) as the voice of God. Now He was saying, "You are to mail that letter, go ahead with the plans to invite John and Gloria. Rolland would have wanted you to do it, and I want you to do it, too." So I did it, inwardly protesting all the while. I was full of misgivings about the whole matter. How would I ever manage with Rolland's funeral just over? Unwittingly, I was on the verge of a great discovery, one that others of God's people had made again and again. The antidote to grief and depression is to lose one's self in service to others. Grief and depression by their very nature can consume us in self-pity, our attention ceaselessly riveted on ourselves, creating a self-perpetuating cycle of torment.

John and Gloria arrived on schedule and for weeks I traveled with them. We rode together to churches and meetings. I introduced them to friends and acquaintances all over southern California. As I listened to their testimonies and watched God at work bringing in their support, my whole life was infused with new joy and all the while I was soaring above my grief, as it were, on angel's wings.

The Key Goose
Mildred Rice

Mark 14:38 **TWO THINGS TO DO** September 17

We examine ourselves, not for our own interest, but to follow the advice and to accomplish the pure will of God. Moreover, we abandon ourselves in his hands, and we are as glad to know ourselves in the hands of God as we should be sorry to be in our own. We do not wish to see anything which it pleases him to hide. As we love him infinitely more than we love our own selves, we sacrifice ourselves unconditionally to his good pleasure. We only think of loving him and of forgetting ourselves. He who thus generously loses his soul will find it for the life everlasting.

Otherwise, in temptations I only know of two things to do. The first is to be faithful to the light within so that we can cut off, with no quarter and no delay, all that we are at liberty to cut off and that can feed or reawaken the temptation. I say all that we are at liberty to cut off because it does not always depend on us to flee the occasions. The temptations which are connected with the state in which Providence places us are not supposed to be in our power. The second rule is to be turned to God's side in temptation, without being upset, without worrying as to whether or not we have given a half-consent to it, and without letting it block our direct approach to God. We should run the risk of returning to temptation, by wanting to examine too closely to see if we have committed any infidelity. The shortest and surest way is to act like a small child at the breast. We show him a horrible beast. He only recoils from it and buries himself in his mother's breast, so that he will see nothing. The practice of the presence of God is the supreme remedy. It sustains. It comforts. It calms. We must not be surprised by temptations, even the most shameful. Scripture says, "Who knows any one who has not been tempted?" And again, "My son, entering into the service of God, prepare thy soul for temptation." We are only here below to be tested by temptation.

Fenelon

September 18
IN DISSIPATION AND SADDNESS
II Corinthian 12:10

It seems to me that you are painfully caught between two things: one, avoiding dissipation; the other, keeping yourself from depression. For dissipation, you will never cure yourself of it by strained reflections. Do not hope to perform the work of grace with the resources and efforts of nature. Content yourself to giving your will to God without reserve, and never envisage any painful state which you do not accept by yielding to divine Providence. Be careful never to go further than this in your thoughts of the cross; but when God permits them to come to you without your seeking them, never let them go by without result.

Accept, despite the revulsion and horror of nature, all that God presents to your mind, as a proof by which he wants to train your faith. Do not trouble yourself to know if you will have, when the time comes, the strength to carry out what you want to do from a distance. The present opportunity will have its grace, but the grace of the moment in which you visualize these crosses is to accept them with a good heart when God gives them to you. Having laid the foundation of abandonment, go on serenely and with confidence. Provided that this disposition of your will is not changed by voluntary attachments to something against the order of God, it will always last.

Fenelon

September 19
THE RIGHT QUESTIONS TO ASK
Job 19:1-7

Catastrophic loss of whatever kind is always bad, only bad in different ways. It is impossible to quantify and to compare. The very attempt we often make in quantifying losses only exacerbates the loss by driving us to two unhealthy extremes. On the one hand, those coming out on the losing end of the comparison are deprived of the validation they need to identify and experience the loss for the bad thing it is. They sometimes feel like the little boy who just scratched his finger but cried too hard to receive much sympathy. Their loss is dismissed as unworthy of attention and recognition. On the other hand, those coming out on the winning end convince themselves that no one has suffered as much as they have, that no one will ever understand them, and that no one can offer lasting help. They are the ultimate victims. So they indulge themselves with their pain and gain a strange kind of pleasure in their misery.

Whose loss is worse? The question begs the point. Each experience of loss is unique, each painful in its own way, each as bad as everyone else's but also different. No one will ever know the pain I have experienced because it is my own, just as I will never know the pain you may have experienced. What good is quantifying loss? What good is comparing? The right question to ask is not, "Whose is worse?" It is to ask, "What meaning can be gained from suffering, and how can we grow through suffering?"

A Grace Disguised
Jerry Sittser

September 20
"WHY WRITE ITS EPITAPH?"
Proverbs 24:14

After a minute of desperate scribbling, he stopped. "It is gone! Why write its epitaph?" As a rule to be applied to accounts, it may not be approved, but as a way of dealing with the little ills of life it is excellent; a bad night, a bad day, a worry, a small pain, a petty annoyance. It is gone. Why write its epitaph?

Why indeed? "A good thing from David today," writes the father of five-year-old David Somervell. "Out of the mouth of babes: When climbing a little hill with me he said, puffing and blowing, but going very strong, 'Nannie always says she wants to stop and get her breath when she's climbing up a hill, but I don't—I only think of getting to the top.'" It is when we stop to "get our breath" that we have time to write epitaphs of past troubles. The best way is little David's as he climbs his infant Everest, "I only think of getting to the top."

And if "the top" means for the reader peace in some long trial of patience and of faith, perhaps this from another letter will be an edelweiss: "Oda has just brought in the verse on her French calendar for today, Proverbs 24:14: 'Know wisdom for thy soul; if thou hast found it, then there is a future and thy waiting shall not be reduced to nothing or be in vain.'" And a letter, quoting a recent *Times*, adds a flower to the cluster: "The grace of final perseverance is that quality of patience which is always equal to the pressure of the passing moment, because it is rooted in that eternal order over which the passing moment has no power."

Gold by Moonlight
Amy Carmichael

Psalm 40:14   **A TERROR OF DARKNESS**   **September 21**

In the night when Charles has the awful terror of darkness, God gave me Psalm 40:14. He is confounding the enemy just as He did in II King 6 and Exodus 14, Acts 27, etc. "The enemy shall come out one way and flee before thee seven ways." I was dazed for loss of sleep but renewed in faith. He was lifting and carrying me forward.

I was awakened by Charles going through an awful thing and is dying. Phoned the doctor and he came right over. Found Charles had had a stroke which paralyzed his left side. He gave him something and it quieted him, but my nerves were shocked and so were Jennie's. I crept out to the sunroom and lay down. Billie came and snuggled up to me and purred. In the early dawn I called mother, got her breakfast, stayed up a time then went back to my bedroom where He conducted me through the Valley of Peace. About midnight he felt he was going and called us together and sang with a clear voice, "Tis so sweet to trust in Jesus, just to take Him at His word, just to rest upon His promise, just to know thus saith the Lord." I felt I had come just so far in the valley with him, and we parted then and at that point he seemed to start on alone and began the song. We sang with him. Then he left messages for many, for all of our church saying that he loved them—the Lairds, the Kimbers, the Clark families, the Revivalist family. Said "Tell them it was their help that did the work in Japan, not ours," and said he loved them. Then to the English sons, our missionaries, and our native helpers, he said, "Tell them to do their very utmost to bring me as many souls as possible." Then to Brother Kilbourne, "We have not only been knit together, but burned together for God's work." Said if anyone had anything against him, he loved them and forgave them. Then he said to Jennie the nurse, "You have been like an angel praying for me under your breath when you did not know that I heard it."

Lettie Cowman Diary, 1924

September 22

SHEER RANDOMNESS

Job 19:8-12

Humans also impose order on the world, as we see, for example, through clocks, schedules, and city planning. But order does not always prevail. A family lives comfortably for 40 years in a Midwestern town. Suddenly a tornado blows through and destroys their home, but leaves every other house on the block untouched. A middle-aged man eats a proper diet and exercises regularly for many years, but a lump in his neck prompts him to visit the doctor, who tells him that he has lymphoma. A woman enjoys years of a career, marriage, and motherhood. Then one day while jogging in a park she is raped by a stranger. Suddenly her world turns ugly, and she turns bitter. She wonders with regret why she was running through the park at just that time and why her assailant was waiting at just that place.

Loss makes the universe seem like a cold and unfriendly place, as if it were little more than trillions of atoms colliding together with no predictability, no design, and no reason to it. Life just happens, whether good or bad. Randomness mandates that we simply live as best we can, but in the end we must realize that what happens is often arbitrary. At such times the universe seems to make about as much sense as a little girl who thinks that her fleeting grudge against a brother is the reason why he got measles.

One of the worst aspects of my experience of loss has been this sense of sheer randomness. The event was completely outside my control—an "accident," as we say. The threat of "anomie," as Peter Berger has called this disorderliness, was and still is almost unbearable to me.

A Grace Disguised
Jerry Sittser

Mark 15:34 ## THE ABSURDITY OF LIFE   **September 23**

For months after the accident, I turned the events of that day over and over in my mind. I kept reliving the day, changing the schedule in some way so that the accident would not occur. I also searched for reasons. I blamed myself for being a selfish husband, an inattentive father, or an aloof son. I wondered if my family had been cursed. I entertained the idea that the accident was a demonic attack. I looked with cynicism on the absurdity of life. Maybe, I thought, there really is no God and no meaning to life. I resigned myself to misery and death, thereby yielding to its inexorability. These machinations of the mind tormented me because I could not discover any explanation that made sense of the tragedy. An answer to the "Why?" question eluded me.

Suffering may be at its fiercest when it is random, for we are then stripped of even the cold comfort that comes when events, however cruel, occur for a reason. To fall while attempting a dangerous climb without ropes leads to one kind of suffering. We shake our heads at the tragedy but realize that the climber should have taken precautions or attempted a climb within his range of ability. What happened constitutes real suffering, but at least it is understandable. Sometimes people do jobs or hobbies that carry an inherent risk of injury or death. But to be killed by a random bolt of lightning or a stray bullet engenders another kind of suffering, in which case we tremble because there is no satisfactory explanation or no sensible pattern. Death just happened. The victim was simply at the wrong place at the wrong time.

A Grace Disguised
Jerry Sittser

Job 1:22   **MORE JUST THAN GOD**   **September 24**

Job did not know why, but he knew why he trusted God who knew why, and in suspending judgment he trusted. The resistance leader knew what he was doing. But this, of course, was only the first round of the testing and, as events unfolded, agony was piled on agony and there was no relief. His wife encouraged him to curse God and die, his friends accused him heartlessly, his brothers held aloof, his relatives faded away, his servants forgot him, his slaves refused to answer him, children despised him, and he came to stink in the nostrils of his own family (Job 19).

Each degree of mounting pressure served to heighten the dilemma. If he trusted God and suspended judgment, he had to be silent. But every moment he continued in silence was taken as a tacit admission of his guilt. Yet to defend himself he had to explain the suffering, and to do this he had to press reason to conclusions he had no desire to entertain and no right to make. This tension was the torturous rack on which Job's faith was stretched to the breaking point. It is little wonder that his self-defense is a demonstration of faith mixed with doubt.

On the one hand, Job's faith reach heights of unrivaled courage, as when he cried, "But in my heart I know that my vindicator lives and that he will rise last to speak in court" (Job 19:25). On the other hand, his chosen style of defense led him into the bitter blackness of self-pity and doubt, as wrong as it is understandable. In his reply God rebuked Job for defending himself in a way that accused God: "Dare you deny that I am just or put me in the wrong that you may be right?" (Job 40:8). In doing this Job had dissolved the moral universe in one stroke and had brought down upon himself even more spiritual agony because he had made himself out to be more just than God.

In Two Minds
Os Guinness

September 25

NONE UNSCATHED

Romans 9:20

Unanswerable intellectual questions . . . tax the power of speculation by pushing it beyond its limits and raising anxiety for faith. (For example, Why did God create man if he knew that . . . ?) There are questions which in this life are unanswerable. There are facts which we cannot explain but must never explain away. Faith can suspend judgment on these. There is no question which we cannot leave with God if he is the Father of Jesus Christ.

It would be tempting to leave the question here but impractical, too, for the essence of suffering is experience, not thought. If the suspended judgment cannot be applied, it is useless. There are two situations where suspended judgment has practical applications. The first is when we suffer because of the injuries or hurts which come from other people.

The Christian view of life is not romantic but realistic. Life in the fallen world involves injuries. No one passes through unscathed. We will all be injured. We will all meet with injustices. Across the fabric of our lives thousands of these "little murders" leave their marks of wear and tear. The challenge each time will be the same: Where we do not know why, will we trust God and suspend judgment or will we demand to know why and go on to say why anyway?

In Two Minds
Os Guinness

September 26
IN THE POWER OF STILLNESS
Mark 15:3

There is no scene in all the Bible more majestic than our Savior remaining silent before the men who were reviling Him. With one quick burst of divine power or one fiery word of rebuke, He could have caused His accusers to be laid prostrate at His feet. Yet He answered not one word, allowing them to say and do their very worst. He stood in *the power of stillness*—God's holy silent lamb.

There is a place of stillness that allows God the opportunity to work for us and gives us peace. It is a stillness that ceases our scheming, self-vindication, and the search for a temporary means to an end through our own wisdom and judgment. Instead, it lets God provide an answer, through His unfailing and faithful love, to the cruel blow we have suffered. Oh, how often we thwart God's intervention on our behalf by taking up our own cause or by striking a blow in our own defense! May God grant each of us this silent power and submissive spirit. Then once our earthly battles and strife are over, others will remember us as we now remember the morning dew, the soft light of sunrise, a peaceful evening breeze, the Lamb of Calvary, and the gentle and holy heavenly Dove.

A. B. Simpson

I remember hearing Bishop Whipple of Minnesota, who was well known as "The Apostle of the Indians," voice these beautiful words: "For the last 30 years I have looked for the face of Christ in the people with whom I have disagreed. When this spirit drives us, we will be immediately protected from a feeble tolerance of others, narrow-mindedness, harsh vindictiveness, and everything else that would damage our testimony for Him who came not to destroy lives but to save them."

W. H. Griffith-Thomas

September 27
BLESSEDNESS OF THE UNOFFENDED
Matthew 11:6

Are you offended with Christ? It is very easy to be when we do not understand His dealings with us. It is very natural, too, when in the midst of the "fiery furnace" of suffering, in some desert of temptation, or some prison house of denied privileges and opportunities, to become offended with the One who could have saved or delivered us from it if only He would! Truly, to take no offense at God's varied and often mysterious dealings with us is one of the marks of genuine piety and spiritual maturity. How few attain!

The context of this passage before us reveals the discouragement, questioning and doubt which had entered the heart of John the Baptist as he languished behind prison bars. John had had a miraculous birth, a divine commission and a mighty message. His was no ordinary ministry, for he had been ordained to announce the coming Messiah and the setting up of His Kingdom, and this significant background of his calling had given him confidence in the message he preached. Doubtless, too, he had looked forward with great anticipation to participating in the affairs of a triumphant King and a victorious nation. And then, like "lightning out of a clear sky," instead of a throne, a prison; instead of freedom, incarceration; and instead of expected blessings, a curse of the direst nature! Of course, he could not understand (who could?) and like myriads of other humans down the long centuries of time, he asked the age-old question, "Why? Why? Why?" God's dealing seemed so contradictory to God's call and his own worthy hopes and ambitions.

Have you, dear reader, ever felt that God's promise had apparently failed, His love had evidently ceased, His pity had been seemingly withdrawn, and His mercy irrevocably cancelled? Sooner or later we all pass this common road of temptation and doubt, and with John we cry from the depths of our heart's anguish, "Why? What can it mean?"

E. M. Beyerle

September 28

EVERYTHING AGAINST ME

Genesis 42:36

And thus, for those who may be questioning God's love in His present dealings with them, we would point to a well-known and much loved passage: "We know that all things work together for good to them that love God, to them who are the called according to His purpose" (Romans 8:28). Have you been "called" to be a follower of the Lord Jesus Christ? If so, then you have been called also for a high "purpose" and that purpose, according to Romans 8:29 is that you may be "conformed to the image of His Son." We are called to no general, indefinite "good" but to one which is specific, well-defined and God ordered.

If we can but believe this plain statement of fact and "cast anchor" (Acts 27:30) during the tempestuous night of misfortune, sickness, prejudice, misunderstanding, abuse, neglect, poverty, or any other of the varied unpleasant experiences of life, it will save us much suffering at the time and much repentance in the future, for we are bound to be distressed when we disbelieve God, and we are equally as bound to undergo the deep anguish of repentance when once we realize the sin of our unbelief.

During trial, especially when it is long drawn out, one is very apt to settle down into a state of hopelessness and despair and say with Jacob of old, when he was about to be bereft of his one remaining joy in life, "All these things are against me" (Genesis 42:36). How much better it would be and how much more pleasing and glorifying to God if we could take our stand with Jacob's well-beloved son, Joseph, and although deprived of everything which life holds sweet and dear, say from a determined and chastened heart, even to the bitterest enemy of our happiness, "As for you, ye thought evil against me, but God meant it for good" (Genesis 50:20).

E. M. Beyerle

September 29
AN INSUPERABLE OBJECTION
Genesis 1:26-27

The case for disbelief in God because of pain and evil in the world was so succinctly put by the late Professor C.E.M. Joad of the University of London that I should like to use it in beginning this chapter. "For many years," said Dr. Joad, "the problem of pain and evil seemed to me to offer an insuperable objection to Christianity. Either God could abolish them but did not, in which case, since He deliberately tolerated the presence in the universe of a state of affairs which was bad, I did not see how He could be good; or He wanted to abolish them but could not, in which case I did not see how He could be all-powerful." It is a problem which has at some time disturbed every thoughtful person.

Dr. Joad went on to say that he had accepted the Christian view of pain as a fact not incompatible with a benevolent God, and stated why. Since C. S. Lewis has said that Dr. Joad's summary is very close to his own position in *The Problem of Pain*, I shall cite him again: "It was of no interest to God to create a species consisting of virtuous automata, for the "virtue" of automata who can do no other than they do is a courtesy title only; it is analogous to the "virtue" of the stone that rolls downhill or of the water that freezes at 32 degrees. To what end it may be asked, should God create such creatures? That He might be praised by them? But automatic praise is a mere succession of noises. That he might love them? But they are essentially unlovable; you cannot love puppets. And so God gave man free will that he might increase in virtue by his own efforts and become, as a free moral being, a worthy object of God's love. . . . Freedom entails freedom to go wrong: man did, in fact, go wrong, misusing God's gift and doing evil. Pain is a by-product of evil, and so pain came into the world as a result of man's misuse of God's gift of free will."

The Christian World of C.S. Lewis
Clyde S. Kilby

September 30

UNEQUAL TRIALS

Daniel 3:17-18

We quickly run into spiritual trouble if we look around at God's dealings with others. Our Lord taught Peter a salutary lesson on this point. He was concerned lest John should receive preferential treatment. Jesus replied sternly, "What is that to thee? Follow thou me." James went from prison to the executioner's block. Peter went from prison to a prayer meeting. Peter won 3,000 souls. Stephen received 3,000 stones. We have to accept the fact that "the ways of the Lord are not equal." He does not deal with us on the mass-production principle. He delivers some from trial. He delivers some in trial.

Do we have a "But if not" in our spiritual vocabulary? Do we have this third resource of faith? Is our faith fireproof? If wars should arise and son, daughter, husband, sweetheart be taken from our side, have we a "But if not" to carry us through that fiery furnace? If business should fail, or financial reverses be experienced? If ill-health grips us? When old age enfeebles us? When bereavement strikes? When desire for a life partner is not granted? When cherished plans are thwarted? If Christian work does not meet with the success we envisaged? When we are not designated to the mission station we expected or to live with the fellow-worker we would choose? Let us emulate the dauntless faith of the noble three who maintained their confidence in God in the face of seemingly unrewarded faith. "But if not, we will still go on trusting God," said the three men. They did not fall into self-pity or unbelief.

We may not always understand God's dealings with us at the time, and He nowhere undertakes to explain Himself. "What I do thou knowest not now, but thou shalt know hereafter," is His promise. In the meantime we learn many lessons in the furnace of testing.

Spiritual Maturity
J. Oswald Sanders

October 1
A RUDE QUESTION
Job 21:22-26

A letter from a friend of many years describes her cancer surgery and its aftermath—an incision that had to be scraped and cleaned daily for weeks. It was so painful that Diana, Jim, Monica, and I prayed while she cleaned it, three times and some days four times. Monica would wipe my tears. Yes, Jesus stands right there as the pain takes my breath away and my toes curl to keep from crying out loud. But I haven't asked, "Why me, Lord?" It is only now that I can pray for cancer patients and know how the flesh hurts and how relief, even for a moment, is blessed.

There are those who insist that it is a very bad thing to question God. To them, "why?" is a rude question. That depends, I believe, on whether it is an honest search, in faith, for his meaning, or whether it is a challenge of unbelief and rebellion. The psalmist often questioned God and so did Job. God did not answer the questions, but answered the man—with the mystery of himself. He has not left us entirely in the dark. We know a great deal more about his purposes than poor old Job did, yet Job trusted him. He is not only the Almighty—Job's favorite name for him—he is also our Father, and what a father does is not by any means always understood by the child. If he loves the child, however, the child trusts him. It is the child's ultimate good that the father has in mind. Terribly elementary. Yet I have to be reminded of this when, for example, my friend suffers, when a book I think I can't possibly do without is lost, when a manuscript is worthless. The three things are not all in the same category. The second and third things have to do with my own carelessness and failure. Yet in all three I am reminded that God is my Father still, that he does have a purpose for me, and that nothing, absolutely nothing, is useless in the fulfillment of that purpose if I'll trust him for it and submit to the lessons. "God disciplines us for our good *that we may share in his holiness.*"

Elizabeth Elliot

October 2
THE PREREQUISITE FOR JOY
John 12:23-24

Discipline very often involves loss, diminishment, "fallings from us, vanishings." Why? Because God wills our perfection in holiness, that is our *joy*. But, we argue, why should diminishments be the prerequisite for joy? The answer to that lies within the great mystery that underlies creation: the principle of life out of death, exemplified for all time in the Incarnation ("that a vile Manger his low Bed should prove, who in a Throne of stars Thunders above," as Crashaw expressed it) and in the cross and resurrection ("who, for the joy that was set before him, endured a cross"). Christ's radical diminishments—his birth as a helpless baby and his death as a common criminal—accomplished our salvation.

It follows that if we are to share in his destiny we must share in his death, which means, for us sinners, the willingness to offer up to him not only ourselves but all that goes with that gift, including the simplest, down-to-earth things. These things may be aggravating and irritating and humiliating as well as mysterious. But is it the very aggravation and irritation and humiliation that we can offer—every diminishment of every kind—so that by the grace of God we may be taught his loving lessons and be brought a little nearer to his loving purpose for us and thus be enlarged.

Somehow it's easy to understand the principle of control and denial and loss in the matter of *self*-discipline. It is perfectly plain to anyone who wants to do a difficult and worthwhile thing that he's got to deny himself a thousand unimportant and probably a few hundred important things in order to do the one thing that matters most. Bishop Stephen Neill said that writing is almost entirely a matter of self-discipline. "You must make yourself write." I know. Alas. Sit yourself down, shut yourself up, restrict your enthusiasms, control your maunderings. Think.

Elizabeth Elliot

October 3
"THAT IS HOW I TREAT MY FRIENDS"
Nehemiah 8:10

Teresa constantly urged the nuns to criticize her own faults as they would those of others. She would also submit to humiliating mortifications with all the meekness that she would expect of her daughters. This would be repugnant if we did not recognize the all-important value she attached to the practice of humility. Humility was the chief of all virtues in her eyes. This was all the more remarkable when we consider a prevailing cultural Spanish characteristic which Clissold discusses:

> In a Spain dominated by the cult of "honor"—pride of lineage, disdain for plebian occupation and manual work, and a touchiness which led to ferocious revenge for every imagined injury—the practice of self-abasement stood in dramatic contrast. Even her pious father and brothers had not been immune from the poisonous obsession with "honor."

Certainly the surest antidote to this terrible obsession was the practice of humility.... A side to Teresa's character which may be related to humility is her incredible sense of humor. She professed to dislike "moody people" and asked to be delivered from "frowning saints." As a matter of fact, at the heart of her life of poverty and penance throbbed a tremendous joy and spontaneity. Furthermore, this profound inner joy seemed to be developed even further by privation. There is her famous dialogue with the Lord, when fighting with a river crossing in her advanced age, she complained to the Lord that she had a sore throat and high temperature. She added, therefore, that this prevented her from enjoying the incidents of the journey as she might. The Lord was alleged to have said, "But this is how I treat my friends." To which Teresa replied, "Yes, Lord and that is why you have so few of them!"

Preface to a Life of Prayer
St. Teresa of Avila

Hebrews 4:1-3 ## THE SWEETEST PART October 4

Said Hudson Taylor in a letter to his sister: "The sweetest part, if one may speak of one part being sweeter than another, is the *rest* which full identification with Christ brings. I am no longer anxious about anything, as I realize this; for *He*, I know is able to carry out *His will*, and His will is mine. It makes no matter where He places me, or how. That is rather for Him to consider than for me; for in the easiest positions He must give me His grace, and in the most difficult His grace is sufficient. It little matters to my servant whether I send him to buy a few cash worth of things, or the most expensive articles. In either case he looks to me for the money and brings me his purchases. So, if God place me in great perplexity, must He not give me much guidance; in position of great difficulty, much grace; in circumstances of great pressure and trial, much strength? No fear that His resources are mine, for He is mine and is with me and dwells in me."

Some around him could hardly understand this joy and rest, especially when fellow-workers were in danger. A budget of letters arriving on one occasion, as Mr. Nicoll relates, brought news of serious rioting in two different stations. Standing at his desk to read them, Mr. Taylor mentioned what was happening and that immediate help was necessary. Feeling that he might wish to be alone, the younger man was about to withdraw, when, to his surprise, someone began to whistle. It was the soft refrain of the well-loved hymn: "Jesus, I am resting, in the joy of what Thou art. . . ."

Turning back, Mr. Nicoll could not help exclaiming, "How can you whistle, when our friends are in such danger?" "Would you have me anxious and troubled?" was the long-remembered answer. "That would not help them, and would certainly incapacitate me for my work. I have just to roll the burden on the Lord."

Elizabeth Skoglund

ONE THING I DREAD

October 5

II Thessalonians 1:5

There were always choices to make. Every day, every hour, offered the opportunity to make a decision, a decision which determined whether you would or would not submit to those powers which threatened to rob you of your very self, your inner freedom; which determined whether or not you would become the plaything of circumstance, renouncing freedom and dignity to become molded into the form of the typical inmate.

Seen from this point of view, the mental reactions of the inmates of a concentration camp must seem more to us than the mere expression of certain physical and sociological conditions. Even though conditions such as lack of sleep, insufficient food and various mental stresses may suggest that the inmates were bound to react in certain ways, in the final analysis it becomes clear that the sort of person the prisoner became was the result of an inner decision, and not the result of camp influences alone. Fundamentally, therefore, any man can, even under such circumstances, decide what shall become of him—mentally and spiritually. He may retain his human dignity even in a concentration camp.

Dostoyevsky said once, "There is only one thing that I dread: not to be worthy of my sufferings." These words frequently came to my mind after I became acquainted with those martyrs whose behavior in camp, whose suffering and death, bore witness to the fact that the last inner freedom cannot be lost. It can be said that they were worthy of their sufferings; the way they bore their suffering was a genuine inner achievement. It is this spiritual freedom—which cannot be taken away—that makes life meaningful and purposeful.

Victor Frankl

October 6

SAFETY FOR HAZARDS
Matthew 10:1

The dynamic periods are those heroic times when God's people stirred themselves to do the Lord's bidding and went out fearlessly to carry His witness to the world. They exchanged the safety of inaction for the hazards of God-inspired progress. Invariably the power of God followed such action. The miracle of God went when and where His people went; it stayed when His people stopped. The static periods were those times when the people of God tired of the struggle and sought a life of peace and security. Then they busied themselves trying to conserve the gains made in those more daring times when the power of God moved among them.

Bible history is replete with examples. Abraham "went out" on his great adventure of faith, and God went with him. Revelations, theophanies, the gift of Palestine, covenants and promises of rich blessings to come were the result. Then Israel went down into Egypt, the wonders ceased for 400 years. At the end of that time Moses heard the call of God and stepped forth to challenge the oppressor. A whirlwind of power accompanied that challenge, and Israel soon began to march. As long as she dared to march, God sent out His miracles to clear the way for her. Whenever she lay down like a fallow field, He turned off His blessing and waited for her to rise again and command His power.

This is a brief but fair outline of the history of Israel and of the Church as well. As long as they "went forth and preached everywhere," the Lord worked "with them . . . confirming the word with signs following." But when they retreated to monasteries or played at building pretty cathedrals, the help of God was withdrawn till a Luther or a Wesley arose to challenge hell again. Then invariably God poured out His power as before.

A. W. Tozer

October 7
MIRACLES FOLLOW THE PLOW
Hosea 10:12

Here are two kinds of ground: fallow ground and ground that has been broken up by the plow. The fallow field is smug, contented, protected from the shock of the plow and the agitation of the harrow. Such a field, as it lies year after year, becomes a familiar landmark to the crow and the blue jay. Had it intelligence, it might take a lot of satisfaction in its reputation; it has stability; nature has adopted it; it can be counted upon to remain always the same while the fields around it change from brown to green and back to brown again. Safe and undisturbed, it sprawls lazily in the sunshine, the picture of sleepy contentment. But it is paying a terrible price for its tranquility. Never does it see the miracle of growth; never does it feel the motions of mounting life nor see the wonders of bursting seed nor the beauty of ripening grain. Fruit it can never know because it is afraid of the plow and the harrow.

In direct opposite to this, the cultivated field has yielded itself to the adventure of living. The protecting fence has opened to admit the plow, and the plow has come as plows always come, practical, cruel, business-like and in a hurry. Peace has been shattered by the shouting farmer and the rattle of machinery. The field has felt the travail of change; it has been upset, turned over, bruised and broken, but its rewards come hard upon its labors. The seed shoots up into the daylight its miracle of life, curious, exploring the new world about it. All over the field the hand of God is at work in the age-old and ever renewed service of creation. New things are born, to grow, mature, and consummate the grand prophecy latent in the seed when it entered the ground. Nature's wonders follow the plow.

A. W. Tozer

October 8

AFRAID OF LIFE

Judges 7:3

In the first place, science most certainly does not free man from fear. Modern man is as full of fear as was his primitive ancestor. On this all the psychologists are agreed. Dr. Oscar Forel, whom nobody can accuse of having a Christian bias, declares roundly that "metaphysical anguish" remains the fundamental human problem. The scientists are as much afraid as the rest. I have already referred to a remark made by Harold Urey, Nobel Prize winner for Physics, one of the inventors of the atomic bomb: "I write in order to make you afraid. I am myself a man who is afraid. All the scientists I know are afraid. The men of science are clearly becoming conscious of the limitations of science; that it is no more than a representation of things—a representation that is most fruitful in practical deductions—but that it tells us nothing of things themselves, not even of matter or energy. It can never then have an answer for the problems that haunt the heart of man."

Tournier

During those last days, Amy Carmichael kept by her side the last stanza of an old hymn which epitomized her source of comfort:

> Green pastures are before me
> Which yet I have not seen,
> Bright skies will soon be o'er me
> Where the dark clouds have been.
>
> My hope I cannot measure,
> My path to life is free,
> My Savior has my treasure,
> And He will walk with me.

Something To Die For
Elizabeth Elliot

October 9

THE HARDEST PLACE
II Corinthians 2:16

Dinapore, Dec. 6, 1806

To the Rev. J. Chamberlain, Katwa,

I find myself here in a sphere so vast that I cry out with unfeigned astonishment, "Who is sufficient for these things?" I am somewhat dispirited at finding myself at a standstill; not knowing what course to take to acquire the language of the people—for the fine language of my Mussulman (Muslim) munshi is as unintelligible as English to the country people, and I have very limited opportunities of being much with them. I cannot be absent a night from this station without permission from the commander-in-chief. However, these are small difficulties. Our great obstacle is the dominion which Satan has obtained over the hearts of men.

Henry Martyn

Dr. Samuel Zwemer met a young medical student who said he would go to Arabia if he could be convinced that it was the hardest mission field in the world. Dr. Zwemer sat down and wrote, "Arabia is the hardest mission field in the world for the following reasons: 1. The climate is the most unbearable. One hundred degrees in the shade is common. It stays hot all night. 2. Arabic is the hardest language of which I know anything. 3. You probably cannot expect any converts to Christianity in your lifetime. All you can do is serve and love and let the results come as God sends them. 4. In addition, our mission has no money. We're not supported by any church board, and we have to raise our own funds. 5. New missionaries must promise not to marry for five years. Life here at this time is too primitive for women and children. Let me know what you decide. The young medical student read the letter and replied, "I am your man." His name was Paul Harrison.

Selected

Philippians 2:7 **SHARE HIS SORROW** October 10

As we develop the characteristics of biblical leadership, we begin to identify with those to whom we minister. Missionaries soon learn this is vital for compassionate, intimate ministry. Like the Baptist missionary couple who went to Sri Lanka a few years ago, taking with them four rooms of furniture. When they set up their home in Colombo, it looked just like the one they had left in America, including a deep freezer, television and microwave. After two years and many urgent appeals for funds from the faithful in the States, they had two or three converts. Disillusioned, they shipped themselves and their possessions home.

William Booth, founder and first general of the Salvation Army, sent a command to all of his missionaries in India: "Go to the Indian as a brother, which indeed you are, and show the love which none can doubt you feel . . . eat and drink and dress and live by his side. Speak his language, share his sorrow." And Count Zinzendorf, the great reformer, sent missionaries around the world with the same instruction: Do not lord it over the unbelievers but simply live among them; preach not theology, but the crucified Christ. Those are good instructions for all of us. For in a post-Christian culture, the church in America is not unlike a missionary outpost. As Dietrich Bonhoeffer put it: "The church is herself only when she exists for humanity. . . . She must take her part in the social life of the world, not lording it over men, but helping and serving them." If the church can only be the church when it exists for others, then the Christian can only be truly Christian when he or she is willing to be emptied out for others. There are no harder words in all of Scripture than Jesus' commandment that we love one another as He loved us—which means love that lays down its life for another. Sometimes that is a commandment we must take literally.

Charles Colson

October 11

"YOU ARE MY MAN"
II Thessalonians 2:13

No preacher in America has moved his generation more deeply than Dr. George W. Truett of Dallas, Texas. His simple eloquence mightily moved great congregations. Few, indeed, knew the personal tragedy in his life that led him into deeper consecration and became the secret of his power. The story is told in his biography by his son-in-law, Dr. Powhatan W. James.

As a younger man, Dr. Truett went out hunting on one occasion with some friends. Truett's shotgun discharged accidentally and wounded his closest friend, a Chief of Police. While the wounded man lingered between life and death, young Truett, together with his whole congregation, interceded for the life of the friend who had been shot. Nevertheless, soon after, Truett saw his friend die. All that night and for days to come the young pastor wrestled with God in prayer. No light came. He told his wife that never again could he go into the pulpit to preach. . . . his ministry was ended. He spent long hours with his Bible and repeatedly uttered these words, "My times are in Thy hands."

Late Saturday night he fell asleep, just before daybreak. Sunday morning there came to him a vision which inspired him to go back into his pulpit to pray and to preach with a fervor and conviction never known before. In his vision he seemed to see Jesus as vividly near as an earthly friend at his side and heard the Master say to him, "Have no fear. You are My man from now on." So vivid was the vision that he awakened his wife immediately and told her. He slept again and the vision was repeated. . . . and then the vision was repeated for the third time. Something revolutionary happened in the soul of George Truett. "You are My man from now on," said Jesus. All who heard Truett speak thereafter went away under the conviction of the Holy Spirit whispering, "Truett is surely God's man."

Benjamin P. Browne

Exodus 32:32   **PRAYERLESS PRAYING**   October 12

If men only prayed on all occasions and in every place where they go through the motion! If there were only holy inflamed hearts back of all these beautiful words and gracious forms! If there were always uplifted hearts in these erect men who are uttering flawless but vain words before God! If there were always reverent bended hearts when bended knees are uttering words before God to please men's ears!

There is nothing that will preserve the life of prayer, its vigor, sweetness, obligations, seriousness and value, so much as a deep conviction that prayer is an approach to God, a pleading with God, an asking of God. Reality will then be in it; reverence will then be in the attitude, in the place, and in the air. Faith will draw, kindle and open. Formality and deadness cannot live in this high and all-serious home of the soul. Prayerless praying lacks the essential element of true praying; it is not based on desire and is devoid of earnestness and faith. Desire burdens the chariot of prayer, and faith drives its wheels. Prayerless praying has no burden because no sense of need; no ardor, because none of the vision, strength or glow of faith. No mighty pressure to prayer, no holding on to God with the deathless, despairing grasp, "I will not let thee go except thou bless me." No utter self-abandon, lost in the throes of a desperate, pertinacious, and consuming plea: "Yet now if thou wilt forgive their sin—if not, blot me, I pray thee, out of thy book"; or, "Give me Scotland, or I die."

Purpose in Prayer
E. M. Bounds

October 13

"TEACH ME TO PRAY"

Luke 11:1

There is probably not a praying soul who has not prayed thus. But most of us do not really know what we are praying for when we ask the Lord to teach us to pray. We are completely surprised, therefore, when the Lord fulfills our petition. He sends us *distress*, for that is the simplest way to teach us to pray. He leads us into *spiritual* distress, hiding Himself from us for a season, thus making plain to us how much our own piety is worth. Our whole spiritual life dries up and withers away; prayer, reading of the Bible, faith, love, repentance, the self-denying attitude of heart, and the willing spirit.

Perhaps He leads us at the same time into *temporal* distress. And when spiritual and temporal tribulations have overwhelmed us, we feel that our cup is filled to overflowing. At such a time every sincere soul becomes acquainted with one of the aspects of prayer with which he has not been particularly well acquainted before. He learns that prayer is to open the heart to Jesus, that He many enter into our every need. If you are praying the Lord to teach you to pray, you must make it clear to yourself that you are praying for distress and tribulation.

Dare you *then* pray: "Lord, teach me to pray"? Well, let us be honest and admit that we are afraid of tribulation and suffering, in fact, that we are afraid even of God. But neither you nor I will be happy until we have committed ourselves into the pierced hands of the Lord Jesus. And in so doing we will enter voluntarily into the school of prayer which the Spirit has established for people who cannot pray as they ought.

O. Hallesby

October 14

"GIVE ME SOULS OR I DIE"
Genesis 32:26

John Smith believed, "When you are with people in distress on account of their sins, you must not only pray for them, but you must throw yourself into their circumstances; you must be a penitent too; they must pray through you, and what you say must be exactly what they would say if they knew how." So he entered vicariously into the sins of others:

> The condition of sinners inspired his heart with an unutterable pity. He entered so fully into their misery and peril, and had so poignant and distressing a sense of the malignity and heinousness of their violations of God's law, as to be often indescribably oppressed. It was a settled principle with him to "confess the sins of the people." "I remember," says Mr. Clarkson (John's close friend), "to have heard him remark that 'unless a preacher carries about with him a daily burden, he is not likely to see many sinners converted to God.'"

Mr. Calder, John's coworker, testified: "I have often seen him (John) come downstairs in the morning, after spending several hours in prayer, with his eyes swollen with weeping. He would soon introduce the subject of his anxiety by saying, 'I am a broken-hearted man; yes, indeed I am an unhappy man; not for myself, but on account of others. God has given me such a sight of the value of precious souls that I cannot live if souls be not saved. Oh, give me souls, or else I die!'"

Heroes of the Holy Life
Wesley Duewel

Romans 3:3

PRAYING HYDE

October 15

Praying Hyde became known as one of the most effective personal soul winners India ever knew, especially in his latter years. Wherever he went he led souls to Christ. He would stop to speak to a stranger, and soon his hand would be on the stranger's shoulder and he would be praying with that person, leading him to Christ.

When John traveled on the crowded Indian trains, he was always trying to lead another person to Christ. Often by the time he reached his destination, he was dealing very directly with another traveler about his salvation but had not yet won him. John would ignore the fact that he was at his destination and would travel farther on the train, witnessing and praying. When he had led the person to Christ, if possible he would baptize him and then return by a later train to his own destination. On one occasion he rode past his stopping place four times in order to win the person to whom he was witnessing. When he finally arrived at this destination, having passed through the station four times already, he found that the engagement he was going to attend was over, but heaven was richer with four new believers he had led to Christ en route.

Praying Hyde's ministry was anointed with tears. He was often seen weeping during private prayer as he interceded for souls. And at times he broke down while praying publicly. As he described the love of Jesus, especially his agony in Gethsemane and Calvary, he would speak with many tears. He believed that Jesus, as he intercedes at the right hand of the Father, prays with great agony for the sins and sinners of our world. This would break John's heart as he shared Christ's burden.

Heroes of the Holy Life
Wesley Duewel

Matthew 27:39-40 ## WHERE IS GOD? **October 16**

Jewish writers are telling the story of the Holocaust in the most vivid and powerful language. And part of that story of unimaginable suffering concerns God and His involvement in places like Auschwitz. Elie Wiesel's works are a good example.... In one tale a boy is suspected of sabotage and is hanged alongside two adults. Wiesel writes: "The SS seemed more preoccupied, more disturbed than usual. To hang a young boy in front of thousands of spectators was no light matter. The head of the camp read the verdict. All eyes were on this child. He was lividly pale, almost calm, biting his lips. The gallows threw its shadow over him.

"The three victims mounted together onto the chairs. The three necks were placed at the same moment within the nooses. 'Long live liberty!' cried the two adults. But the child was silent. 'Where is God? Where is He?' someone behind me asked. At a sign from the head of the camp, the three chairs tipped over. Total silence throughout the camp. On the horizon the sun was setting. 'Bare your heads!' yelled the head of the camp. His voice was raucous. We were weeping. 'Cover your heads!' Then the march past began. The two adults were no longer alive. Their tongues hung swollen, blue tinged. But the third rope was still moving; being so light, the child was still alive.... For more than half an hour he stayed there, struggling between life and death, dying in slow agony under our eyes. And we had to look him full in the face. He was still alive when I passed in front of him. His tongue was still red, his eyes not yet glazed.

"Behind me, I heard the same man asking, 'Where is God now?' And I heard a voice within me answer him, 'Where is He? Here He is—He is hanging here on this gallows.'"

James Londis

October 17
SWEET AS WELL AS BITTER
Jeremiah 9:1

The accident itself bewilders me as much today as it did three years ago. Much good has come from it, but all the good in the world will never make the accident itself good. It remains a horrible, tragic, and evil event to me. A million people could be helped as a result of the tragedy, but that would not be enough to explain and justify it. The badness of the event and the goodness of the results are related, to be sure, but they are not the same. The latter is a consequence of the former, but the latter does not make the former legitimate or right or good. I do not believe that I lost three members of my family *in order that* I might change for the better, raise three healthy children, or write a book.

Yet the grief I feel is sweet as well as bitter. I still have a sorrowful soul; yet I wake up every morning, joyful, eager for what the new day will bring. Never have I felt as much pain as I have in the last three years; yet never have I experienced as much pleasure in simply being alive and living an ordinary life. Never have I felt so broken; yet never have I been so whole. Never have I been so aware of my weakness and vulnerability; yet never have I been so content and felt so strong. Never has my soul been more dead, yet never more alive. What I once considered mutually exclusive—sorrow and joy, pain and pleasure, death and life—have become parts of a greater whole. My soul has been stretched. Above all, I have become aware of the power of God's grace and my need for it. My soul has grown because it has been awakened to the goodness and love of God. God has been present in my life these past three years, even mysteriously in the accident. God will continue to be present to the end of my life and through all eternity. God is growing my soul, making it bigger, and filling it with himself. My life is being transformed. Though I have endured pain, I believe that the outcome is going to be wonderful.

A Grace Disguised
Jerry Sittser

October 18
WHAT ABOUT AFTERWARDS?
Psalm 34:22

On this day many years ago, I went away alone to a cave in a mountain called Arima, in Japan. I felt many feelings of fear about the future. That was why I went there. I wanted to be alone with God.

The devil kept on whispering, "It's all right now, but what about afterwards? You are going to be very lonely." And he painted pictures of loneliness. I can see them still. Then I turned to my God in a kind of desperation and said, "Lord, what can I do? How can I go on to the end?" And He said, "None of them that trust in Me shall be desolate" (Psalm 34:22).

That word has been with me ever since, and I give it to you now. It has been fulfilled to me. It will be fulfilled to you. Only live for Him who redeemed you and trust Him to take care of you, *and He will.*

That day the words "not only but also" were given to me, too. There is not only joy but also sorrow in every life, but in the end—O in the end—we shall see His face and we shall serve Him together.

Amy Carmichael

October 19

PEACE IN TRIBULATION
John 16:25-33

Here is a strange medley of experiences! I am to enjoy the gift of peace, and yet I am to be smarting under tribulation! When the Holy Spirit is my guest, I am to enjoy the gift of peace. "I have told you these things, so that in me you may have peace." The life of the soul is to move without jar or discord. It shall be like a quiet engine-house, in which every wheel cooperates with every other wheel, and there is no waste or friction in the holy place. "All that is within me" blesses God's holy name.

And yet, while peace reigns within, there may be tribulations without! "In the world you will have trouble." Here is a peace which is not broken by the noise and assault of brutal circumstances. The moist tempestuous wind cannot disturb the quiet serenity of the stars. When the world stones me, not one grain of its gritty dust need enter the delicate workings of my soul. That was the peace of my Lord, and it is my Lord who says to me: "My peace I give you." So, "be of good cheer," my soul. Thy Lord has "overcome the world," and you shall share His victory.

J. H. Jowett

October 20

DECENTRALIZATION

Philippians 1:6

In bringing an individual into the likeness of His son, God must decentralize him. Decentralization begins in the crisis of justification and the new birth and continues in the crisis of sanctification or the filling with the Holy Spirit.

Of necessity it does not end there. These are only beginning experiences similar to a vestibule, which is a good place to enter but a poor place to stay. The work of sanctification by which the self is decentralized is both instantaneous and progressive. It is both a crisis and a process which continues throughout life. "Being confident of this very thing, that he which hath begun a good work in you will perform it until the day of Jesus Christ" (Philippians 1:6).

If God's net purpose in saving an individual is just to get him to heaven, He would probably take him to glory immediately. But God wants to prepare him for rulership in an infinite universe that demands character. Progress in sanctification, in the development of Godlike character and agape love, is impossible without tribulation and chastisement.

"Not only so, but we also rejoice in our sufferings, because we know that suffering produces perseverance; perseverance, character; and character, hope."

> I walked a mile with pleasure;
> She chattered all the way,
> But left me none the wiser
> For all she had to say.
>
> I walked a mile with sorrow;
> And ne'er a word said she;
> But, O, the things I learned from her
> When sorrow walked with me.

Paul E. Billheimer

October 21
THE PURPOSEFULNESS OF SUFFERING
Hebrews 2:10

This explains Paul's inspired revelation: "If we suffer, we shall also reign with him" (II Timothy 2:12). According to Romans 5:3-5 suffering issues in character (agape love), and character is a prerequisite to rulership. Because there is no character development without suffering, suffering is a necessary preparation for rulership.

One of the most amazing commentaries on the purposefulness of suffering in the economy of God is set forth in Hebrews 2:10: "For it became him, for whom are all things, and by whom are all things, in bringing many sons unto glory, to make the captain of their salvation perfect through sufferings." "Though he were a son, yet learned he obedience by the things which he suffered" (Hebrews 5:8). In Christ's case, according to Maclaren, "His perfecting was not the perfecting of moral character but the completion of His equipment for His work as Leader and Originator of our salvation. Before He suffers He has the pity of God. After He suffers He has the compassion of a man."

The New Testament and Wycliffe Bible Commentary say: "By suffering His human experience was made complete.... Because He suffered He is now fully qualified to serve as captain (archegos, leader) of man's salvation." If the "many sons" whom Christ was to bring to glory and rulership had to be prepared and perfected for that glory by suffering, their Captain must lead the way by having His human experience perfected in the same way. The fact that Christ's human experience had to be perfected by suffering proves that no suffering is purposeless, but that it is an essential part of God's economy.

Paul E. Billheimer

October 22
DON'T WASTE YOUR SORROWS
Isaiah 53:4-6

It is clear from the foregoing and other similar passages of Scripture that sorrow, suffering, tribulation, and pain which come to the believer are not primarily for punishment but for child training. They are not purposeless. Earthly parents may make mistakes in their chastisement—and often do. But not God. He is preparing the believer for rulership in a universe so vast that it appears infinite. It seems that God cannot fully decentralize fallen man, even though born again, sanctified or filled with the Holy Spirit, without suffering.

Watchman Nee says that we never learn anything new about God except through adversity. Some consider this an exaggeration, but it does seem that few seek a deeper walk with God except under duress.

Christ's suffering only matured and perfected His human experience. It purged nothing from His moral nature even as a man because He was unfallen. No stain of sin ever marred His humanity. But not so with fallen man. There is no way that Christlike character can be formed in man without suffering because he cannot be decentralized otherwise. If he will not suffer, if he determines to evade it, if he refuses to allow the life of nature and of self to go to the cross, to that extent he will remain hard, self-centered, unbroken, and therefore unChristlike.

"Whole, unbruised, unbroken men are of little use to God" (J. R. Miller). By his self-will, one may escape a certain quality of pain, that which accompanies voluntary self-sacrifice, but in so doing he becomes the victim of a far greater pain, that of self-worship. He cannot escape both. Someone has said, "There are things which even God cannot do for us unless He allows us to suffer."

Paul E. Billheimer

October 23
"SHALL I LEAVE YOU ALONE"
John 15:2

A child of God was once overwhelmed by the number of afflictions that seemed to target her. As she walked past a vineyard during the rich glow of autumn, she noticed its untrimmed appearance and the abundance of leaves still on the vines. The ground had been overtaken by a tangle of weeds and grass, and the entire place appeared totally unkempt. While she pondered the sight, the heavenly Gardener whispered such a precious message to her that she could not help but share it.

The message was this: "My dear child, are you questioning the number of trials in your life? Remember the vineyard and learn from it. The gardener stops pruning and trimming the vine or weeding the soil only when he expects nothing more from the vine during that season. He leaves it alone because its fruitfulness is gone and further effort now would yield no profit. In the same way, freedom from suffering leads to uselessness. Do you now want me to stop pruning your life? Shall I leave you alone?" Then her comforted heart cried, "No!"

Homera Homer-Dixon

It is the branch that bears the fruit,
  That feels the knife,
To prune it for a larger growth,
  A fuller life.
Rejoice, though each desire, each dream,
  Each hope of thine
Will fall and fade; it is the hand
  Of Love Divine
That holds the knife, that cuts and breaks
  With tenderest touch,
That you, whose life has borne some fruit,
  Might now bear much.

Annie Johnson Flint

October 24
SICKNESS AMONG CHRIST'S FRIENDS
John 11:1-16

And so sickness can enter the circle of friends of the Lord. "The one You love is sick." My sicknesses do not mean I have lost His favor. The shadow is His, as well as the sunshine. When He removes me from the glare of boisterous health, it may be because of some spiritual fern which needs the ministry of the shade. "This sickness . . . is for God's glory." Something beautiful will spring out of the shadowed seclusion, something which shall spread abroad the name and fame of God.

And, therefore, I do not wonder at the Lord's delay. He did not hasten away to the sick friend: "He stayed where He was two more days." Shall I put it like this: the awakening bulbs were not yet ready for the brighter light—just a little more shade! We are impatient to get healthy; the Lord desires that we become holy. Our physical sickness is continued in order that we may put on spiritual strength.

And there are others besides sick Lazarus concerned in the sickness; "and for your sake I am glad I was not there." The disciples were included in the Divine scheme. Their spiritual welfare was to be affected by it. Let me ever remember that the circle affected by sickness is always wider than the patient's bed. And may God be glorified in all!

J. H. Jowett

October 25

A BIGGER PICTURE

Isaiah 42:10-16

I have often imagined my own story fitting into some greater scheme, the half of which I may never fathom. I simply do not see the bigger picture, but I *choose to believe* that there is a bigger picture and that my loss is part of some wonderful story authored by God himself. Sometimes I wonder about how my own experience of loss will someday serve a greater purpose that I do not yet see or understand. My story may help to redeem a bad past, or it may bring about a better future. Perhaps my own family heritage has produced generations of absent and selfish fathers, and I have been given a chance to reverse that pattern. Perhaps people suffering catastrophic loss will someday look to our family for hope and inspiration. I do not know. Yet I choose to believe that God is working toward some ultimate purpose, even using my loss to that end.

Thornton Wilder suggests in *The Eighth Day* that we should understand our lives as a great landscape that extends far beyond what the eye of our experience can see. Who knows how one experience, so singularly horrible, can set in motion a chain of events that will bless future generations? Loss may appear to be random, but that does not mean it is. It may fit into a scheme that surpasses even what our imaginations dare to think.

A Grace Disguised
Jerry Sittser

Isaiah 61:1-2   **THE SADDEST WEEK**   **October 26**

Yangzhou as "home" to the Taylors, though they had so seldom lived there, held all Maria's possessions, and Hudson Taylor had to spend a few days disposing of them. Two days before Christmas he wrote, "Last week was perhaps the saddest I have passed since my dear wife's removal. I was going over many of her things—our betrothal presents, her wedding dress, and many things . . . connected with the birth and death of some of the dear children and with my darling wife herself." A flood of memories had been inescapable.

He had asked Emily Blatchley to compile materials for a memoir of Maria for the children and then to write it herself. She began but as her health failed had to put it aside. Little survives, but scattered reminiscences and tributes in letters of sympathy confirm the impression of a highly competent, caring and self-effacing wife, mother and missionary colleague. James Williamson recalled her constant attention to the single men's clothes, keeping them laundered and mended. Charles and Elizabeth Judd knew her only from the six weeks they were together in Hangzhou, and then in Zhenjiang after the riots, when Hudson Taylor was down with dysentery. In spite of her injuries Maria had risen to the occasion and struck Judd as being "the backbone of the Mission at that time." A false inference has been drawn from his remark—that without Maria, Hudson Taylor would have been weak—but throughout the collected correspondence (her own, the Bergers' and Hudson Taylor's) the clear impression is given of a consistently unobtrusive but positive personality supporting her husband loyally and obediently, in his strong leadership, never asserting her own opinions when they occasionally differed from his.

Hudson Taylor and China's Open Century
A. J. Broomhall

October 27
RADICAL RECONSTRUCTION
Matthew 5:12

Matthew 5 describes God's radical reconstruction of the heart. Observe the sequence. First, we recognize we are in need (we're poor in spirit). Next, we repent of our self-sufficiency (we mourn). We quit calling the shots and surrender control to God (we're meek). So grateful are we for his presence that we yearn for more of him (we hunger and thirst). As we grow closer to him, we become more like him. We forgive others (we're merciful). We change our outlook (we're pure in heart). We love others (we're peacemakers). We endure injustice (we're persecuted). It's no casual shift of attitude. It is a demolition of the old structure and a creation of the new.

The Applause of Heaven
Max Lucado

The gossamers are hung today
Outside my window, see them play.
Descending from up there somewhere
They slide along their path of air
Where spiderlings are bound to sail
The heights above my woodland trail.

Now, dawning sunbeams in caress
Come gliding on their silkiness
And slide their whisperings of light
In gentle gleamings soft and bright.

Those fairy cable cars seem weak!
And yet so strong, so smooth and sleek;
A filament more fine than hair
Yet carries sunlight sweetly fair

And more than this! My load of care
They strangely whisk away somewhere.
For when the gossamers are here,
How could I help but have good cheer?

Lois Kempton

October 28
IN THE PRESENCE OF ETERNITY
Psalm 103:15

It is he who every moment produces and renews the breath of life which animates us. It is he who has counted our days, who holds in his powerful hands the keys of the tomb, to open it or to close it. That which strikes us the hardest is nothing in the eyes of God. A little more or a little less of life are differences which disappear in the presence of his eternity. What does it matter if this frail vessel, the body of clay, should be broken and reduced to ashes a little sooner or a little later?

O, how short and deceiving our sight is! We are in consternation to see a person die in the prime of life. "What a horrible loss," we say. But why is it a loss? What does he who dies lose? Some years of vanity, illusion, and of danger of eternal death. God lifts him from the midst of sin and snatches him from the corrupt world and from his own weakness. What do the people lose by whom he was loved? They lose the toxin of worldly happiness. They lose a perpetual inebriation. They lose the forgetfulness of God and of themselves, into which they were plunged, or rather they gain, by virtue of the cross, the blessing of detachment. The same blow which saves the person who dies, prepares the others to detach themselves by suffering, to work bravely for their salvation. O, how true it is then that God is good, that he is tender, that he is merciful to our true ills even when he seems to crush us, and even when we are tempted to pity ourselves because of his sternness.

What difference do we find now between two people who lived a hundred years ago? One died twenty years before the other, but after all both died. Their separation, which seemed at the time so long and so hard, seems to us now, and really was, only a brief separation. Soon what is separated will be united, and no trace of that so short separation will appear.

Fenelon

October 29

A FEATURELESS PAIN

Psalm 23:1-4

The routines of life called for decisions, always decisions; but I had lost confidence in my ability to make even the simplest decisions. Being decisive required mental energy, and there was no energy to draw from. I was weary. It was an effort just to arrange my jumbled thoughts long enough to solve the most mundane problems. I went through the day's schedule like a robot.

"What, Lord, has happened to my joy, my enthusiasm, my motivation?" I cried out. In the same friendly office, the friendliest face was missing. By contrast, everything seemed cold and lifeless. The little house, where friends used to gather for boisterous, fun-filled evenings, now seemed empty and bare. *If only,* I thought, *Henry could once again walk in that door.* But Henry would never again do that. The thought unleashed waves of depression and self-pity.

The world around me had turned into a featureless plain. People I passed on the streets had no faces; I hardly saw them. Driving over the familiar concrete stretches of the Los Angeles freeway, crowded with automobiles, I felt more isolated than on the country farm where I grew up. On one particular day, absorbed in the tangle of my own thoughts, I missed my turn-off, suddenly discovering that I did not know where I was, not even sure how to get back home. It seemed somehow symbolic. My life had become like that—a long dull stretch of road that I was traveling, hardly knowing where I was going, or where to get off.

Thrice Through the Valley
Valetta Steel

John 6:63 **IN NO WAY EXEMPT** **October 30**

I have shared all of this as frankly as I know how to underscore a plain truth: Christians are in no way exempt from the tragedies of life. We share in the curses and frailties of that nature common to all men. Death, that savage intruder, has the power to break our heart, to leave us demoralized and, for a time, under the tyranny of despair.

And yet, when the worst that can happen has indeed happened, when the heart is broken, the tears have flowed, and unanswered questions have been wrung in anguish from the soul—a discovery comes. To some it comes sooner, and to some later.

The discovery is simple. God has not left his children without resources. I had known the comfort of his Word when I cradled my dying son in the little Sherwood parsonage, through the night hours when I tried to quench his unquenchable thirst. Yes, God had spoken then. I had known it in the guest room in Korea as I listened to my husband struggling to draw breath into his tormented lungs; God had spoken both times, and my heart had been at peace. Now he was gently instructing again.

To my surprise and delight, I discovered the Scriptures did indeed bring healing for my latest grief. Every cliché that I had ever heard about his Word was true, really true. It was light in the darkness, bread to the hungry, a staff to the weak, water for parched lips. "The words that I speak unto you," Jesus said, "They are spirit, and they are life." How true.

Thrice Through the Valley
Valetta Steel

October 31

GOLD BY MOONLIGHT
Proverbs 20:24

I learned, as Amy Carmichael expressed it, to find "gold by moonlight." I started a special notebook in which I stored up my treasures. Many of these verses, long-familiar mottos, were now peculiarly apt, as though the Holy Spirit were fitting them like a skillful tailor to every dimension of my life: "Weeping may endure for a night, but joy cometh in the morning" (Psalm 30:5). "Since the Lord is directing our steps, why try to understand everything that happens along the way?" (Proverbs 20:24, TLB). "For it is God who works in you to will and to act according to his good purpose" (Philippians 2:13). "We can make our plans, but the final outcome is in God's hands" (Proverbs 16:1, TLB). "Commit your work to the Lord, then it will succeed" (Proverbs 16:3, TLB). "We should make plans—counting on God to direct us" (Proverbs 16:9, TLB). "The Lord destroys the possessions of the proud but cares for widows" (Proverbs 15:25, TLB).

In the valley of the shadow, like the Psalmist, I had discovered that God's rod and staff—his Word—were indeed my comfort (Psalm 23:4). And like the shepherd's instrument, God used his rod not only for comfort and safety, but also for guidance and correction. God knew there were faulty areas in my life that needed correction. Lovingly, he brought the chastening rod of his Word to bear on those deficiencies.

Thrice Through the Valley
Valetta Steel

November 1

WEAK ENOUGH
II Corinthians 4:7-8

Mr. Taylor's humility was certainly a striking feature of his character. Some years ago dear Elder Cumming told me of a conversation he had had with Mr. Hudson Taylor. Remembering that, I wrote to Elder Cumming the other day and asked him if he could give me just a brief record of it, and he wrote me as follows: "At Dr. Somerville's funeral in Glasgow, Mr. Hudson Taylor and I were together and alone in the same carriage. After talking of dear old Dr. Somerville and of other subjects, I ventured to speak of the China Inland Mission and to say that he must often have felt the wonderful honor that God had put upon him as the founder of the Mission, and that I doubted whether any one then living had had a greater honor. He turned to me and, with a voice trembling with suppressed feeling, said that he sometimes thought that God must have looked into the various countries and places to find someone weak enough to do such a work, so that none of the glory could go to the man himself, and then when He alighted upon him, God said, 'This man is weak enough. He will do.'"

W. B. Sloan

A. B. Simpson did not employ the means men use to achieve leadership. He neither exalted himself nor would he allow others to exalt him. He did not exploit the public. The tricks of the advertiser he despised. He did not lay stress on organization; in fact, he determinedly opposed the introduction of much machinery. In his dedicatory address of the Madison Avenue Tabernacle, he said: "I am afraid of human greatness; I am afraid of the triumphs of human praise; I am glad to have the work of God beginning in lowliness." But he believed that God had sent him on a definite mission and for a specific ministry and lived and loved and labored in the unconquerable courage and invincible strength of a true apostle.

A. E. Thompson

November 2
GOD'S MEGAPHONE
Genesis 50:20

At Peace Ledge we were alone with our heavenly messengers and our questions. "When a man is to be hanged in a fortnight, it concentrates his mind wonderfully," Samuel Johnson said more than two centuries ago. Although I wasn't due for a hanging, I sometimes felt like it was what I deserved. And in that prevailing mood the mind was concentrated. It was time to search for more substantial truths about God and about self than we ever had before. We determined to do it.

Out of that came the Peace Ledge Principle: Somewhere in those early days we equated the principle of being silent with listening. We wish to be listeners to the deep sources where certain kinds of heavenly truth are tapped only by those who have a heart to be attentive. Usually those are the hearts of the suffering or the hearts of broken-world people in search of a rebuilding effort.

We wanted to look at pain the way Joseph looked at it when he scanned the many years of slavery, imprisonment and ill-treatment and said, "You meant evil against me; but God meant it for good" (Genesis 50:20, NKJV). Our questions were another version of that. How do you take an evil event and its consequences and squeeze good out of it? Can the worst that human beings do be forced to render something good?

Gordon MacDonald

No doubt pain, as God's megaphone, is a terrible instrument; it may lead to final and unrepented rebellion. But it gives the only opportunity the bad man can have to amendment. It removes the veil; it plants the flag of truth within the fortress of the rebel soul.

C. S. Lewis

November 3

THE KEY TO SUCCESS
I Corinthians 12:25-26

Physical pain is effective because it forces the body to cease other activities and attend to the reason for the pain. We can become the emotional incarnation of Christ's risen body. Just as the world will never learn the Good News apart from our efforts, the church of Christ will never experience a healing response to suffering unless we learn to focus on the body's pains and act as healing agents. Dr. Paul Brand has developed this idea as a key part of his personal philosophy:

> Individual cells had to give up their autonomy and learn to suffer with one another before effective multicelled organisms could be produced and survive. The same designer went on to create the human race with a new and higher purpose in mind. Not only would the cells within an individual cooperate with one another, but the individuals within the race would now move on to a new level of community responsibility, to a new kind of relationship with one another and with God. As in the body, so in this new kind of relationship the key to success lies in the sensation of pain. All of us rejoice at the harmonious working of the human body. Yet we can but sorrow at the relationships between men. In human society we are suffering because we do not suffer enough. So much of the sorrow in the world is due to the selfishness of one living organism that simply doesn't care when the next one suffers. In the body if one cell or group of cells grows and flourishes at the expense of the rest, we call it cancer and know that if it is allowed to spread the body is doomed. And yet, the only alternative to the cancer is absolute loyalty of every cell in the body, the head. God is calling us today to learn from the lower creation and move on to a higher level of evolution and to participate in this community which He is preparing for the salvation of the world.

Philip Yancey

November 4
"WHY IS IT DOING THIS?"
Romans 8:17-18

When the world deals with us harshly, it makes us ask "Why is it doing this?", and we have got our answer, "It is doing this to us because we are Christians." And that makes us remember that because we are Christians we are receiving the same treatment as Christ received. And as verse 17 has said, "If we suffer with him," we shall be "glorified together." The world persecuted Him, and it is persecuting us. So persecution, far from getting us down, reminds us that we are aliens in the world; we are but "strangers and pilgrims." We do not belong to this world, "as he was so are we in this world."

Trials and tribulations also force us to think of the glory which is awaiting us. In thought, we are back again to verse 18: "For I reckon that the sufferings of this present time are not worthy to be compared with the glory which shall be revealed in us." The trials drive us to think in these terms and in terms of all that follows in Romans 8:19-32. They turn our attention to the promised glory. We know something of the following, "We ourselves also, which have the first fruits of the Spirit, even we ourselves groan within ourselves, waiting for the adoption, to wit, the redemption of our body. For we are saved by hope, but hope that is seen is not hope, for what a man seeth, why doth he yet hope for? But if we hope for that we see not, then do we with patience wait for it." These trials and troubles and tribulations turn our minds to the glory that awaits us, and the moment they do so they become as nothing. So we are "more than conquerors" . . . His mark is upon us. He has set His heart upon us. He has a purpose for us.

Martyn Lloyd-Jones

Luke 10:41   **SAINTS OR CYNICS**   **November 5**

Trouble does not automatically sanctify. Sometimes it does the opposite. Sometimes it breeds not saints but cynics. Sometimes it does not soften the spirit but makes it hard and bitter. The fact is trouble in itself is neutral. It needs something else—it needs the Spirit of God—to make it not neutral but positive and creative. We have an Indian fern whose frond changes as it grows. As the forces of life play upon it and work within it, each little pinna divides and subdivides till, in the end, the frond is a fan of delicate lace, a feather fan.

"What has been the effect upon him of all the trouble?" we asked a guest who had been telling us of her father and of how he had suffered from injustice. "It has left him unable to think an unkind thought of anyone," she answered. The frond of that fern had been perfected.

If the wear and tear of life on a soul do not make for beauty, the process of the fern is reversed. The multitude of insignificant, trying things that are sure to come fret it into a ragged selfishness, and rough blows coarsen its texture. Or if it be otherwise fashioned it reacts to the touch like a jarred sea-anemone, gathering itself within itself. Then (unlike the anemone, which, if left in peace, opens again) the jarred soul gradually closes completely and hardens, till it acquires the power to jar others even as it was jarred. So there is loss. Fellow-lovers, who were meant to meet, pass each other coldly. They do not even recognize each other as members of the family. Each is frozen in his own ice. But the love of God shed abroad in our hearts (not filtered through various screens) can melt us and love us out of fretfulness and out of hardness. It was said of one who lived this life, "Love gladdened him. Love quickened him. Love set him free." Love sets us free to love. And having been set free it is impossible to be bound any more.

                                                              Amy Carmichael

November 6

YOU'VE GOT GOD
Psalm 95:2

Say! You've struck a heap of trouble—
 Bust in business, lost your wife;
No one cares a cent about you,
 You don't care a cent for life;
Hard luck has of hope bereft you,
 Health is failing, wish you'd die—
Why, you've still the sunshine left you
 And the big, blue sky.

Sky so blue it makes you wonder
 If it's heaven shining through;
Earth so smiling 'way out yonder,
 Sun so bright it dazzles you;
Birds a-singing, flowers a-flinging
 All their fragrance on the breeze;
Dancing shadows, green, still meadows—
 Don't you mope, you've still got these.

These, and none can take them from you;
 These, and none can weigh their worth.
What! You're tired and broke and beaten?—
 Why, you're rich—you've got the earth!
Yes, if you're a tramp in tatters,
 While the blue sky bends above
You've got nearly all that matters—
 You've got God, and God is love.

Robert W. Service

Only he who gives thanks for little things receives the big things. We prevent God from giving us the great spiritual gifts he has in store for us because we do not give thanks for daily gifts.

Detrich Bonhoeffer

Psalm 40:1-2 **BLESS YOU PRISON** November 7

Crisis crushes. And in crushing, it often refines and purifies. You may be discouraged today because the crushing has not yet led to a surrender. I've stood beside too many of the dying, ministered to too many of the broken and bruised to believe that crushing is an end in itself. Unfortunately, however, it usually takes the brutal blows of affliction to soften and penetrate hard hearts even though such blows often seem unfair.

Charles Swindoll

The thing that helped me personally more than any thing else to come to a conviction of God was an experience some years ago. I went to a saintly Christian pouring out my troubles, expecting she would take a great interest in me and do all she could to help me. She listened and then said, "Yes, all you say may be very true but then, in spite of it all, there is God." Every time I went to see her, her answer was the same. "After all, there is God." At last because she said it so often and seemed so sure, I began dimly to wonder whether after all God might not be enough, even for my need, overwhelming and peculiar as I felt it to be. From wondering I came gradually to believing that being my Creator and Redeemer, He must be enough; and at last a conviction burst upon me that He really was enough and my eyes were opened to the fact of the absolute and utter all-sufficiency of God.

Hannah Whithall Smith

November 8

AN ILLUMINATION

James 5:10

The best remedy—I do not say for getting rid of trouble, for I know of none for that, but for enabling the soul to endure it—is to occupy oneself with external things and with works of charity, hoping in God's mercy. His mercy is never lacking to those who trust in Him. May He be blessed forever.

St. Theresa of Avila

Suffering is an essential element in the Christian religion, as it is in life. After all, the cross itself is the supreme example. If Christ hadn't suffered, do you imagine that anyone would have paid the slightest attention to the religion he founded? Not at all.

It's a mystery in a sense, but just imagine the opposite. Supposing you eliminated suffering, what a dreadful place the world would be! I would almost rather eliminate happiness. The world would be the most ghastly place because everything that corrects the tendency of this unspeakable little creature, man, to feel over-important and over-pleased with himself would disappear. He's bad enough now but he would be absolutely intolerable if he never suffered. However, we needn't fear that.

Malcolm Muggeridge

November 9

HAST THOU NO SCAR?

John 20:27-28

Hast thou no scar?
No hidden scar on foot, or side, or hand?
I hear thee sung as mighty in the land,
I hear them hail thy bright ascendant star,
Has thou no scar?

Hast thou no wound?
Yet I was wounded by the archers, spent,
Leaned Me against a tree to die; and rent
By ravening beasts that compassed Me, I swooned.
Hast thou no wound?

No wound? No scar?
Yet, as the Master shall the servant be,
And pierced are the feet that follow Me;
But thine are whole: can he have followed far
Who has no wound nor scar?

Amy Carmichael

The higher a person hath advanced in the Spirit, so much the heavier crosses he oftentimes findeth; because the grief of his banishment increaseth with his love to God.

Nevertheless this man, though so many ways afflicted, is not without refreshing comfort, for that he perceiveth very much benefit to accrue unto him by the bearing of his own cross.

For whilst he willingly putteth himself under it, all the burden of tribulation is turned into the confidence of divine comfort.

Thomas a Kempis

THE BEAUTIFUL FOLIAGE
November 10

Isaiah 30:18

The greenest grass is found wherever the most rain falls. So I suppose it is the fog and mist of Ireland that makes it "the Emerald Isle." And wherever you find the widespread fog of trouble and the mist of sorrow, you always find emerald green hearts that are full of the beautiful foliage of the comfort and love of God.

Dear Christian, do not say, "Where are all the swallows? They are gone—they are dead." No, they are not dead. They have simply skimmed across the deep, blue sea, flying to a faraway land; but they will be back again soon.

Child of God, do not say, "All the flowers are dead—the winter has killed them, so they are gone." No! Although the winter has covered them with a white coat of snow, they will push up their heads again and will be alive very soon.

O believer, do not say that the sun has burned out, just because a cloud has hidden it. No, it is still there, planning a summer for you; for when it shines again, it will have caused those clouds to have dropped their April showers, each of them a mother to a sweet mayflower.

Above all, remember—when God hides His face from you, do not say that He has forgotten you. He is simply waiting for a little while to make you love Him more. And once He comes you will rejoice with the inexpressible "joy of the Lord" (Nehemiah 8:10). Waiting on Him exercises your gift of grace and tests your faith. Therefore continue to wait in hope, for although the promise may linger, it will never come too late.

Charles H. Spurgeon

November 11
AMID YOUR DASHED HOPES
Joshua 1:1-2

Yesterday you experienced a great sorrow, and now your home seems empty. Your first impulse is to give up and to sit down in despair amid your dashed hopes. Yet you must defy that temptation, for you are at the front line of the battle, and the crisis is at hand. Faltering even one moment would put God's interest at risk. Other lives will be harmed by your hesitation, and His work will suffer if you simply fold your hands. You must not linger at this point, even to indulge your grief.

A famous general once related this sorrowful story from his own wartime experience. His son was the lieutenant of an artillery unit, and an assault was in progress. As the father led his division in a charge, pressing on across the battlefield, suddenly his eye caught sight of a dead artillery officer lying right before him. Just a glance told him it was his son. The general's fatherly impulse was to kneel by the body of his beloved son and express his grief, but the duty of the moment demanded he press on with his charge. So after quickly kissing his dead son, he hurried away leading his command in the assault.

Weeping inconsolably beside a grave will never bring back the treasure of a lost love, nor can any blessing come from such great sadness. Sorrow causes deep scars and indelibly writes its story on the suffering heart. We never completely recover from our greatest griefs and are never exactly the same after having passed through them. Yet sorrow that is endured in the right spirit impacts our growth favorably and brings us a great sense of compassion for others. Indeed those who have no scars of sorrow or suffering upon them are poor. "The joy set before" (Hebrews 12:2) us should shine on our griefs just as the sun shines through the clouds, making them radiant. God has ordained our truest and richest comfort to be found by pressing on toward the goal. Sitting down and brooding over our sorrow deepens the darkness surrounding us, allowing it to creep into our heart. And soon our strength has changed to weakness. But if we will turn from the gloom and remain faithful to the calling of God, the light will shine again and we will grow stronger.

J. R. Miller

>Lord, You know that through our tears
>   Of hasty, selfish weeping
>Comes surer sin, and for our petty fears
>   Of loss you have in keeping
>A greater gain than all of which we dreamed;
>   You knowest that in grasping
>The bright possessions which so precious seemed
>   We lose them; but if, clasping
>Your faithful hand, we tread with steadfast feet
>   The path of Your appointing,
>There waits for us a treasury of sweet
>   Delight, royal anointing
>With oil of gladness and of strength.

Helen Hunt Jackson

November 12
WAITING FOR THE FIRST GLIMMER OF DAWN
Job 35:10

Do you ever experience sleepless nights, tossing and turning and simply waiting for the first glimmer of dawn? When that happens, why not ask the Holy Spirit to fix your thoughts on God, your Maker, and believe He can fill those lonely, weary nights with song?

Is your night one of bereavement? Focusing on God often causes Him to draw near to your grieving heart, bringing you the assurance that He needs the one who has died. The Lord will assure you He can call the eager, enthusiastic spirit of your departed loved one to stand with the invisible yet liberated, living and radiant multitude. And as this thought enters your mind, along with the knowledge that your loved one is engaged in a great heavenly mission, a song begins in your heart.

Is your night one of discouragement or failure, whether real or imagined? Do you feel as if no one understands you, and your friends have pushed you aside? Take heart; your Maker "will come near to you" (James 4:8) and give you a song—a song of hope, which will be harmonious with the strong, resonant music of His providence. Be ready to sing the song your Maker imparts to you.

Selected

The strength of a ship is only fully demonstrated when it faces a hurricane, and the power of the gospel can only be fully exhibited when a Christian is subjected to some fiery trial. We must understand that for God to give "songs in the night," He must first make it night.

Nathaniel William Taylor

Job 5:17

THE TAPESTRY

November 13

I stood one day with a friend in Marshall Fields in Chicago where magnificent tapestries were on display. In front of us was one whose rare beauty of design and marvelous skill in execution made it particularly impressive. Curious about its cost, I stepped over and turned up the corner to see if I could find a price mark. I found it—$6,000. But I found something else. I made the discovery that this expensive tapestry had two sides and that if Marshall Fields had hung it up wrong side out it would not have brought six dollars. The back side was utterly without design. Threads ran crazily in this direction and that. It all looked like the work of a nitwit. Yet those were the very threads that, worked by the masterly hand of the artist had produced the exquisite picture that appeared on the other side.

Paul Rees

When God has a particularly great task for a man to perform, He generally does try him. I care not which biography you pick. You may take the life of any man who has been signally used by God and you will find that there has been a severe time of testing and of trial in his experience.

D. Martyn Lloyd-Jones

Suppose that what you are up against is a surgeon whose intentions are wholly good. The kinder and more conscientious he is, the more inexorably he will go on cutting. If he yielded to your entreaties, if he stopped before the operation was complete, all the pain up to that point would have been useless. But is it credible that such extremities of torture should be necessary for us? Well, take your choice. The tortures occur. If they are unnecessary, then there is no God or a bad one. If there is a good God, then those tortures are necessary. No . . . good Being could possible inflict them if they weren't.

C. S. Lewis

November 14
OUT OF THE CESSPOOL OF HISTORY
Psalm 119:9-11

Can the world claim to have passed on beyond the ethical standards of the New Testament and to have disproved the perfection of those standards? The honest student must confess that modern man would be happier and more blessed if he would or could live up to the ethics and morals of this great Book. And yet consider the condition of the ancient ages during which the Bible was written! The lechery and incest of both Greece and Rome are known to all students of history. Women were chattels in those days, and maidens were guarded jealously because they brought a high cash price in the marts of trade. A father not only felt justified when he sold a daughter for a high price, but he was the recipient of congratulations for his astuteness in business. Adultery was a definite practice in many of the temples, and the philosophies that men studied were expressed in the vilest and most vulgar terms.

Out of the cesspool of history there flowered the lily of New Testament teachings. A standard of thinking and conduct so high and holy that the godliest man cannot meet its stern demands today was set up in an age when lechery was rife and shame had lost her blush. When Jesus said, "Whosoever looketh on a woman to lust after her hath committed adultery with her already in his heart," He was far ahead of His generation as He is ahead of ours.

If and when the "perfect state" is erected and the "golden age" of human government dawns upon this earth, that state will be ruled and planned according to the political standards of the New Testament.

Ernest E. Lott

November 15
THE AGELESS AND ETERNAL BOOK
Psalm 119:89-90

Because Jesus is the theme of the Bible, we have an acceptable explanation of the great power of this Book. It has been the most potent influence ever exerted in human annals. It has changed the flow of history, erected empires, and cast down conquerors and kings, bringing blessing and success to those who obeyed its precepts, and death and oblivion to those who fought against it. The highway of human events is strewn with the wrecks of time, while the ageless and eternal Book survives.

Harry Rimmer

The light of the Divine countenance, which the Apostle himself says "no man can approach unto" is like an inexplicable labyrinth to us, unless we are directed by the thread of the Word.

The basis of Calvin's theology, therefore, is the belief that through the Bible alone can God be known in His wholeness as the Creator, Redeemer and Lord of the world. He is not so discernible in any other place—in the creation, or in man's conscience, or in the course of history and experience. And since, if we are to know of God, we must go to the place where He is to be found; it is to the Scriptures that we must go, and there we shall find Him as He is. If a man asks us to meet him in Piccadilly Circus, it is there (if he will and can keep his word) that we shall find him, and not in Trafalgar Square. The Scriptures are not man's guesses about the mystery of God, nor are they the conclusions that men have drawn from certain data at their disposal. On the contrary, they are the unveiling of the mystery of God by God Himself; God's gracious revelation of Himself to ignorant and sinful men. Far from being a stage, even the last stage, on man's quest for the well at the world's end, the Bible is the place where God comes from above and beyond the world to show Himself to His people.

T. H. L. Parker

Psalm 73:24   **THE MAGNETIC FIELD**   **November 16**

Cancer is bad enough in itself. But the person who has to struggle with the question of why God permits it besides has something even harder to bear. In such life situations, which we all know, we are basically having it out with God. Anybody who once meets God can never again do anything else but constantly come to grips with God in every situation of his life; on the one hand thanking him for the many fulfillments in his life, but on the other hand also protesting when God appears to be refusing him, praying to him when we have wishes, but also warning him in case he should not grant them. The Bible, this so thoroughly human book, is literally filled with a buzzing confusion of voices, of sounds of joy and quarreling, of gratitude and protest, of despair and praise. And the reason is that the men of the Bible—Adam and Abraham, Job and Isaiah, Peter and Judas, all the rest of them—could never do anything else but accept from God everything they experienced and endured, or refuse to accept it and thus go on strike. They cannot simply accept things as they are and simply go jogging on, presenting a thick and callous skin to the accidents and inevitabilities of life. No, everything that happens to them gets caught up in the magnetic field of their encounter with God. And that makes it easier for them, but sometimes harder, too. Once God has become the theme of a man's life it becomes tremendously exciting, even adventurous. For one never knows how God will lead him and what he has in mind. And it can be very exciting, even dramatic, to reflect that on the one hand God wants to be my Father and be faithful to me, and that on the other hand much that I go through seems to prove just the opposite and looks more like fate and accident than purposeful guidance. When God becomes the theme of a man's life, everything that happens to him becomes both a question and a call to trust. That's why the Christian's life is so exciting and that's why he is a stranger to the nihilist's boredom.

Helmut Thielicke

November 17

SHOW ME THY FACE
II Corinthians 3:18

I would now plead with believers. Some of you have really been brought by God to believe in Jesus. Yet you have no abiding peace and very little growing in holiness. Why is this? It is because your eye is fixed anywhere but on Christ. You are so busy looking at books, or looking at men, or looking at the world that you have no time, no heart for looking at Christ. No wonder you have little peace and joy in believing. No wonder you live so inconsistent and unholy a life. Change your plan. Consider the greatness and glory of Christ, who has undertaken all in the stead of sinners, and you would find it quite impossible to walk in darkness or to walk in sin. Oh, what mean, despicable thoughts you have of the glorious Immanuel! Lift your eyes from your own bosom, downcast believer—look upon Jesus. It is good to consider your ways, but it is far better to consider Christ.

Robert Murray McCheyne

> Show me Thy face—one transient gleam
>   Of loveliness divine,
> And I shall never think or dream
>   Of other love save Thine;
> All lesser light will darken quite,
>   All lower glories wane,
> The beautiful of earth will scarce
>   Seem beautiful again.
>
> Show me thy face—my faith and love
>   Shall henceforth fixed be,
> And nothing here have power to move
>   My soul's serenity.
> My life shall seem a trance, a dream
>   And all I feel and see,
> Illusive, visionary—Thou
>   The one reality.

Selected

GOD MOVES IN MYSTERIOUS WAYS
November 18
Isaiah 55:8-9

William Cowper, a poet and hymn writer from the eighteenth century, sometimes wrote what he could not quite believe. He suffered from severe mental illness. His mother died when he was six years old, his classmates often teased him at school, and his father prevented him from marrying the woman he loved. He panicked when he learned, at the very end of his course of study to earn a law degree, that he would have to take his bar exam before the House of Lords. He tried to commit suicide. After spending a year in an insane asylum, he moved in with a Christian couple who cared for him. Mental illness continued to plague him, and he often fell into a deep depression. Perhaps that is why he could write such superb poetry. The following lines from his most famous hymn, "God Moves in a Mysterious Way," illustrate his confidence, often fragile, in God's benevolent sovereignty:

> Judge not the Lord by feeble sense,
> But trust Him for His grace;
> Behind a frowning providence
> He hides a smiling face.
> His purposes will ripen fast,
> Unfolding every hour;
> The bud may have a bitter taste,
> But sweet will be the flower.
> Blind unbelief is sure to err
> And scan His work in vain;
> God is His own interpreter,
> And He will make it plain.

A Grace Disguised
Jerry Sittser

November 19
A CONSTANT SENSE OF DESOLATION
Job 36:15

All of us suffer disappointments in life. Sometimes the effect upon us can be minor. At other times our lives can be devastated. Loneliness, for instance, may be so intense that proper functioning as a man or woman is almost impossible. Shortly after her beloved consort Prince Albert died, Queen Victoria is reported to have confided in her trusted friend, Dean Stanley, that she was "always wishing to consult one who is not here, groping by myself, with a constant sense of desolation." Many of you are suffering from *rejection*, a hurt which causes great damage, for it affects us deep within. Possibly a girlfriend or boyfriend has dropped you for someone else. Or your marriage is breaking up over a third party. Possibly you have been interviewed for an important job and been turned down.

Billy Graham

It was not until Beethoven had become so deaf he could not hear the fortissimo of a full orchestra that he composed his chief oratorio. It was not until John Milton had become stone blind that he could dictate the sublimest poem of the ages. It was not until Walter Scott was kicked by a horse and confined to the house for many days that he could write the "Lay of the Last Minstrel." The painter who mixes his colors with blood from his own broken heart makes the best pictures. The mightiest men of all ages have been mightiest in their agonies.

Talmage

The real difficulty is (isn't it?) to adapt one's steady beliefs about tribulation to this particular tribulation: for the particular, when it arrives, always seems so peculiarly intolerable. I find it helpful to keep it very particular—to stop thinking about the ruin of the world, etc., for no one is going to experience that—and to see it as each individual's personal sufferings.

C. S. Lewis

November 20
LITTLE BIRDS AND LITTLE GIRLS
Revelation 21:4

How sweet the light when morning creeps
   Into the woods in spring!
And Heaven downward dips awhile
   When thrushes start to sing.
And birds, and little singing girls
   With sunshine in their hair
Can lift your heart on wings of love
   Into that Other-where—
That place, long hidden from our sight
   Where pain cannot assail.
Your song, so fleeting, for a bit
   Drew back the hindering veil.

But little birds and little girls
   Will someday fly away.
The winter winds sweep o'er the land,
   And skies are cold and grey.
On earth, the spring will come again,
   And little birds return.
But little girls may find that place
   Beyond the stars that burn,
Where joy is so intense and sweet,
   They never do come back.
We look aloft, and moan within
   Our loneliness and lack.

Oh, little girl! Let birds return;
   But keep your splendor new.
I'll fly one day to that far height
   And sing your joy with you.

                Farewell to Coralie, May 24, 2005
                                Lois Kempton

Psalm 121:6

GOD OF THE NIGHT ALSO
November 21

God is with us as much in our perplexity as in our prosperity. If we trust Him no matter what may come, He will prove to us that He is always there. The widow of a martyred missionary in Africa wrote, "I felt like a bird in a cage. But I determined to be a canary, singing, rather than a starling, beating his wings on the cage.... It has been the crowning blessing of my life." Here was a Christian who realized that the One in control when the sun shines is still in control when darkness engulfs the soul.

A songwriter expressed the Christian's response to trial like this:

> I will believe, though dark the way may be,
> Though naught but shadowed specters now I see.
> I will believe, of nothing be afraid,
> For fiery darts of doubts are often made.
> I will believe, for God is on my side,
> And Jesus for my sins was crucified.
> The cross, the empty tomb, assurance bring,
> And on His mighty arm my soul does cling.

Have you suddenly been thrust into the darkness of a difficult trial? Take heart! He who walked with you in the light is still with you in the dark. You can trust Him to lead you safely through. The God of the day is the God of the night also.

Our Daily Bread
Paul Van Gorder

> Songs in the night—ah, such songs the Lord gives,
>   He the great Comforter who ever lives.
> Though dark without, He sheds wonderful light,
>   Thus making possible songs in the night.

Brondsema

November 22

NEARING HOME
II Timothy 4:1-8

There is a most valiant pilgrim nearing home! By the mercy of Christ he can look back upon a brave day and there's a fine hopeful light in the evening sky. He has fought well! "I have fought the good fight." And his has been a hard field. The enemy has ever regarded him as a leader in the army of the Lord and against him has the fiercest fighting been waged. But he has never lost or stained his flag.

And he has run well! "I have finished the race." There was no melancholy turning back when the feverish start had cooled. There was no shrinking when the biting wind of malice and persecution swept across his track. On and on he ran, with increasing speed and ardour, until he reached the goal.

And well had he guarded his treasure! "I have kept the faith." He was the custodian of "unsearchable riches," and he watched, day and night, lest any infernal burglar should despoil him of his wealth. He guarded his gospel, his liberty, his hope, as the sentinels guard the crown jewels in the Tower.

And now the hard day is nearly over. "Now there is in store for me the crown of righteousness, which the Lord, the righteous Judge, will award to me on that day."

J. H. Jowett

November 23

A RELIGION OF HOPE
I Corinthians 15:19

Christianity is a religion of hope. It is noteworthy that historically the doctrine of Christian hope has flourished in direct proportion to the amount of suffering men were having to endure. Some of us, however, are grateful that our hope is not the outgrowth of suffering but of believing steadily a "more sure word of prophecy." We have hope because of the Word of God. But this glorious hope must not be an escape from reality *now*! To the Christian, hope is a force with which he nerves the daily endeavor. It is essentially unchristian to use this hope as an escape from facing today's challenge. Any emphasis upon the return of our Lord which relieves us of responsibility for trying to change our present evil society is an unworthy escape.

Salvation as a present, living, vital matter must be rooted in the Cross. The Cross of sublime memory is not enough. It must become a part of our present, living moment of experience. It is easy to sing about glorying in the Cross of Christ which towers above the wrecks of time, and all the while refuse to take it up for today's walk. We have too many decorative crosses: stained glass windows, cruciform cathedrals, jewelry, and the like. Beautiful crosses! But without sweat, and dirt, and blood, and agony. Gaylord B. Noyce suggested that the Cross has become so idealized that to preserve its offense we had better use a noose instead! We need the Cross as a way of living experience in the salvation that is *now*! The Cross enters our Christian experience at the point where we surrender our efforts to impress God with our goodness and kneel to receive the forgiveness of our sins, being reconciled with Him through the offering of Christ's blood. This is the objective Cross. It appears again when we yield ourselves a living sacrifice unto God. It persists as we face the world and the things that are in the world.

The Spirit of Holiness
Everett Cattell

November 24

LETTER TO MRS. T. (I)

Daniel 6:19-22

My Dear Madam,   March 12, 1774

My heart is full, yet I must restrain it. Many thoughts which crowd on my mind, and would have vent were I writing to another person, would to you be unseasonable. I write not to remind you of what you have lost, but of what you have, which you cannot lose. May the Lord put a word in my heart that may be acceptable; and may his good Spirit accompany the perusal, and enable you to say with the apostle, that as sufferings abound, consolations also abound by Jesus Christ. Indeed I can sympathize with you. I remember, too, the delicacy of your frame and the tenderness of your natural spirits; so that were you not interested in the exceeding great and precious promises of the Gospel, I should be ready to fear you must sink under your trial. But I have some faint conceptions of the all-sufficiency and faithfulness of the Lord, and may address you in the king's words to Daniel: "Thy God, whom thou servest continually, he will deliver thee."

Motives for resignation to his will abound in his Word; but it is an additional and crowning mercy that he has promised to apply and enforce them in time of need. He has said: "My grace shall be sufficient for thee;" and "as thy day is so shall thy strength be." This I trust you have already experienced. The Lord is so rich and so good that he can easily compensate his children for whatever his wisdom sees fit to deprive them of. If he gives them a lively sense of what he has delivered them from and prepared for them, or of what he himself submitted to endure for their sakes, they find at once light springing up out of darkness, hard things become easy, and bitter, sweet.

                               Collected Letters of John Newton

November 25
LETTER TO MRS. T. (II)
Psalm 107:1-14

I remember reading about a good man in the last century, who, when his beloved and only son lay ill, was for some time greatly anxious about the event. One morning he stayed longer than usual in his closet; while he was there his son died. When he came out, his family were afraid to tell him; but, like David, he perceived it by their looks; and when upon inquiry they said it was so, he received the news with a composure that surprised them. But he soon explained the reason, by telling them that for such discoveries of the Lord's goodness as he had been favored with that morning, he could be content to lose a son every day. Yes, Madam, though every stream must fail, the fountain is still full and still flowing. All the comfort you ever received in your dear friend was from the Lord, who is abundantly able to comfort you still; and he is gone but a little before you. May your faith anticipate the joyful and glorious meeting you will have in a better world. Then your worship and converse together will be to your great advantage, will be perfect and will have no end. Then all tears shall be wiped away, and every cloud removed; and then you will see that all your concerns here below (the late afflicting dispensation not excepted) were appointed and adjusted by infinite wisdom and infinite love.

The Lord, who knows our frame, does not expect or require that we should aim at a stoical indifference under his visitations. He allows that afflictions are at present not joyous, but grievous; yet, he was pleased when upon earth to weep with his mourning friends when Lazarus died. But he has graciously provided for the prevention of the anguish and bitterness of sorrow, which is, upon such occasions, the portion of such as live without God in the world; and has engaged that all shall work together for good and yield the peaceable fruits of righteousness. May he bless you with a sweet serenity of spirit and a cheerful hope of the glory that shall shortly be revealed.

Collected Letters of John Newton

Psalm 139:1-12 ## THOUGHTS AFAR OFF **November 26**

"You know my thoughts from afar." That fills me with awe. I cannot find a hiding place where I can sin in secrecy. I cannot build an apparent sanctuary and conceal evil within its walls. I cannot with a sheep's skin hide the wolf. I cannot wrap my jealousy up in flattery and keep it unknown. "You are the God who sees me." He knows the bottom thought that creeps in the basement of my being. Nothing surprises God! He sees all my sin. So I am filled with awe.

"You know my thoughts from afar." This fills me also with hope and joy. He sees the faintest, weakest desire, aspiring after goodness. He sees the smallest fire of affection burning uncertainly in my soul. He sees every movement of penitence which looks towards home. He sees every little triumph and every altar I build along life's way. Nothing is overlooked. My God is not like a policeman, only looking for crimes: He is the God of grace, looking for graces, searching for jewels to adorn His crown. So am I filled with hope and joy.

J. H. Jowett

Galatians 2:20 ## MY RIGHT TO MYSELF November 27

We are dealing with fundamental pain, the basis of which is tragedy—all the forces making for disaster. "I have been crucified with Christ"—crucifixion is a painful thing. It means, not in the theological sense, but in the spiritual sense, being made one with Jesus Christ, and that costs *me* pain. I have deliberately to be willing to give up my right to myself; that has now been put to death by mine own determination, and "the life which I now live in the flesh I live by faith in the Son of God." Literally, the faith that was in Jesus Christ is now in me.

There are three big fundamental things in our human life, and the basis of each is pain. They are not things to preach about, but rather matters for our consideration. In the light of this terrible tragedy of war where pain is sweeping the whole universe until there is scarcely a home that has not been touched by it, there is again a chance to witness the incoming of the quiet power of our Lord Jesus Christ. I do not believe we shall see the incoming power of denominationalism or "Churchianity" or creed, but I do believe that the Spirit of God is pushing His way into people's lives on the only line of emancipation there is, namely, through the cross. We are realizing that the revelation given to us of God is of a God who suffers. We see more into the real tragedy of life when we have great elemental pain that has shocked the externals. The human mind instantly says, "Why should these things be?" They are unreasonable. Emphatically so, we may rage as we choose, but we come to the conclusion that the Bible is right—the basis of things is tragic, not mathematical. As soon as we recognize that life is based on tragedy, we won't be too staggered when tragedy emerges, but will learn how to turn to God.

The Place of Help
Oswald Chambers

November 28
WHERE SATAN CONFRONTS GOD
Job 1:6-12

In my imagined rectangle where Satan confronts God throughout all time and space, I picture Satan as saying to God, "If a woman had five sons who died in a war, she couldn't keep on trusting You." God would then reply, "There is Mrs. _____ whose five sons died in World War One, and she did keep on trusting Me." And then Satan might say, "Ah, but if a young man lost his wife and child during the first year in the mission field, that man would stop trusting You." And the reply would come: "There is Mr. _____ who went through exactly that in 1906 in Africa and still loved Me." Satan: "But if a woman had her first son born dead, and then her husband died three weeks later, she would become bitter." God answers, "Look at Jessie Green who went to Bible school and prepared for work in China in 1896, although she had just gone through these tragic losses. She loved Me and spent her life trusting Me in China." Satan: "If a young man saw his parents and friends tortured and killed in Cambodia, he could never trust You and love You." God says to the accusation: "There is a sad Cambodian boy in 1977 who is going on after just that experience, trusting Me, and continuing to ask Me for help." Another challenge by Satan: "If a woman prayed for her alcoholic husband to change, and he kept on beating her for fifteen years, she would stop trusting You." And God would point out exactly the woman who had gone through that combination of frustrated sadness, and yet still remained faithful to Him.

Affliction
Edith Schaeffer

November 29

A PAIN THAT IS TERRIFIC
I Peter 2:21

We make calls out of our own spiritual consecration, but when we get right with God He brushes all these aside and rivets us with a pain that is terrific to one thing we never dreamed of, and for one radiant flashing moment we see what He is after, and we say—"Here am I, send me."

This call has nothing to do with personal sanctification but with being made broken bread and poured-out wine. God can never make us wine if we object to the fingers He uses to crush us with. If God would only use His own fingers and make me broken bread and poured-out wine in a special way! But when He uses someone whom we dislike, or some set of circumstances to which we said we would never submit and makes those the crushers, we object. We must never choose the scene of our own martyrdom. If ever we are going to be made into wine, we will have to be crushed; you cannot drink grapes. Grapes become wine only when they have been squeezed.

I wonder what kind of finger and thumb God has been using to squeeze you, and you have been like a marble and escaped? You are not ripe yet, and if God *had* squeezed you, the wine would have been remarkably bitter. To be a sacramental personality means that the elements of the natural life are presenced by God as they are broken providentially in His service. We have to be adjusted into God before we can be broken bread in His hands. Keep right with God and let Him do what He likes, and you will find that He is producing the kind of bread and wine that will benefit His other children.

My Utmost for His Highest
Oswald Chambers

November 30
TALKING ABOUT OUR SUFFERINGS
Romans 8:18

Suffer without imposing on others a theory of suffering, without weaving a new philosophy of life from your own material pain, without proclaiming yourself a martyr, without counting out the price of your courage, without disdaining sympathy and without seeking too much of it.

We must be sincere in our sufferings as in anything else. We must recognize at once our weakness and our pain, but we do not need to advertise them. It is well to realize that we are perhaps unable to suffer in grand style, but we must still accept our weakness with a kind of heroism. It is always difficult to suffer fruitfully and well, and the difficulty is all the greater when we have no human resources to help us. It is well, also, not to tempt God in our sufferings, not to extend ourselves, by pride, into an area where we cannot endure.

We must face the fact that it is much harder to stand the long monotony of slight suffering than a passing onslaught of intense pain. In either case what is hard is our own poverty, and the spectacle of our own selves reduced more and more to nothing, wasting away in our own estimation and in that of our friends.

We must be willing to accept also the bitter truth that, in the end, we may have to become a burden to those who love us. But it is necessary that we face this also. The full acceptance of our abjection and uselessness is the virtue that can make us and others rich in the grace of God. It takes heroic charity and humility to let others sustain us when we are absolutely incapable of sustaining ourselves.

We cannot suffer well unless we see Christ everywhere—both in suffering and in the charity of those who come to the aid of our affliction.

No Man Is An Island
Thomas Merton

December 1
A TERRIBLE NIGHTMARE (I)
Job 19:7-10

The years passed full of happiness and fruitfulness, our marriage and family blessed with the joy of the Lord. And then I began to sense a dark shadow falling across our lives. At this time, Arthur was pastor of Pittsboro United Methodist Circuit, which included Brown's Chapel and Pleasant Hill Church. We loved the churches and to this day have many wonderful friends in the area. Things went well at first. Then the first familiar clues that signal problems in a marriage. Arthur began to absent himself from home for long periods of time, using the excuse of committee meetings, ministry preparation for services, etc. Before long I was hearing rumors of a friendship with a young lady. When I confronted him, he denied it. But there was something in his demeanor, the look in the eyes, the hard lines in his face that told a different story. I would go to our bedroom and fall on my knees, weeping and praying, asking the Lord to somehow convict him, show him his mistake, bring him back to me. How deeply I loved him. But this was not to be.

Arthur was away Labor Day weekend, 1977, on a fishing trip at the coast. When I welcomed him back as lovingly and warmly as I knew how, his curt, harsh response sent a shaft of pain into my heart. Then one day he said, "It's all over, Mary. I'm leaving." Thus began a separation which ended in divorce two years later. We had been married 28 years. I was crushed, dazed, as though I had been caught in a terrible, unexplainable nightmare. "Lord," I cried, "can this actually be happening to me? I've loved You all my life, served You as a missionary. Arthur and I have had wonderful years of joy and fruitfulness in Your service and now this." Always an extremely sensitive person, these tragic circumstances sent me into a dark pit of depression which, try as I might, it seemed impossible to climb out of. Truly, if ever, this was my dark night of the soul. I devoutly longed for death, an extinction now of this horrible, incredible nightmare.

I had a few friends with whom I could share the awful depths of my depression, but, foolishly, I contrived to hide the whole matter from my family, although they sensed something was wrong. Now, when I most needed their prayers, compassion and solace, I could not bring myself to share with them the terrible shame of our broken marriage. Finally, at the suggestion of a friend, I went to a counselor at Duke University for about six months. He was an excellent psychiatrist and born-again Christian. He gave helpful counsel and put me on medication for depression.

Under His Wings
Mary Payseur

December 2

A TERRIBLE NIGHTMARE (II)
Job 19:21

During the next two to three years, I gradually began to emerge from that dark night. I was still active in the church, even teaching the adult Sunday school class. I also continued my teaching in public schools which I had commenced following our return from Taiwan. Now I was learning a lesson which I had observed in the life of my dear mother, who in her hour of trial, resolved to keep busy. The requirement of going to school every day and facing a class, continuing teaching no matter what, was proving to be my salvation. I had earlier received a degree in special education, helping students with learning disabilities, which gave me great joy. During these years I taught at Goldston Elementary in Chatham County, North Carolina. In my desperately painful and wounded condition, this proved marvelous therapy provided by God. The principal had so much confidence in me that, when he encountered special problems in the school, he would call me over the intercom and ask me to talk with him between my classes. Thus, in time, the sun began to shine again.

Another wonderful resource and comfort to me during those hard years were Christian books. I voraciously devoured wonderful devotional books like *Streams in the Desert* and all sorts of literature that strengthened my faith. But, above all, I was nourished on the Word of God. I continued the life-long habit of memorizing scripture, and now I wrote out verses and put them on index cards on the dashboard of my car. As I drove along, I would pray and repeat again and again those wonderful promises. I added to this visitation to the sick and needy in the community. The more I focused on Christ and ministered to others the less I was obsessed with my own problems.

Under His Wings
Mary Payseur

December 3

A TERRIBLE NIGHTMARE (III)
Job 19:25-26

A special friend at this time was Ruth Thomas, a wonderful Christian lady who had been ill for years, cared for by her daughters. Ruth was finally diagnosed with Lou Gehrig's Disease and near the end could not walk. Yet she wanted to be where the action was, sitting in the kitchen or living room with family or friends. I went to see Ruth every few days and what a wonderful blessing she was to me. In the midst of all her pain, she was always smiling. I never once heard her complaining about her condition or speaking unkindly of anyone. I thought I would go to cheer her up, but I was the one to have my spirits lifted and receive a special blessing from her. Ruth's teenage daughters, Kay, Marcia and Lynda, were so faithful in taking care of their mother and had the same loving attitude as she, always smiling, never complaining about anything.

Thank the Lord for those dear ones He uses in our lives to be a blessing to us when we are going through the valleys. We can always look around and see those whose needs are greater than our own. In my thoughts and prayers, I would sometimes go up and down the roads in the community, stopping at each house to pray for every member of the family. The more I ministered to others, it seemed, the more the Holy Spirit restored to me joy, peace and emotional health.

Under His Wings
Mary Payseur

December 4
THE LAZINESS OF GRIEF
II Corinthians 4:9

No one ever told me about the laziness of grief. Except at my job—where the machine seems to run on much as usual—I loathe the slightest effort. Not only writing but even reading a letter is too much. Even shaving. What does it matter now whether my cheek is rough or smooth? They say an unhappy man wants distractions—something to take him out of himself. Only as a dog-tired man wants an extra blanket on a cold night; he'd rather lie there shivering than get up and find one. It's easy to see why the lonely become untidy, finally dirty and disgusting. Meanwhile, where is God? This is one of the most disquieting symptoms. When you are happy, so happy that you have no sense of needing Him, so happy that you are tempted to feel His claims upon you as an interruption, if you remember yourself and turn to Him with gratitude and praise, you will be—or so it feels—welcomed with open arms. But go to Him when your need is desperate, when all other help is vain, and what do you find? A door slammed in your face and a sound of bolting and double bolting on the inside. After that, silence. You may as well turn away. The longer you wait, the more emphatic the silence will become. There are no lights in the windows. It might be an empty house. Was it ever inhabited? It seemed so once. And the seeming was as strong as this. What can this mean? Why is He so present a commander in our time of prosperity and so very absent a help in time of trouble?

I tried to put some of these thoughts to C. this afternoon. He reminded me that the same thing seems to have happened to Christ: "Why hast thou forsaken me?" I know. Does that make it easier to understand? Not that I am (I think) in much danger of ceasing to believe in God. The real danger is of coming to believe such dreadful things about Him. The conclusion I dread is not "So there's no God after all," but "So this is what God's really like."

A Grief Observed
C. S. Lewis

Psalm 31:15 NO DATE FOR RELEASE **December 5**

Grief still feels like fear, perhaps more strictly, like suspense, or like waiting, just hanging about waiting for something to happen. It gives life a permanently provisional feeling. It doesn't seem worth starting anything. I can't settle down. I yawn, I fidget, I smoke too much. Up till this, I always had too little time. Now there is nothing but time, almost pure time, empty successiveness.

A Grief Observed
C. S. Lewis

Former prisoners, when writing or relating their experiences, agree that the most depressing influence of all was that a prisoner could not know how long his term of imprisonment would be. He had been given no date for his release. (In our camp it was pointless even to talk about it.) Actually a prison term was not only uncertain but unlimited. A well-known research psychologist has pointed out that life in a concentration camp could be a called a "provisional existence." We can add to this by defining it as a "provisional existence of unknown limit." New arrivals usually knew nothing about the conditions at a camp. Those who had come back from others camps were obliged to keep silent, and from some camps no one had returned. On entering camp a change took place in the minds of the men. With the end of uncertainty, there came the uncertainty of the end. It was impossible to foresee whether or when, if at all, this form of existence would end. The unemployed worker, for example, is in a similar position. His existence has become provisional and in a certain sense he cannot live for the future or aim at a goal. . . . Prisoners, too, suffered from this strange "time-experience." In camp a small time unit, a day for example, filled with hourly tortures and fatigue, appeared endless. A larger time unit, perhaps a week, seemed to pass very quickly.

Man's Search for Meaning
Victor Frankl

Proverbs 26:24-26
IT MASQUERADES WELL
December 6

Hostility masquerades very well. "A man with hate in his heart may sound pleasant enough, but don't believe him, for he is cursing you in his heart. Though he pretends to be so kind, his hatred will finally come to light for all to see. . . . Flattery is a form of hatred and wounds cruelly (Proverbs 26:24-26, 28 TLB). One of the first things we all learned to do with our hostility, because it got us into trouble, was to pretend that it wasn't there. Only occasionally does hostility emerge in all of its cruelty. Usually it masquerades as something else. The more hostile and angry a person is, the more he develops the skills of disguise. This becomes a problem when it makes us wonder how to interpret people's motives when they are nice to us.

There are a couple of symptoms that can guide us in learning whether a lot of hostility is found in a personality. Most analysts of human behavior say the rigidity of personality, woodenness, inability to bend and make changes, are symptoms of suppressed rage. The person who can never change a schedule, the person who can never compromise a viewpoint or a method, is an angry person. Rigidity is a symptom which shows that a person is working very hard to control his rage; he's afraid it will break open on him. When Jesus attacked Pharisaism, He was saying, "This rigidity is covering up an awful lot of hate; it's laced up with all these tight rules that can never be bent." Another symptom of hostility is "opinionation." As one of the most opinionated men I know, I speak from authority. We betray the hostility within us by our vehemence over little things. I'm not talking about the great issues of life because we need to take a stand for truth. I don't think we should confuse low adrenalin and a lack of conviction with Christian virtue. But some of these little tiny questions can be argued with the same vehemence as the great issues. Some people can't seem to see things in their proper proportions.

Paul Larsen

December 7

PROFOUND SECRETS

Hebrews 12:5-6

We must bear in mind that the discipline of our Father's hand is to be interpreted in the light of our Father's countenance, and the deep mysteries of His moral government to be contemplated through the medium of His tender love. If we lose sight of this, we shall be sure to get into a spirit of bondage as respects ourselves, and a spirit of judgment as respects others, both of which are in direct opposition to the spirit of Christ. All our Father's dealing with us are in perfect love. When He furnishes us with bread, it is in love; and when He takes down the rod, it is in love also. "God is love." It may frequently happen that we are at a loss to know the why and the wherefore of some special dispensation of our Father's hand. It seems dark and inexplicable. The mist which enwraps our spirits is so thick and heavy as to prevent our catching the bright and cheering beams from our Father's countenance. This is a trying moment—a solemn crisis in the soul's history. We are in great danger of losing the sense of divine love through inability to understand the profound secrets of divine government.

Satan, too, is sure to be busy at such a time. He will ply his fiery darts and throw in his dark and diabolical suggestions. Thus, between the filthy reasonings which spring up within and the horrible suggestions which come from without, the soul is in danger of losing its balance and of getting away from the precious attitude of artless repose in divine love, let the divine government be what it may.

C. H. Mackintosh

Psalms 46:10

SILENT SPACES

December 8

The soul needs its silent spaces. It is in them we learn to pray. There, alone, shut in with God, our Lord bids us pray to our Father which is in secret and seeth in secret. There is no test like solitude. Fear takes possession of most minds in the stillness of the solitary place. The heart shrinks from being alone with God that seeth in secret! Who shall abide in His Presence? Who can dwell with God who is shadowless light? Hearts must be pure and hands clean that dare shut the door and be alone with God. It would revolutionize the lives of most men if they were shut in with God in some secret place for half an hour a day. . . . For such praying all the faculties of the soul need to be awake and alert.

One cannot emphasize too much the necessity of doing spiritual work in spiritual ways and with spiritual tools. For instance, we say that we believe in prayer. We say that prayer is more important than anything else. But how many of us actually put it first in our programs.

It was my privilege for 20 years to belong to a fellowship in a mission in India that literally tried to put prayer first. We met for as many days as a situation required, often for three or four days. We gave ourselves to the Word and to prayer—and prayed as long we were burdened to do so. No one worried whether we had better get on with "business." Prayer was our business.

Prayer is our first business. The Apostolic pattern of spiritual leaders giving themselves "to prayer and to the ministry of the word" is an absolute necessity for spiritual growth in the church.

Samuel Chadwick

December 9

A DESPONDENT STATE
I Kings 19:3-5

Then followed weary days of waiting, and the days grew to weeks. The strain of the three dreary months of disappointment and anxiety had undoubtedly told upon Carey, and after the first flush of joy at the news from Thomas, there followed a period of acute reaction. The daily entries in his journal during this time of suspense reveal the despondent state into which he had come. "I mourn my barrenness and the foolish wanderings of my mind," he wrote. "Surely all the sweetness that I have formerly felt has gone." Two days later he wrote: "In the morning, had a very miserable, unhappy time for some hours." Another day we have this entry: "I am very defective in all duties. . . . In prayer I wander and am formal. . . . I soon tire; devotion languishes; and I do not walk with God." On Sunday, March 16, he wrote, "Another such Sabbath I hope shall never pass." Then on March 20: "A most unhappy day." Two days later: "Still in suspense, waiting in daily expectation of a letter from Malda." And again: "Long delay and unsettlement have filled me with discouragement and drunk up my spirit."

After four weeks of waiting, he actually so lost count of the days that he mistook Saturday for Sunday and kept it as such! He began to realize what it was to be deprived of the refreshment of Christian worship and fellowship, and he felt that with so little Bengali on the tongue he was doing little or nothing for God. He recalled the old Sabbaths in England with the joy of preaching, and the six days of the week spent in ministering to his flock at Moulton and Leicester. Here he seemed to be idle. Many a young missionary since that day has passed through a similar experience.

William Carey, Father of Modern Missions
F. Deaville Walker

December 10

EVEN THERE

Philippians 4:4

    Then one insidious, Despair his name,
His nature venomous, of torturers chief,
Approached me, and with ancient subtle darts
Assailed me inwardly: "Dost thou believe? . . .
Thou art cut off; thy hope clean gone forever.
For God—He hath forgotten to be gracious;
In anger He hath shut His tender mercies.
God—doth He reign? How canst thou
    know He reigneth
Is the world God's or Devil's?"

    Thou hast touched
The deep place than which deeper there is not;
Thou has touched bottom. Oh, in such an hour
Of sudden fallings off of trusted things,
Of gloom, of moonless night appalling thee,
And winds tempestuous, tell me if thou didst then
Perceive a light, a glorious certainty?
Feel under thee the Rock of ages, know
It stood unshakable? Discover God,
The living God? . . .

    His hand shall lead thee,
His right hand shall hold thee
Until the path, compassed so far by Him
Whom thy soul loveth, turn, and lead thee straight
Home to Land Celestial, where unveiled
He welcometh His travelers, healing them
By the sweet welcome of all weariness.

                              Amy Carmichael

Colossians 1:24   **NO HOPE OF REVENGE**   **December 11**

In order to give glory to God and overcome suffering with the charity of Christ:

Suffer without reflection, without hate, suffer with no hope of revenge or compensation, suffer without being impatient for the end of suffering.

Neither the beginning of suffering is important nor its ending. Neither the source of suffering is important nor its explanation, provided it be God's will. But we know that He does not will useless, that is to say sinful, suffering. Therefore in order to give Him glory we must be quiet and humble and poor in all that we suffer, so as not to add to our sufferings the burden of a useless and exaggerated sensibility.

In order to suffer without dwelling on our own affliction, we must think about a greater affliction and turn to Christ on the Cross. In order to suffer without hate, we must drive out bitterness from our heart by loving Jesus. In order to suffer without hope of compensation, we should find all our peace in the conviction of our union with Jesus.

No Man Is An Island
Thomas Merton

Human life is becoming richer as the generations pass because each contributes its special ingredient to the general sum of good. The leaves fall unnoticed on the forest floor and rot, but the soil grows richer. All suffering rightly borne fills up that which is behind the sufferings of Christ and helps (though it has no substitutionary value) to hasten the redemptive processes that work out from His cross.

F. B. Meyer

Ephesians 3:10-11 ONE THING I DO December 12

I often think how wonderful it is to have nothing to think of, no care in all the world but to do His will and finish His work. There are sorrows—there must be in a world so full of sorrow—but "This one thing I do" can be our word. And there is joy in that.

I have been reading Ephesians 3:10-11. "The powers in the heavenly places" are real powers. If only we by the grace of God live lives that glorify our Lord, if only we are not overcome by griefs and trials such as those we are passing through now, but look above them and go on in peace, then something of the wonderful wisdom of God will be shown to those Unseen Watchers. It is a solemn thought, for of course the opposite is true. If we are "overcome of evil," we show nothing of His love and grace and all that is meant by His "manifold wisdom." Oh, may He help us not to lose this opportunity to glorify His Name.

The salvation of a single child—who can measure what that may mean not only here but There? You can't do everything. "After it, follow it, follow the Gleam." For us the Gleam is the salvation of children, and it involves the prosaic towel. "He took a towel." So we won't mind if our feet are bound, for it is Love that binds them. (Tamil proverb: "Children bind the mother's feet.") His were bound on the cross.

Amy Carmichael

December 13
HE TOOK THE CUP
Mark 10:38-39

Charles Cowman took the cup that God gave, quaffed its bitter dregs and stood calmly beneath His chastening rod, subdued, but not cast down. During those years, although extremely broken in body, he kept an oversight of the home office and every department of the work on the field; and in the midst of suffering was dictating letters by the hundreds. They were so full of old-time fire, cheer and enthusiasm, that the recipients little imagined that they came from a hopelessly sick man. With his exceedingly limited strength he was making an appeal to the strong to keep the missionary vision; not to grow cold or lukewarm in the task of evangelizing the Orient. . . . Once, after an unusual battle with pain, Charles said to the one sitting beside him, "God gave me a song in the night, and I have found sweet music even in the solitude of the sick room."

Why not leave the story of his life just as it stands—bright, beautiful, full of life and glow? I would be untrue to my subject were I to omit the shadows which give to the picture balance and tone. But why record this? For one reason only, that some dear missionaries away from their flocks, shut up in sick rooms, or in lonely deserts, may catch the echo of a wonderful note of triumph, and through it may also learn to discover streams gushing forth in the desert place.

Charles Cowman was great as a business man; he was great before his audiences, he was great on the mission field, but he was greatest when shut away alone with God in the loneliness of the desert. All the interests that had been so dear to him were shut out from his life, yet he never lived so deeply, so triumphantly, as during those six pain-filled years. I shall ever thank God for the privilege which He gave me in being close by, to witness the anointing of that life in the twilight hour.

Missionary Warrior
Lettie Cowman

December 14
WHEN GOD DOESN'T MAKE SENSE
II Timothy 2:3-4

We hear often about the blessings and benefits of devotion to the Master, and they are incalculable. But less is said about the cost of discipleship. Jesus left no doubt about Kingdom priorities when He said, ". . . anyone who does not take his cross and follow me is not worthy of me" (Matthew 10:38).

The Apostle Paul later used another analogy to express a similar concept. He instructed believers to "endure hardship with us like a good soldier of Christ Jesus. No one serving as a soldier gets involved in civilian affairs—he wants to please his commanding officer" (II Timothy 2:3-4). These short verses have intrigued me for years. What do you suppose Paul meant by his reference to military service? How is the training of a soldier relevant to the life of a Christian? And what does it mean to "endure hardship like a good soldier"?

We have all seen John Wayne movies that made combat look like a romantic romp in the park. Men who have been through it tell a different story. The most graphic descriptions of battle I've read came from Bruce Catton's excellent books on the American Civil War, including *The Army of the Potomac*. They provide a striking understanding of the toughness of both Yankee and Rebel soldiers. Their lives were filled with deprivation and danger that is hardly imaginable today. It was not unusual for the troops to make a two-week forced march during which commanders would threaten the stragglers at sword point.

The men were often thrown into the heat of a terrible battle just moments after reaching the front. They would engage in exhausting combat for days, interspersed by sleepless nights on the ground—sometimes in freezing rain or snow. During the battle itself, they ate a dry, hard biscuit called hardtack, and very little else. In less combative times, they could add a little salt pork and coffee to their diet. That was it! As might be expected, their intestinal tracks were regularly shredded by diarrhea, dysentery and related diseases that decimated their ranks. The Union Army reported upwards of 200,000 casualties from disease, often disabling up to 50 percent of the soldiers. The Confederates suffered a similar fate.

Combat experience itself was unbelievably violent in those days. Thousands of men stood toe to toe and slaughtered one another like flies. After one particularly bloody battle in 1862, 5000 men lay dead in an area of two square miles. Twenty thousand more were wounded. One witness said it was possible to walk on dead bodies for 100 yards without once stepping on the ground. Many of the wounded remained where they fell among dead men and horses for 12 or 15 hours, with their groans and cries echoing through the countryside.

While their willingness to endure these physical deprivations is almost incomprehensible, one has to admire the emotional toughness of the troops. They believed in their cause, whether Union or Confederate, and they committed their lives to it. Most believed that they would not survive the war, but that was of little consequence.

Please understand that I do not see unmitigated virtue in the heroic vision of that day. Indeed, men were all too willing to put their lives on the line for a war they poorly understood. But their dedication and personal sacrifice remain today as memorials to their time.

When God Doesn't Make Sense
James Dobson

December 15
A FORM OF SELF-PUNISHMENT
Matthew 6:12

Loss can be transformative if it causes us to seek the forgiveness of God. Sometimes the stalled motion picture reminds us of how far short we fell prior to the loss and how poorly we responded to it. The snapshot exposes our inner selves. We are forced to face the ugliness, selfishness, and meanness of our own lives. Then what? In this case, there are no second chances. We are left only with the bitter memory of our failures or even of the good intentions we had but failed to live up to. But God promises to forgive those of us who confess our failures . . . and to make right what we are sorry for doing wrong.

The gift of divine forgiveness will help us to forgive ourselves. Without it, regret becomes a form of self-punishment. We see the evil we have done and the pain we have inflicted on others. We feel an acute sense of guilt. We loathe our selfishness and foolishness. And we know that there is nothing we can do to reverse the consequences of our actions. Yet a holy God imparts forgiveness if we sincerely ask for it; a just God shows us mercy and embraces us in love. If such a God can forgive us, then surely we can forgive ourselves. If such a God lavishes us with grace, then surely we can stop punishing ourselves and live in that grace. Divine forgiveness leads to self-forgiveness. God's forgiveness will show us that he wants to take our losses and somehow bring them back upon us in the form of a blessing. This work of grace will not erase the loss or alter its consequences. Grace cannot change the moral order. What is bad will always be bad. But grace will bring good out of a bad situation; it will take an evil and somehow turn it into something that results in good. That is what God accomplished through the crucifixion. He turned the evil of an unjust murder into the good of salvation. God can do the same for us as well.

A Grief Disguised
Jerry Sittser

December 16
IN THE DAY OF TROUBLE (I)
Psalm 27:5

I firmly believe in healing and was twice miraculously healed, from cholera and typhoid in China. These healings had come without any doubt in answer to my prayers and the prayers of God's people.

During those early years in Taiwan, I claimed God's many promises for healing and gave myself to fasting and prayer, fully convinced that I could serve God better in a body healthy and free from pain. Certainly, I felt, it was His will to touch and heal the tormenting arthritis.

Though God had done so much for me, caring for me through three wars and answering my prayers in spectacular fashion, apparently He has not willed to deliver me from this infirmity or spare me the discomforts of other illnesses. I have repeatedly been hospitalized and operated on 14 different times. After prolonged fasting and prayer for a cure for my arthritis, God gave me two verses, one the familiar II Corinthians scripture, words given to St. Paul when God declined to remove his thorn in the flesh: "My grace is sufficient for you, for my strength is made perfect in weakness."

The second scripture was John 13:7, the same verse God had given the wife of OMS founder, Charles Cowman, during the terrible years of his invalidism due to an agonizing heart condition. Through the six-year crucible of suffering, neither her prayers nor that of thousands of others apparently were answered and in 1924, after months of indescribable suffering, Charles Cowman died. In the mist of this trial, God had given Lettie these same words spoken by Christ to Peter at the last supper, "What I do now thou knowest not, but afterwards thou shalt know" (John 13:7).

In the Day of Trouble
Flora Chen

December 17
IN THE DAY OF TROUBLE (II)
Hebrews 12:6

As I now reflect on the role of suffering in the life of God's children, I am convinced that illness and affliction, even tragedies, are often divine and purposeful gifts. It is an absolute truth that there is much that God cannot accomplish in human life apart from pain and testing. This is the clear message of Hebrews 12:6, "Whom the Lord loves He chastens and scourges every son whom He receives."

St. Teresa of Avila, weak and physically afflicted all her life, claimed to actually cherish suffering, testifying that in pain Christ draws nearer than at any other time and ministers His precious, intimate, indescribable blessings. This, too, has been my experience. When I am suffering physically, I definitely feel the presence of the Lord in a very tender and special way. During these long, dark hours, I am blessed with a kind baptism of His love and peace. I often testify to friends, "Though my body is in pain, I have no worry or fear—none. God fills my heart to overflowing with His peace." So suffering, without question, has helped me to know God more and more deeply. This is His essential school without which we so often cannot grow in grace.

After that early period in Taiwan when God gave me His definitive answer to my prayer for healing from arthritis, I never again asked Him to deliver me from that affliction.

In the Day of Trouble
Flora Chen

IT'S DONE

December 18

Mark 9:23

I seldom have heard a better definition of faith than that given in one of our meetings by a sweet, elderly black woman, as she answered a young man who asked, "How do I obtain the Lord's help for my needs?" In her characteristic way, pointing her finger toward him, she said with great insistence, "You just have to believe that He's done it and it's done." The greatest problem with most of us is, after asking Him to do it, we do not believe it is done. Instead, we keep trying to help Him, get others to help Him, and anxiously wait to see how He is going to work. Faith adds its "Amen" to God's "Yes" and then takes its hands off, leaving God to finish His work.

I simply take Him at His word, I praise Him that my prayer is heard, I claim my answer from the Lord, I take, He undertakes.

Active faith gives thanks for a promise even though it is not yet performed, knowing that God's contracts are as good as cash. Passive faith accepts the Word as true—But never moves. Active faith begins the work to do, And thereby proves. Passive faith says, "I believe it! Every word of God is true."

Well I know He has not spoken what He cannot, will not, do. He has instructed me, "Go forward!" but a closed-up way I see. When the waters are divided, soon in Canaan's land I'll be. Lo! I hear His voice commanding, "Rise and walk; take up your bed;" And, "Stretch to Me your withered hand!" which for so long has been dead. When I am a little stronger, then, I know I'll surely stand; When there comes a thrill of healing, I will use with ease my reclaimed hand. Yes, I know that "God is able" and full willing all to do; I believe that every promise, sometime, will to me come true.

Streams in the Desert
Lettie Cowman

December 19

STEPPING STONES

Hebrews 11:6

We all need faith for desperate days and the Bible is filled with accounts of such days. Its story is told with them, its songs are inspired by them, its prophecy deals with them, and its revelation has come through them. Desperate days are the stepping-stones on the path of light. They seem to have been God's opportunity to provide our school of wisdom.

Psalm 107 is filled with stories of God's lavish love. In every story of deliverance, it was humankind coming to the point of desperation that gave God His opportunity to act. Arriving at "their wits' end" (Psalm 107:27) of desperation was the beginning of God's power.

Remember the promise made to a couple "as good as dead," that their descendants would be "as numerous as the stars in the sky and as countless as the sand on the seashore" (Hebrews 11:12). Read once again the story of the Red Sea deliverance and the story of how "the priests who carried the ark of the covenant of the Lord stood firm on dry ground in the middle of the Jordan" (Joshua 3:17). Study once more the prayers of Asa, Jehoshaphat, and Hezekiah when they were severely troubled, not knowing what to do. Go over the history of Nehemiah, Daniel, Hosea, and Habakkuk. Stand with awe in the darkness of Gethsemane, and linger by the tomb in Joseph of Arimathea's garden through those difficult days. Call to account the witnesses of the early church and ask the apostles to relate the story of their desperate days.

Desperation is better than despair. Remember, our faith did not create our desperate days. Faith's work is to sustain us through those days and to solve them. Yet the only alternative to desperate faith is despair. Faith holds on and prevails.

Streams in the Desert
Lettie Cowman

December 20

A FOUL, STINKING DOG
II Corinthians 11:27-28

Japanese antagonists paraded the streets calling Francis "a foul, stinking dog, the most beggarly fellow alive, and a devourer of dead men's carcasses"—the old, horrible calumny. Pinto too gives an exciting but incredible story of a great argument between Francis and the bonzes which lasted five days, with the daimio as referee! On one occasion Duarte went ashore in a small boat to bring Francis back to safety on the ship and found him instructing a catechuman in a poor house. He told him his life would be forfeit if he did not escape at once. The answer was typical: "I for my part know well I am not worthy of so great an honor." All told, the Christians in Japan numbered between 1500 and 2000—about a thousand at Yamaguchi, a few hundred at Bungo and Hirado, the little group at Ichicu, and less than 200 at Kagoshima. Through the varying fortunes to come, the loyalty and courage of his Japanese children were splendidly to justify Francis's belief in them. Priests and laymen remained faithful through the most ghastly tortures and horrible deaths. In 1643 the last European Jesuit to land was burnt alive, yet for over two centuries the Christians of Japan, cut off from all communication with the world, deprived of all human teaching, kept the faith alive and supplied the church with one of the most wonderful pages of her history.

St. Francis Xavier – Apostle of the East
Margaret Yeo

I have no fellow-Christians to whom I might unbosom myself. . . . I live poorly with regard to the comforts of this life. . . . I lodge in a bundle of straw. My labor is hard and extremely difficult, and I have little appearance of success to comfort me. . . . Farewell friends and earthly comforts, the dearest of them all—the very dearest, if the Lord calls for it, I will spend my life to my latest moments in caves and dens of the earth.

David Brainerd

December 21
THE COMMONPLACE OF DEATH
Luke 7:11-17

Death is never a commonplace. We never become so accustomed to funerals as not to see them. Everybody sees the mournful procession go along the street. A momentary awe steals over the flippant thought, and for one brief season the superficial opens into the infinite abyss.

And yet, while a thousand are arrested, only a few are compassionate. There can be awe without pity; there can be interest without service. When this humble funeral train trudged out of the city of Nain, our Lord halted and His heart melted! There was an "aching void," and He longed to fill it. There was a bleeding, broken heart, and He yearned to stand and heal it. He found his own joy in removing another's tears, His own satisfaction in another's peace.

"The Lord has come to help His people!" That is what the people said, and I do not wonder at the saying! And let me, too, be a humble visitor in the troubled ways of men. Let my heart be a well of sweet compassion to all the sons and daughters of grief! Like Barnabas, let me be "a son of encouragement."

J. H. Jowett

Isaiah 49:13 **CONFIDENT IN THE FATHER** **December 22**

If you'll celebrate a marriage anniversary alone this year, God speaks to you. If your child made it to heaven before making it to kindergarten, he speaks to you. If your dreams were buried as they lowered the casket, God speaks to you.

He speaks to all of us who have stood or will stand in the soft dirt near an open grave. And to us he gives this confident word: "I want you to know what happens to a Christian when he dies so that when it happens, you will not be full of sorrow as those are who have no hope. For since we believe that Jesus died and then came back to life again, we can also believe that when Jesus returns, God will bring back with him all the Christians who have died" (I Thessalonians 4:13-14 TLB).

When Christ Comes
Max Lucado

Among the parables that Chinese teachers use is the story of a woman who lost an only son. She made her sorrow a wailing wall. Finally she went to a wise old philosopher. He said to her, "I will give you back your son if you will bring me some mustard seed. However, the seed must come from a home where there has never been any sorrow." Eagerly she started her search and went from house to house. In every case she learned that a loved one had been lost. "How selfish I have been in my grief," she said. "Sorrow is common to all."

How to Face Life
Author Unknown

December 23
ASLEEP WITH LULLABIES
John 16:20

Tragedy struck opera singer Beverly Sills when her first child was born almost totally deaf. This little child would never hear the beautiful voice of her mother or the lovely sounds of a soft forest. Shortly after discovering the deafness, Mrs. Sills gave birth to a second child, only to find that this son was mentally retarded.

So great was the sorrow of her life that she took off a full year from her profession to work with her daughter and son, trying to come to terms with the double tragedy.

Later when asked how she learned to cope, the famed songstress said. "The first question you ask is, Why me? Then it changes to Why them? It makes a complete difference in your attitude."

C. R. Hembree

> Here a pretty baby lies
> Sung asleep with lullabies;
> Pray be silent and not stir
> Th' easy earth that covers her.

The old words are new somewhere every day.... There are darker woods than illness, poverty, bereavement. There is the gloom wrapped about every thought of some catastrophe that has shaken the fabric of life to its foundations. There has not yet been full recovery from that shock. Broken hearts are everywhere in this world of tragedies: "How many there are, like the king in Samaria, wearing hidden sackcloth. Outside, the gay purple robe which rent reveals the secret. The people looked and behold, he had sackcloth within upon his flesh."

Gold By Moonlight
Amy Carmichael

Galatians 2:20 ## THE UNKNOWN MILE **December 24**

Frank went to meet Mother and Charlie was all ready to see her. *She had prayed that he might live and that she might hear him say "Mother."* That was granted and they visited all day long. It was the loveliest and most restful day—a hush over everything and a sweet brooding rest. Dr. Baldwin came in and thought he was better, but I thought of the word, "When the wind blows softly, look out; there is a tempest ahead."

Charles slept through the night, wakened once and wanted to sing. So he sang, "Keep on believing Jesus, keep on believing, there is nothing to fear, keep on believing. This is the way, truth in the night as well as the day." Then went to sleep until a.m. The Lord whispered to me three or four times, "Child of my love, dread not the unknown mile or the new demands life makes of thee." Asked for a word and picked up Murray's book and opened to Galatians 2:20, "I live by the faith of the Son of God." It seems prophetic. I'm carried along on His own inbreathed faith, not my own, but His own faith. There is a hush and peace indescribably resting upon everything and God is here! It seems that we have started to walk out of the valley, but it is yet dim as a morning before the dawn breaks. . . . About three Charles wakened suddenly with the awfulest attack. He fought for life and it was a terrific struggle, and I thought he was dying. Called the doctor quickly and he rushed over and gave him hypos. It quieted him. Then we found that it was a stroke which paralyzed his right side. His legs are swollen above the knee, and death creeps on. We called W.J.C. and told him to bring Corneal and Mrs. Clark. They were soon here. I went to Mother as we had not told her Charlie was dying. I got her some breakfast. Before this I lay in the sun room and Billie came and snuggled up to me, then purred. I lay in the steamer chair and got very quiet.

Lettie Cowman Diary, 1924

December 25
TO ONE AFRAID OF FAILING
I Peter 1:8-9

It is those who never fear a fall who fall most terribly. "Hold thou me up and I shall be safe." Not for one moment is our own power enough.

I think our Lord demands all. I see nothing less in His words about taking up the cross. It is all or nothing. I don't mean that one sees all there is to see at first, or even at last, but only that all we know is given because we want to give all.

> And faith shall sing a joyous Yes
> To every dear command of Thine

He poured out all for us. Can we measure our offering to Him? Don't be anxious. It is not what we feel that is important. By His grace, who has grace sufficient for the weakest of us, do you will to do His will? Do you will to do it even if it brings sorrow and pain and weariness? Yes, and dullness? If you can say, "He enabling me, that is my desire," then you need not fear. You will not fail.

Amy Carmichael

When I was a very young boy, a dear neighbor who lived two doors down the street experienced a great sorrow. She often played and sang at her piano, but after this tragedy struck in her life, the first song with which she would open her "daily concert" was the lovely hymn, "I Must Tell Jesus." The words made a deep impression upon me as a child.

H. G. Bosch

Isaiah 40:8   **"WHAT DOES IT MEAN?"**   **December 26**

A certain Frenchwoman while still a child was haunted by an odd question: What is the meaning of our actions? "What does it mean," she wondered, "if I go to the left and not to the right, do this rather than that?" At the age of twelve she experienced an inner illumination. It happened one day in the middle of a bridge over the Rhone. All at once she felt filled with joy. She had found the answer to her persistent question. She realized that any act, however trivial, could have meaning only if it fitted in with the meaning of the whole world.

She questioned her parents, asking them where she might find the meaning of the world. Unbelievers, they replied that the question was an absurd one. She went on asking the same question of all sorts of people. Several years later someone answered, "In the Bible." She bought a Bible and began reading it.

She had been given the only sensible answer to her question. Neither science, philosophy or the human mind can teach us the meaning of things for the good reason that it is a secret that belongs only to the author of all things, and we can know only what He chooses to reveal to us of His plan and purposes.

Paul Tournier

December 27
ALWAYS IN HIS HAND
I Peter 1:25

Praying Hyde loved God's Word. From the time he arrived in India, he felt it absolutely essential that he really know the Bible. Over the years his love for the Word became deeper and deeper. Throughout the day, from his first cup of tea in the early morning, whenever possible his Bible was in his hand. When he witnessed to people, when he prayed with people, the Bible was always in his hand or close beside him. Usually when he knelt to pray in his tent, in his room, or in a prayer room, the Bible lay open before him. Often his hands rested on it as he claimed the promises of God and grounded his whole praying upon them. The Bible was his constant strength.

Another source of repeated renewal of strength was his joy in the Lord. In the midst of tremendous wrestling in prayer, he would often break out into songs of joy. Sometimes in prayer he would be so thrilled by the presence and promises of God and so filled with faith that he would break out into holy laughter. He was very much at home with the Indian custom of praising the Lord by calling "Bol! Yisu Masih, Ki Jai!"—"Shout victory to Jesus!"

During revival times at Sialkot, when John led someone to victory in the prayer room, he would stand up, smile, and begin to sing, "Tis done, the great transaction's done" (from the hymn, "O Happy Day!"). Often he became so full of joy that he would clap his hands or even leap for joy. . . .

John Hyde expressed the hope that other people would not try to duplicate his life. He knew his was a special call from God, and he was faithful unto death. Our responsibility is to be faithful to God's call for our lives. God needs only one John Hyde, but he needs many others to become mighty intercessors in the service of Christ. . . .

Heroes of the Holy Life
Wesley Duewel

December 28
THE GREAT RESERVOIR OF POWER
Psalm 119:163-168

The great reservoir of the power that belongs to God is His own Word—the Bible. If we wish to make it ours, we must go to that Book. Yet people abound in the church who are praying for power and neglecting the Bible. Men are longing to have power for bearing fruit in their own lives and yet forget that Jesus has said: "The seed is the Word of God" (Luke 8:11). They are longing to have power to melt the cold heart and break the stubborn will of those to whom they witness, and yet forget that God has said: "Is not My Word like as a fire? . . . and like a hammer that breaketh the rock in pieces?" (Jeremiah 23:29).

If we are to obtain fullness of power in life and service, we must feed upon the Word of God. There is no other food so strengthening. If we will not take time to study the Bible, we cannot have power, any more than we can have physical power if we will not take time to eat nutritious food.

In Acts 2:37 we read, "Now when they heard this, they were pricked in their heart, and said unto Peter and to the rest of the apostles, 'Men and brethren, what shall we do?'" If we look back and see what it was they had heard that produced this deep conviction, we find that it was simply the Word of God. If you will read Peter's sermon, you will find it one of the most biblical sermons ever preached. It was scripture from beginning to end. It was, then, the Word of God, carried home by the Spirit of God, that pricked them to the heart. If you wish to produce conviction, you must give men the Word of God.

R. A. Torrey

December 29
POWER TO PRODUCE FAITH
Romans 10:17

You can never get faith by merely praying, nor can you ever get it by any effort of the will. You can never get it by trying to pump it up in any way. Faith is the product of a certain cause, and that cause is the Word of God.

It is so, for example, with saving faith. If you want a man to have saving faith, simply give him something definite from God's Word upon which he can rest. The Philippian jailer asked, "Sirs, what must I do to be saved?" (Acts 16:30), and Paul answered: "Believe on the Lord Jesus Christ, and thou shalt be saved and thy house" (Acts 16:31). But Paul did not stop there. Read verse 32: "And they spake unto him the Word of the Lord and to all that were in his house." They did not merely tell the Philippian jailer to believe on the Lord Jesus Christ, and then leave him floundering in the dark without giving him something to believe, or something for his faith to rest upon. They gave that which God has ordained to produce faith. Here we often make a mistake. We tell people, "Believe, believe, believe," but do not show them how, do not give them anything definite to believe. Give him Isaiah 53:6 and thus hold up Christ crucified or give him I Peter 2:24. Here he has something for his faith to rest upon. Faith must have a foundation.

Not only saving faith comes through the Word of God, but prevailing faith in prayer does also. Suppose I read Mark 11:24: "What thing soever ye desire, when ye pray, believe that ye receive them, And ye shall have them." I used to say, "The way to get anything I want is to believe I am going to get it." I would kneel down and pray and try to believe, but I did not get the things that I asked for. I had no real faith. Real faith must have a warrant. Before I can truly believe I am to receive what I ask, I must have a definite promise of God's Word, or a definite leading of the Holy Spirit, to rest my faith upon.

R. A. Torrey

December 30
POWER TO CLEANSE
Ephesians 5:25-26

The Word of God has power not only to take impurity out of the heart, but to cleanse the outward life as well. If you wish a clean outward life, you must wash often by bringing your life in contact with the Word of God. If one lives in a city whose atmosphere is polluted with smoke, when he goes into the streets, his hands will become dirty. He must wash frequently if he wishes to keep clean.

In Ephesians 5:25-26 we read, "Husbands, love your wives, even as Christ also loved the church, and gave Himself for it; that he might sanctify and cleanse it with the washing of water by the Word." We all live in a world whose atmosphere is polluted, a very dirty world. As we go out from day to day and come in contact with this dirty world, there is absolutely only one way to keep clean, and that is by taking frequent baths in the Word of God. You must bathe every day and take plenty of time to do it. A daily, prolonged, thoughtful bath in the Word of God is the only thing that will keep a life clean. "Wherewithal shall a young man cleanse his way? By taking heed thereto according to Thy Word" (Psalm 119:9).

In Acts 20:32 we read, "I commend you to God and to the Word of His grace, which is able to build you up." We hear a great deal about character building. The Word of God is that by which we must carry it on if it is to be done right. In II Peter 1:5-7 we have a picture of a 70-story and a basement Christian. The great trouble today is we have so many one-story Christians, and the reason is neglect of the Word. If we are to grow, we must have wholesome, nutritious food and plenty of it. "As newborn babes, desire the sincere milk of the Word, that ye may grow thereby" (I Peter 2:2). A Christian can not more grow as he ought without feeding frequently, regularly, and largely upon the Word of God than a baby can grow as he ought without proper nutriment.

R. A. Torrey

Revelation 7:14
THE DOOR TO TRIUMPH
December 31

Tribulation is the door to triumph. The valley leads to the open highway, and tribulation's imprint is on every great accomplishment. *Crowns are cast in crucibles,* and the chains of character found at the feet of God are forged in earthly flames. No one wins the greatest victory until he has walked the winepress of woe. With deep furrows of anguish on His brow, the "man of sorrows" said, "In this world you will have trouble." But immediately comes the psalm of promise, "Take heart! I have overcome the world." The footprints are visible everywhere. The steps that lead to thrones are stained with spattered blood, and scars are the price for scepters. We will wrestle our crowns from the giants we conquer. It is no secret that grief has always fallen to people of greatness.

    The mark of rank in nature
      Is capacity for pain;
    And the anguish of the singer
      Makes the sweetest of the strain.

Tribulation has always marked the trail of the true reformer. It was true in the story of Paul, Luther, Savonarola, Knox, Wesley, and the rest of God's mighty army. They came through great tribulation to their point of power. . . . "These are they who have come out of the great tribulation." In spite of his blindness, wasn't Homer the unparalleled poet of the Greeks? And who wrote the timeless dream of *Pilgrim's Progress*? Was it a prince in royal robes seated on a couch of comfort and ease? No! The lingering splendor of John Bunyan's vision gilded the dingy wall of an old English jail in Bedford, while he, a princely prisoner and a glorious genius, made a faithful transcript of the scene.

    Great is the easy conqueror;
      Yet the one who is wounded sore,
    Breathless, all covered o'er with blood and sweat,
      Sinks fainting, but fighting evermore,
    Is greater yet.

                                        Selected

ACKNOWLEDGMENTS

We gratefully acknowledge permission granted by the following publishers to use excerpts from their copyrighted publications.

Alfred A. Knopf
Days of Grace by Arthur Ashe

Augsburg Publishers
God's Word for Today by O. Hallesby

Baker Book House
Listening to the Giants by Warren Wiersbe

Barclay Press
Over the Teacup by Catherine Cattell

Beacon Hill Publishers
The Spirit of Holiness by Everett Cattell

Christian Literature Crusade
Write the Vision by A. J. Appasamy
God by Moonlight by Amy Carmichael

Christian Publications
The Divine Conquest by A.W. Tozer
The Rest of Righteousness by A.W. Tozer

Cityhill Publishers
China Miracle by Arthur Wallis

Collins Fontana Books
Jesus Rediscovered by Malcolm Muggeridge

David Cook Publishers
The View from the Hearse by Joseph Bayly

Daybreak Books
Still Higher for His Highest by Oswald Chambers

Dell Publishing Company
No Man is an Island by Thomas Merton

Discovery House Publishers
The Place of Help by Oswald Chambers

William Eerdmans Publishers
The Christian World of C.S. Lewis by Clide Kilby

Fleming H. Revel
Whatever Happened to the Human Race? by Francis Schaeffer

Focus on the Family
Letter by James Dobson

Fontana Books
A Plain Man Looks at the Beatitudes by William Barclay

Francis Asbury Society Press
This Day with the Master by Dennis Kinlaw

Steve Griffith
In Two Minds by Os Guinness

Harold Shaw Publishers
The Miracles of Our Lord by Rolland Hein

Harper Brothers Press
Where is God when it Hurts? by Philip Yancey
Christ and the Meaning of Life by Helmut Thielicke
Songs of Hope by Grace Noll Crowell

Harvard University Press
Book of Abigail and John by John Butterfield

Harvest House Publishers
Seeking the Face of God by Gary Thomas

Hodder and Stoughton
Affliction by Edith Schaeffer
Hudson Taylor and the Open Century by A.J. Broomhall

Inter Varsity Press
Death in the City by Frances Schaeffer

D. James Kennedy
 The Grestest Book in the World by D. James Kennedy

John Knox Press
 To Resist or to Surrender by Paul Tournier

Moody Press
 Spiritual Maturity by J. Oswald Sanders
 The Miracle Book by Ernest Lott

Muhlenberg Press
 How the World Began by Helmut Thielicke

Multnomah Press
 Encourage Me by Charles Swindol
 Simply Jesus by Joseph Stowel

Navpress
 Disciples in Action by Leroy Eims

The Overcomer Literature Trust
 Life out of Death by Jessie Penn Lewis

OMS International, Inc.
 Another Valley, Another Love by Valetta Steel Crumley
 The Key Goose by Mildred Rice
 Missionary Warrior by Lettie Cowman
 The Story Behind Stream in the Desert by Lettie Cowman and Ed Erny
 Under His Wings by Mary Payseur
 Under Sentence of Death by Valetta Steel

Radio Bible Class
 Our Daily Bread by Paul Van Gorder, H.G. Bosch

Scripture Press (Victor Books)
 Living with Your Dreams by David Seamands
 Be Mature by Warren Wiersbe

Simon and Schuster Publishers
 Man's Search for Meaning by Victor Frankl

Elizabeth Skoglund
 Hudson Taylor by Elizabeth Skoglund

Thomas Nelson Publishers
The Applause of Heaven by Max Lucado
A Gentle Thunder by Max Lucado
When Christ Comes by Max Lucado
Malcolm Muggeridge – A Life by Ian Hunter

The Warner Press
More Prayer Meeting Topics by Vivian Ahrendt
David's Song by Maurice Berquist

Zondervan Press
Heroes of the Holy Life by Wesley Duewel
A Grace Disguised by Jerry Sitser

OTHER BOOKS BY ED ERNY

NO GUARANTEE BUT GOD
With Esther Erny

Brief biographies of the founders of The Oriental Missionary Society (OMS International)—converted Western Union executives, Charles Cowman and Ernest Kilbourne; Lettie Cowman, famed author of *Streams in the Desert*; dynamic Japanese pastor and evangelist, Juji Nakada.

THE STORY BEHIND STREAMS IN THE DESERT
With Lettie Cowman

The diary of Lettie Cowman for the year 1924, the final year of her husband Charles' life, provides a window into the crucible of physical pain and emotional and spiritual turmoil from which emerged the classic devotional *Streams in the Desert*, destined to bless millions of sufferers.

THIS ONE THING

The biography of missionary leader and statesman, Eugene Erny. A member of the famed Asbury College Missionary team, he held evangelistic meetings throughout Asia in 1929-30. In China he met, courted and won the hand of a young missionary with The Oriental Missionary Society (OMS International), Esther Helsby. Together they served in China and India until 1950 when Eugene was elected president of the mission, a position he held until 1969.

NOBIE
By Nobie Pope Sivley with Ed Erny

A life begun in shame and remorse finds beautiful fulfillment as a young lady travels from West Texas to the remote waterways of Colombia, South America, to offer healing and the message of salvation.

UNDER THE SENTENCE OF DEATH
By Valetta Steel with Ed Erny

The epic story of a young pastor, Henry Steel, who upon learning that he is dying of Hodgkin's disease, determines to give himself unreservedly to reaching the nations for Jesus Christ.

TWICE THROUGH THE VALLEY
By Valetta Steel with Ed Erny

Valetta Steel, widow of Henry Steel (*Under the Sentence of Death*), tells of the series of tragedies which bereft her of her entire family, testing her faith to the limits of human endurance but also leading to unprecedented joy and fruitfulness.

YIPPEE IN MY SOUL
By Margaret Bonnette with Ed Erny

An adventuresome young woman, determined to live life to the hilt, Margaret was once engaged to three men at the same time! Later, with her beloved husband's death, she finds her dreams shattered and her life empty. Her search for God eventuates in a life-changing encounter and a date with destiny as God's healer in the remote mountains of Haiti.

HE GOES BEFORE THEM
By Meredith and Christine Helsby with Ed Erny and Carroll Hunt Rader

A young missionary family caught in the cross currents of war find themselves Japanese prisoners of war in China during World War II. A moving story of God's miracle provision and quiet courage in the darkest days of the 20th century.

THE QUEST

A small booklet explaining in simple language what one needs to do to be a Christian. More than 100,000 copies in print, *The Quest* has also been translated into a number of foreign languages.

THE KEY GOOSE (And Other Lessons God Taught Me)
By Mildred Rice with Ed Erny

Rich spiritual lessons seasoned with humor, gleaned from a lifetime of missionary service in China, Japan and Taiwan.

PRINCESS IN THE KINGDOM
By Evelyn Bellande with Ed Erny

Born into a wealthy, aristocratic family, a young lady finds her dreams broken by a failed marriage and the dark diagnosis of cancer. In her despair, she discovers life and a mission to her own people.

"LORD, THIS IS NOT WHAT I HAD IN MIND"

A series of essays detailing humorous and embarrassing episodes in the lives of missionary families.

WHAT NOW, LORD?
By Margaret Brabon with Ed Erny

The story of Harold and Margaret Brabon who helped pioneer the work of The Oriental Missionary Society in Colombia, South America, during the dangerous years of "La Violencia." This is a true romance in which a beautiful, idealistic college coed, engaged to a ministerial student, improbably falls in love with a brilliant young chemist working for Henry Ford.

TO INDIA WITH LOVE
By Esther Close with Ed Erny

The story of an intrepid missionary nurse in the villages of India.

LEGACIES OF FAITH, VOLUME I, II, III, IV, and V

Daily devotional readings from great Christian authors, arranged by subject matter and indexed for the benefit of pastors, evangelists, teachers, and Christian workers.

UNDER HIS WINGS
By Mary Payseur with Ed Erny

The story of a North Carolina farm girl called of God to serve as a missionary in China where she was imprisoned during World War II.

IN THE DAY OF TROUBLE
By Flora Chen with Ed Erny

The courageous story of a Christian woman caught in the horrors of three wars.

NOTES

NOTES

NOTES

NOTES

NOTES